HEROES ARE FOREVER

Heroes Are Forever

The Life and Times of Celtic Legend Jimmy McGrory

JOHN CAIRNEY

MAINSTREAM
PUBLISHING
EDINBURGH AND LONDON

**To my uncle,
Philip Cairney (1913–74),
who played the game all his life.**

First published in Great Britain in 2005 by
MAINSTREAM PUBLISHING COMPANY (EDINBURGH) LTD
7 Albany Street
Edinburgh EH1 3UG

ISBN 1 84018 933 9

A catalogue record for this book
is available from the British Library

Typeset in Baskerville Book and Stone Sans
Printed and bound in Great Britain by
William Clowes Ltd, Beccles, Suffolk

Acknowledgements

This book could not have been begun without Jimmy McGrory's own story, *A Lifetime in Paradise*, as told to Gerald McNee in 1975, and Mr McNee's other writings on Celtic, such as *The Story of Celtic 1888–1978*. Similarly, David Potter's work on William Maley and Bob Crampsey's on Jock Stein have been invaluable, not to mention *An Alphabet of the Celts* compiled by Eugene MacBride and his team. Other football writers to whom I am indebted are Harry Andrews, Ian Archer, Peter Burns, Tom Greig, Jack Harkness, Rex Kingsley, Archie Macpherson and Hugh Taylor, as well as football authorities like James Farrell, Richard M. Fearon, Jim Friel, John Livingston, Stuart Marshall, Richard McBrearty, Jack McGinn, Bill Murray, Jack Murray and Dean Parker, and players Jim Craig and Billy McNeill MBE, who talked to me at length. Celtic supporters from all over the world wrote to me with their, or their fathers' and grandfathers' McGrory memories, and friends and family also rallied round with contributions – Bob Adams, Jim Cairney, Jonathan Cairney, Sean Cairney, Gordon Cockburn, Alison Hill, Liam Hill, Iain Livingstone, Jane Livingstone, Frank McAteer, Brian McGeechan, Dr Gerald McGrath, Frank McGuire, James Murray, Ray Neale, Graham Roxburgh and, particularly, my dear wife, Alannah O'Sullivan. Without this support the project would have been impossible.

I am grateful also to Anthony Green for comments regarding his family and to the McGrory children: Maria, Elizabeth and especially Jimmy's son, James McGrory, for all his work on my behalf, for his kindness, cooperation and encouragement and for permitting the use of personal material and family photographs.

Appreciation is due to the staff of the Mitchell Library, Glasgow, and to the editors of the Glasgow *Evening Times*, the *Celtic View*, the *Scottish Banner*, the *Ayrshire Advertiser* and *Ayrshire Post* for allowing me the courtesy of their columns to contact McGrory friends and Celtic supporters everywhere.

I have to thank Tom Campbell, a Celtic scholar and gentleman whose hands-on assistance and positive suggestions were pertinent and invaluable, my copy-editor Nick Davis for his keen eye and insight, and to Graeme Blaikie, Deborah Warner and Ailsa Bathgate, and the rest of the magnificent support team at Mainstream Publishing. Last of all and most of all, I extend my sincere gratitude to Pat Woods, a Celtic historian, for his sheer industry in connection with the project.

CONTENTS

PREFACE

The best you can say for football is that it has given the
working man a subject for conversation.

James Hamilton Muir, author, 1901

As I sat down to begin this book on Thursday, 1 September 2004,
the centenary year of Jimmy McGrory's birth, the BBC World
Service, in its early-morning radio news bulletin, carried the story of
Wayne Rooney's transfer to Manchester United. He was signed from
Everton for a fee which could rise to £30 million over six years,
giving an eighteen-year-old boy a weekly wage which is as incredible
as it is obscene. Is there this much money in the game, much less one
club? What price now his frequently expressed loyalty to the club he
has supported all his extremely short life? Or that his labourer father
bought him an Everton shirt on the day he was born? It now seems
a meaningless gesture in the face of such a monstrous tidal wave of
money engulfing the lad. The hope expressed by Sir Alex Ferguson,
the United manager, is that Rooney's partnership with the club's
other star striker, Ruud van Nistelrooy, might yield at least 40 goals
in the season just opened.

The parallels with Jimmy McGrory are irresistible. Except that he
got 50 goals in his second-last playing season and might have got
more but for injury – and he did so on a weekly wage of £8 a week.
He took a whole career to make what young Wayne will make just
reporting for training. Of course, it's another world we live in but all

the money in the world can't buy a player's heart and soul. It hires only his head and feet. And for a very fleeting time at that. Good luck to the prodigious and talented Mr Rooney and to the lawyers, managers and agents who have helped him to his lottery-like windfall – but long live the severely underpaid Jimmy McGrory who remains, for all real lovers of the beautiful game, a continuing legend and a true football immortal. One wonders if the young Mr Rooney will be similarly remembered a hundred years from now.

McGrory's lasting status was confirmed on Monday, 8 November 2004, when he was inducted into the inaugural Scottish Football Hall of Fame at Hampden Park, Glasgow. His son, James, attended the evening reception with his own children, Jamie and Lisa, and his sister, Maria. Later in the same month, James went through to Edinburgh with his other sister, Elizabeth, to see their father installed on 25 November in the Scottish Sports Hall of Fame at the Royal Museum of Scotland. The honour was thus seen properly as a family occasion and a matter of some pride to the McGrory children and grandchildren more than 20 years after his death and nearly 70 since he stopped playing.

These ceremonies gave football its place as part of the very fabric of Scottish national identity, and the name of James Edward McGrory stepped out of history to take up a permanent place in the public record. Chronologically speaking, Jimmy McGrory is so far in the past he might be termed an Ancient among so many Moderns. The nearest in time to him were Bill Shankly and Sir Matt Busby and even they now seem distant. Of course we *are* dealing with history here, but it was noticeable that among the famous sportsmen chosen the bias was towards personally known and near contemporaries. This is the drawback of any public poll, but it makes McGrory's inclusion all the more telling because those who actually saw him play must be few today.

It was also noticed that half of the original inductees had a Celtic connection. There were the inevitable Lisbon Lions led by captain Billy McNeill – Bobby Murdoch, Jimmy Johnstone and, of course, Jock Stein. Danny McGrain and Kenny Dalglish represented the next generation and both Billy Bremner and Matt Busby were known Celtic supporters. Rangers also had a strong team out with Jim Baxter, John Greig and Graeme Souness representing the recent past and Willie Woodburn for the old-timers, but where was Alan Morton or Davie Meiklejohn? Sir Alex Ferguson was there more for his Manchester United association than for his Scottish football pedigree. For the others, Gordon Smith and Dave Mackay represented Hibs and Hearts and Willie Miller was Aberdeen's contribution.

The unveiling was done by another Aberdeen link, the inimitable Denis Law, who still typifies the Scottish player in the modern age. All these famous names deserved to be honoured but you can be sure there were some ghosts flitting about Hampden that night looking for frames to fill. Jimmy Delaney, for instance, or even Jerry Dawson and what about John Thomson? Nor was R.S. McColl, the 'Prince of Centre-forwards' in his day, represented. There are so many great names from Scottish football's past, so many memories, it would need a stadium like Hampden Park itself to hold them all rather than a few rooms under the Main Stand.

The sole reason for the Football Museum, and for this book, is that people still remember and revere the sporting icons of their youth and carry this nostalgia into their middle years as a banner to remind them that football was once very important to them. Perhaps, to borrow from a famous Bill Shankly quote, it is even more important than that.

When football began with its ten association rules at Cambridge around the middle of the nineteenth century, there was little difference between it as a game and rugby, as we now know it. However, the simple game became slightly more complicated as it developed throughout Victorian times, although it still featured a pack and its first purpose was a mad scramble to get at the ball by both teams. It was much like any street game as the older reader will remember it – in order to get a game you had to get the ball. Gradually, a greater precision was arrived at, especially when the passing game was introduced by Queen's Park. This allowed the better ball players to flourish and the best player in the team was generally in the centre of things directing operations from the middle of the field. He was the pivot around which everything and everyone revolved.

Then, as skills and tactics grew more sophisticated into the twentieth century it became obvious that it was goals that mattered and the scoring of them. That's what made the game the attraction it is and drew the crowds, and what eventually allowed the round ball to roll around the world and become *the* international sport. By the time of the Kaiser's War in 1914, the onus for any side's effectiveness had changed from a central pivotal control to a forward central spearhead backed up by wingers either side and inside-forwards behind him. Later, the pivot became a third defender with the full-backs, in front of the goalkeeper, who was then, as now, the last resort. With the emphasis now changed to individual attack rather than a general forward movement en masse, the centre-forward, or striker, evolved and he has been with us ever since.

He is the *prima ballerina assoluta* of the football team – the front-man, the flashpoint of the attack, the leader of the line, the idol of the terraces and the cynosure of all eyes throughout the match. Even in the modern game, his is still seen as the glamour position. By very definition, the centre-forward is always at the centre of the attack – in and around the goalmouth – and a great centre-forward is gold to any team. The current European Footballer of the Year, Andriy Shevchenko, is a striker, like so many winners of the same award were before him – Alfredo Di Stefano, Marco van Basten and Ronaldo. The centre-forward is every boy's hero, whatever team he plays for.

The good striker gets as much adoration as any matador although his activity around the goalmouth more often resembles the bull than the man with the sword and cape. McGrory himself at his peak was said to have had 'shoulders like a young Clydesdale and a neck like an Aberdeen Angus' but what was also true was that he had a lion's heart, a panther's leap and a tiger's courage. Altogether, he was an enviable football animal and, in the football sense, he came from prime stock.

Even early in Scottish football we could boast such centre-forwards as the aforementioned R.S. McColl, Jimmy Quinn of Celtic and Hughie Gallacher of Airdrie and Newcastle, who was McGrory's exact contemporary and his own worst enemy. The poor wee man ended up throwing himself under a train but McGrory, the man he kept from so many caps, was content throughout his career to go along with the train of events. However slowly, it got him to where he is now, an inaugural member of the Scottish Football Museum's Hall of Fame and the subject of this biography.

Edson Arantes do Nascimento, otherwise known as Pele, arguably the best-known player in the world, is credited by the International Football Federation of History and Statistics with 1,281 goals in 1,363 games in *all* categories. This includes tours, friendlies, exhibition matches, etc. – and Pele certainly played in a lot of these – whereas in strictly competitive matches at the highest grade Pele's statistics are 541 goals in 560 games, which is just under a goal a game. McGrory's figures are 550 goals in 547 first-class games, giving him an average of just *over* a goal per game in a career of 15 playing seasons. This is why James Edward McGrory is a Celtic legend and why, as these pages will show, he is remembered today as the greatest goal-scorer in the history of British football.

His rate of scoring showed a truly remarkable consistency and set a level that would be difficult to maintain in today's tightly marked, tactical game. In his era the game, if slower, was tougher, the ball used was smaller and heavier and the playing surfaces were less refined. He was also encumbered by steel-capped boots and bulky shinguards, not to mention some very doughty defenders. Given these conditions, you had to be tough just to play the game, never mind score. This fact alone makes his goal feats all the more remarkable.

The record books will tell you all about the other great goal-scorers from Arthur Friedenreich to Steve Bloomer, from Dixie Deans to Arthur Rowley and on up to the incomparable Pele, but their achievements, however great, are at a distance from the hero of this book. The aim here is to chronicle the deeds of a local boy who made good with the team he supported all his life, and to whom he gave that life as player, manager and, finally, as public relations officer.

His appeal, however, is more than a matter of record-book statistics. Jimmy McGrory exemplified all that Celtic meant to a large section of Glasgow's poorest citizens, the non-playing thousands who followed the club down the years. He knew instinctively what the game and the team meant to them because he shared the same emotional and cultural ties that bound them to a football club and the supporters respected him for this. He had earned this respect not only by his flamboyant deeds on the park but also by his loyalty and total commitment to traditions, which both he and they valued and revered. Even more, he was a flesh-and-blood man with whom the man on the terracing could identify. He was an instant Saturday hero and his goals were the very stuff of legend.

Jimmy McGrory was more than a professional footballer, he was a people's player in a people's club, a beacon who lit up many a winter Saturday for so many in an age when football was a simple opiate for the masses huddled on their stepped hillsides. They had little else to feel good about in the week. At least they could forget it on a Saturday. It was the working man's revenge on a soulless six-day week. He might be fixed on the bottom rung, but if his team was playing well, a man could face a bleak Monday morning in better heart. A winning team could put fire into an empty belly and lift a tired step.

Jimmy McGrory, both as a player and a man, was a typical product of the troubled decades between the two world wars. In a depressing age when wages were low and work was scarce, his feats on the field brought a welcome and much-needed escape for thousands of ordinary, cloth-capped, Scottish working men (in Celtic's case, of mainly Irish descent), who packed the dirt terracings to cheer his every move on the field.

When McGrory started his football career after the First World War, the game had a very different meaning for those involved with it at whatever level, either as player or spectator. The sport had not yet become the board game of bored billionaires. Local clubs still attracted local players and local supporters. The club was the centre and focus of so many lives, and allegiance was almost a parochial matter. Loyalties were unquestioned and fathers passed on to sons their love of the game and their love of the club. Every Glasgow boy grew up playing in the street knowing that, with a bit of luck, he might graduate to grass one day and join that pantheon of the gods he considered the team he supported to be. Few attained their dream, but James Edward McGrory did.

His story is an unfashionable one. There were no great scandals in his private life and he certainly did not make his football fortune. He worked for a weekly wage that wasn't so far above the average supporter's but his qualities were such that he did not need the trappings or appurtenances that are supposed to be part of any success in the public eye. He was glad to be able to work at, and within, his chosen football field all his working life. His trade was playing football and playing it for the club he supported as a boy and served as an adult. He was good at what he did. His job was to score goals and, as already noted, he scored plenty.

His story is worth the telling for several reasons. We need to be reminded, in the material times we live in, that money isn't everything and that fame is really so much hot air – a breeze that blows away as suddenly as it blows up – and that status is something more than the house you live in or the car you drive. We all pay lip service to these self-evident truths but, just the same, we scramble for our share of the goodies. Life is short and a footballer's life is even shorter so the player himself can't be blamed for trying to make the best of what might land at his feet. Jimmy McGrory typified another breed, one that may already have gone the way of the dodo. He couldn't believe his luck in being paid for doing what he would have done for nothing and, for all his fame and goals, he never took anything for granted. He was always on tenterhooks at the end of each season until he was re-signed for the next.

Yet throughout his career he remained the same man that was the boy: modest, undemanding, fiendishly loyal and deeply committed to his Catholic faith and to the football cause that was Celtic's. McGrory wore his heart on his green-and-white sleeve for everyone to see and the Celtic support loved him for it. In him, they saw one of their own. His story was their story, because he was just like them, in every respect, except for a particular skill in steering a leather ball into the back of a net with head or foot. By doing so, and often doing it spectacularly, he lifted the hearts of his countrymen and raised the spirits of a nation.

To begin our consideration of the life and times of the Celtic legend that is Jimmy McGrory we have to start in the native city he never left – Glasgow. Move up the High Street from Glasgow Cross, past the Royal Infirmary and go over the M8 motorway at Townhead to Royston, formerly the Garngad, which for years was known variously as 'Nazareth', 'The Garden of God' or 'Little Ireland'. This is where it all started for Jimmy McGrory and, if we are to fully understand the man, we must appreciate his roots. These went down through the asphalt streets of Glasgow, across the Irish Sea and into the bog soil of old Ireland; and it is there, in what is now called Eire, we must look for the real beginning of the McGrory story.

INTRODUCTION

> History, tradition, rivalry, culture and habit are every bit as important to the game as any yardstick set by quality of players, teams and facilities . . . There is more to football than football.
>
> Tom Watt, actor and author, 2003

The first Scots were an Irish tribe from Ulster who settled in Dalriada (Argyle) sometime in the sixth century. (This fact may be commemorated today in Dalriada Street, which runs behind the Lisbon Lions' Stand at Celtic Park, linking Janefield Street to London Road.) The mass migration by the Irish to Scotland in the middle of the nineteenth century and on up until the First World War was not, therefore, the first movement of peoples from Ireland to Scotland. In the Irish diaspora that took place after what they called 'An Gorta Mor', the Great Hunger, in the years between 1845 and 1851, the better class of Irishman took his family to America, or, if he could afford the £12 passage money, to New Zealand, where he could grow a better class of potato.

For the poorer classes, however, it was a case of finding fourpence to get them and what they could carry across the water by cattle boat (standing room only on deck) to the Broomielaw on the Clyde. The vast majority, estimated at more than 100,000 people, made it to Glasgow in this fashion. They flooded into the city and the surrounding countryside, and before long whole new districts were springing up that were, to all intents and purposes, Irish enclaves. From the Gorbals to the Calton and out to Coatbridge and Carfin a whole lot of 'Little Irelands' emerged and the Garngad, between Springburn and Dennistoun, on the north-east side of the city, hemmed in by the Monkland Canal and the Caledonian Railway works, was one of these.

At that time, it could hardly be seen for smoke. The St Rollox Chemical Factory boasted tall chimneys (one of them, Tennant's Stalk, being among the highest brick-built structures in Europe) which belched out either looming smokescreens offering a hiding place to the incoming Irish, or they were seen as brick sentinels stationed to keep them out. Whatever they were, they were certainly not health-giving. Breathing was a feat on days when the factories were busy, but the same fumes represented work for people and what was a touch of bronchitis compared with the prospect of a weekly wage? Which was why Glasgow in Victorian times had the highest infant mortality in the country, and why in 1898, Jimmy McGrory lost an infant brother, John.

Tenement people got by through scrimping on every penny and by sharing what little they had with neighbours as poor as themselves. When people have little they have no alternative but to share. Apart from the demands of the factor for his weekly rent, the main strain felt by these recent immigrants was the determined antagonism of the native Scots, or rather, Glasgow Presbyterian Protestants, who didn't take too kindly to this sudden influx of rosary beads, and quite ignored the fact that St Patrick himself was a Scot, born in that very Dalriada to which the original Scots first came. Such historical niceties, however, were lost in the immediate wave of anti-Catholicism which rose up on all sides and threatened to engulf the latter-day Paddies.

The trouble was that the newcomers could not forget their Irishness. After all, it's hard to shake off an inherited pedigree of more than a thousand years just because of a bit of sectarian hostility. Strangeness fostered suspicion on both sides, which propagated misunderstanding and so the divide inevitably built up into open animosity. The ground was prepared for a long war. The trenches of bigotry were dug deep and both sides were wary of raising their heads above the parapet. The Irish retreated to their chapels and the Protestants to their kirks and thus both sides allowed 'No Man's Land' to build up between them. Apartheid had come to the west of Scotland. There is no other word that explains the 'separateness' that so quickly emerged between the two communities and was to foster the hostility that led to so many later, and tragic, misunderstandings. The reasons for this were complex but basically it was economic more than religious and more cultural than racist.

The Scots felt themselves threatened in their own country by intruders they regarded at best as 'foreigners' and at worst as little more than 'white Negroes'. Yet these same lower-caste subjects acknowledged a common throne, and gave their lives for the one Government in campaigns that took Irish and Scots alike to Afghanistan and the North-West Frontier, to Sudan and the Veldt. Unfortunately, this larger view was lost in the short-tempered, short-sighted attitude adopted by the bigots for their own immediate ends. For the moment, as far as the Scottish establishment was concerned, the enemy was Celticism (pronounced with a soft 'C') which was the word coined for Irishism, which was now seen as a dangerous wave of anti-British nationalism breaking on Scottish shores. Anything Celtic was automatically unpatriotic.

In February 1887, Edinburgh Hibernian came through to Glasgow and, to the surprise of the nascent football world in Scotland and the great delight of the Catholic fraternity, they beat the favourites, Dumbarton, in the final of the Scottish Cup. There was an after-match celebration in St Mary's Hall hosted by the Glasgow parish during which the Edinburgh team and officials were fêted. In an emotional speech afterwards, their match secretary, John McFadden, called on his Glasgow cousins to follow Edinburgh's example and start a football club for Irish Catholics in the city as Hibernian had done in 1875. At the same time, he stressed, it would put some much-needed money into the local Catholic community through paid admission to arranged matches. This call did not fall on deaf ears.

In the audience was Andrew Kerins, aka Brother Walfrid, a teaching Marist at St Mary's, and a Sligo man, born there in 1840. He was headmaster of the new school in the Sacred Heart parish in Bridgeton and had been appalled at the deprivation of Catholics, especially among children in his area, and was always looking for some means of amelioration. He had noticed in Bridgeton the activities of some zealots of the Protestant establishment who, as good Christians, provided soup kitchens for the Catholic hungry. They, however, could only avail themselves of this nourishment by renouncing their Celticism and that meant Romanism to non-Catholic eyes. Some pour souls were so desperate that they swallowed their pride with the hot soup. 'Taking the soup' became the saying in the East End.

19

However, bearing in mind the Hibernian's success, Walfrid also realised that the new football team might be a focus for the young men of the parishes and give them a Catholic bulwark against this kind of soft oppression and the more usual hard antagonism Catholics then experienced in Glasgow. This was a very real problem for Catholic youth in Victorian times. They needed a focus of identity greater than an Irish name or red hair and freckles. A football club would also serve as a cultural rallying point for their energies. Thousands of these underprivileged citizens of Irish birth or blood were beginning to feel beleaguered in their own city, under siege behind the walls of the faith they had been born with. They needed to feel proud again about their heritage. All it needed was Edinburgh's challenging example to set the Glasgow wheels in action. Suddenly, a football team seemed to be the answer.

Several meetings were held in the area, culminating in one held in St Mary's Hall on Sunday, 6 November 1887 at which the Celtic Football Club was officially formed for the ostensible purpose of feeding the poor children of the East End. It did not stipulate that only Catholic children need apply. However, its original intentions could not have been more specific, as was made clear in a circular distributed early in 1888:

> The main object of the club is to supply the East End conferences of the St Vincent de Paul Society with funds for the maintenance of the 'dinner tables' of our needy children in the missions of St Mary's, the Sacred Heart and St Michael's. Many cases of sheer poverty are left unaided through lack of means. It is therefore with this object we have set afloat the 'Celtic'.

Three weeks later, the *Scottish Umpire* of 29 November announced Celtic's *official* foundation as of 6 November 1887 (as opposed to 1888, the date of their first match):

> We learn that the efforts which have lately been made to organise in Glasgow a first-class football club have been successfully consummated by the formation of the 'Glasgow Football and Athletic Club' under influential auspices. They have secured a ground in the east end and which they mean to put in fine order. We wish the Celts all success.

The first intention of the men of St Mary's was to form the Glasgow Hibernians, a natural enough name for an Irish club, but it was Brother Walfrid who suggested 'Celtic' (with a soft 'C') as an alternative. In this way, perhaps, the club could also embrace the Celts (with a hard 'C'), that all-embracing mother-strain that, according to the Declaration of Arbroath of 1320, included everybody from Ethiopians, Moors, Catalans, Bretons, Cornishmen and the Welsh before becoming Irish and later the premier Scots of Dalriada.

This is highly fanciful no doubt, but what is true about the Celtic Football Club adjacent to Dalriada Street was that from the very beginning, they were practical in a very Scottish way. While proudly acknowledging their Irish, and therefore Catholic, roots they refused to limit their choice of players to Irishmen or Catholics. This was a wise and far-reaching decision, and they acted on it at once by going through to Edinburgh and robbing Hibernian of their best players. This was not quite what the Edinburgh Irishmen had intended when they called on their Glasgow counterparts to follow their example and a very robust exchange took place between the two branches of the family. As in many families, this led to bad blood but the plundering Glaswegians were not to be denied. Celtic were professional from the kick-off.

Driven by John Glass, subscriptions were raised from all quarters, and every Irish labourer, none of whom could offer a penny to the cause, gave thousands of free hours of muscle and sweat into levelling ground and upgrading the playing field just off Dalmarnock Street (now Springfield Road) which led down from Parkhead Cross to London Road. The work continued, weather permitting, throughout the winter and was finished by May Day 1888. Their first competitive game was set for Monday, 28 May against Rangers. So, in white shirts with green collars the infant Celtic toddled on to that original Celtic Park before 2,000 paying spectators, a large crowd for those times, each player sporting over his heart a Celtic cross in red and green. There was no doubt where these 'bhoys' were coming from.

This fact has rankled with some Scots ever since – even expatriate Scots. One such, a certain Billy Bulloch, now living in Canada, wrote to the letter page of the *Scottish Banner* in March 2005, protesting at the inclusion of Celtic football books and videos in the paper's advertising section, saying:

> [The *Banner*] is a Scots newspaper for Scottish people . . .
> Celtic Football Club is Irish, Irish owned, Irish founded, Irish
> managed, fly Irish flags, Irish crest, Irish colours, Irish turf on
> their centre circle, and let's be honest, half the support is Irish,
> so let's have a Scottish *Banner* for Scots to enjoy.

This attitude to Celtic's ethnic dichotomy is something that Celtic,
and Jimmy McGrory throughout his sporting life, have had to deal
with; but what we have to bear in mind is that the development of
Celtic was essential to the development of the young McGrory. Each
is inextricably intertwined in a mutual narrative and one cannot
discuss one without the other, as will be seen as his life story unfolds.
Whatever his roots, Jimmy McGrory was a proud Scot who learned
his football in Scotland, played his football in Scotland, and never left
Scotland. And some of his best friends in football played for Rangers.
By the way, after that very first match, won by Celtic 5–2, both teams
adjourned to St Mary's Hall for a cooked supper and a convivial
singsong. Would Mr Bulloch have approved?

ONE

Garngad – the Good and the Bad

> Players have to remember it's more than just a football
> team they're playing for. They're playing for a cause and
> a people.
>
> Tommy Burns, former Celtic player and manager, 2001

On 25 September 1887, Henry McGrory married Catherine Coll, daughter of Hugh Coll and Catherine Whittaker, at St Johnstone, Donegal, in the north of Ireland. In the year before, George Green had married Ann Jane Bradley in Preston, Lancashire, an event that was also to have future bearing on the McGrory story, but for the moment, the north-west of England was a long way away from the north-west of Ireland.

Harry and Kate McGrory had their first child, Hugh, in 1890, by which time things were not good on the family farm, so they did what so many of their generation were forced to do – they took the cheapest way out and, in 1891, they joined what seemed like the rest of rural Ireland in the queue for the cattle boat that would take them to Glasgow. For them, this meant to the Garngad – the 'Garden of God' to Irish eyes, although its Gaelic derivation – *garn* for 'rough ground' and *gad* for 'burn' – seems nearer the mark.

Once there, the McGrorys would squeeze in with relatives or close friends, as others had done, until they found their own corner of the grubby rabbit warren that was the Victorian tenement. In true Bethlehem fashion, Harry had to find his wife and child a room. This

23

would most likely be a single-end, as the one-room apartments were called, hovering high over the back-court wash houses and middens. Here, a young couple would start their family and begin to gather some belongings. Such a room was duly found at 764 Garngadhill, and the next day Harry was out looking for work. Another child was already on the way, so paying work was a matter of some urgency.

As a fit young man, he would do anything that would bring in a crust but first he had to find the Catholic foreman at the Caledonian railway works, or the St Rollox Chemical Works, or the Blochairn steelworks, or even the docks at Partick – wherever he could find the hand into which he could slip the precious, saved half-crown and thus open the door to some kind of regular employment. He was to find that it wasn't easy to be Irish in Glasgow at the turn of the century. La belle époque it was not, but then it hadn't exactly been idyllic in Ireland either.

The nerve centre of any Irish community then was the local chapel – which also served as clothes shop, post office, soup kitchen and, as a last resort, spiritual home for practising Catholics – and many who didn't. All house moves and job changes were guided by intelligence, and occasionally financial help, received from this active source. At this time, Garngad didn't have its own church, although there had been a St Roche Chapel in the area in 1506 and this had given the name to the district. In 1904, the nearest Catholic church for the McGrorys was St Mungo's in Parson Street, just down the road at Townhead. The church stood next to the Marist St Mungo's Academy, which was to serve as the football cradle for so many future Celtic players – but not Jimmy McGrory.

By the time Elizabeth, their first daughter, was born to Kate McGrory, her husband Harry had found a job as a labourer in the local steelworks and the family had moved to a bigger flat at 150 Millburn Street, off Garngadhill. For the next ten years house moves kept pace with babies as new McGrorys came off the family production line with all the efficiency of the factories surrounding them. After Elizabeth came Catherine in 1893, then Mary Josephine in 1895. The family returned to 764 Garngadhill in 1898 where John was born but he died at 13 months in hospital of meningitis – not uncommon among babies in the tenements. Frances arrived in the following year and by the time Henry Junior was born in 1902 they were living at 258 Garngadhill. The next flitting took them to 179 Millburn Street, and it was here that Jimmy was born on Tuesday, 26 April 1904.

According to custom, he was christened soon afterwards, being duly baptised James Edward by Father Sherwood at St Mungo's on 2 May. The birth certificate was registered in 'Dennistoun in the County of Lanarkshire' and it shows that Harry McGrory signed as the father with his mark – a cross. The godparents were the Hilleys (formerly the Healeys), who were good friends and the parents of Hugh and Cornelius Hilley, who were both to be future teammates of the infant McGrory.

Even with their own happy brood crowding the house, the McGrorys had to take in lodgers. One was a relative of Kate's from Ireland, Minnie Colquhoun, and before the growing McGrory children claimed all the beds, there were young Irish labourers like Patrick Boyle, Peter Quinn and John McFadden to fit in at various times. These men all remained friends with the family even after they had moved on, especially John McFadden.

With the McGrory house bursting at the seams, the children, especially the boys, spent as little time as possible inside. There were only so many chairs available round the kitchen range, so that indoors as far as most city children were concerned, in those vanished pre-radio and television days, was where you went to sleep and eat. Otherwise, you stayed out in the street for as long as there was light, which was not very long in the Garngad.

While the girls played with rag dolls or made chalk games on the pavement or skipped with ropes, the boys played football in the street between the lamp-posts. There were no parked cars then, only the occasional cart and horse, so there was always room for a game. It was always football – only football. That is, as long as the local bobby, big John Henderson, didn't show up at the corner when someone's ground-floor window was broken. Many of the neighbours had grandstand views from their windows one storey up and very often a boy would emerge from one of these windows and shin down a drainpipe to join in. You had to be in on the team selection.

This was when the best player in the street stood with the boy whose ball it was and each was given a choice of player from the boys gathered until the group was used up. The better players always went quickly and the two most hopeless cases were always put in goal between the lamp-post and the tenement wall, or between the two piles of jackets and jerseys on the asphalt if a lamp-post wasn't available. If there was anybody left, they were made linesmen or cop-watchers. The smallest boys were tolerated and allowed to scamper after the bigger lads, as long as they didn't get in the way. Without a doubt, this was how Jimmy McGrory was first introduced to football.

The games were endless and uncompromising and generally played with a 'tanner ba' – that is a rubber ball bought for sixpence – a 'tanner' being the colloquial name for the sixpenny coin. The blown-up, leather equivalent was well beyond the reach of Garngad boys. Only properly organised football teams could afford the real thing. As a little boy, Jimmy would have watched his big brother, Hughie, who was much older, play in the street with the big lads. Hughie didn't play much after boyhood. Although he was later to play right-back for St Roch's in the Charity Cup final of 1926 at Cathkin, his appearances were sporadic. There was a Hugh McGrory from Garngad who went on to play for Burnley as a professional, but he wasn't our Hugh McGrory. Harry, though, who was two years older than Jimmy, played really well when young and might have made it in the professional game but he was badly hit by rheumatic fever as a boy and had to give up playing all games. Jimmy always held that Harry was a far better player than he was until he got sick. It was just another part of the Garngad legacy.

As the boys grew older, games were played on a stretch of open space at the top of Garngadhill bounded by Millbank Street and Rosemount Street called the Brickfield, or the Brickies. This was really 'rough ground' in the Gaelic sense but was where all the Garngad boys developed their football skills. For more sophisticated matches they walked north to the Daisy Park where there were real goalposts, and games would go on there as long as there was light. These encounters were fought out as if they were cup finals, as if they were playing for Celtic – as, in fact, many were to do. The Garngad alumni included not only McGrory and his friend Hugh Hilley, but later Jonny Connor, the classy Malcolm 'Calum' MacDonald and wee John Fitzsimons (who also became the Celtic club doctor). Other luminaries who came still later included Joe Baillie and Stevie Chalmers, the 'Lisbon Lion' and Scotland centre-forward, whose father, Davie Chalmers, had played with McGrory at Clydebank. Peter Buchanan of Chelsea was another Garngader who made it to the top and also played for Scotland. Jim Forrest and Alex Willoughby of Rangers were also from the same busy streets.

Just like the Boys' Guild teams from St Roch's and St Anthony's, juvenile sides in the area like the Germiston Star, the Bellevue Hearts or the Townhead Emerald were nurseries for junior teams who, in turn, were stepping stones to the senior ranks. The supply line from the Brickfields was endless. In this way, boys came to the top level as young men having come gradually through the ranks. This graded process was invaluable and by the time the better players turned professional, they were ready.

When rain stopped play, or for any reason they couldn't get on to the street, the boys would split into pairs, or foursomes if there was room, and go under cover in the close-mouths or landings to play 'headers', which was played in two versions. 'Long heidies' was where the ball (now a tennis ball) was thrown up in the air by the player and headed towards the other player in an attempt to get it past him between the walls of the close walls, whilst 'wee heidies' was a pursuit for the soloist when there was no one else to play with. You just bounced the ball against the wall and headed it back until you were tired – or inadvertently headed the wall. Mrs Mamie Gallacher of Balornock is sure that McGrory's later heading skills were honed at these games of headers in the close. She writes:

> I was brought up in the same street as Jimmy McGrory. [He] lived with his aunt, Mrs Elliott, in the same tenement as my own aunt and I remember well watching Jimmy playing 'Headers' on the landing with his nephew, Jimmy Elliott. They played on the stairhead landing between two [doors]. The landing was about 12 to 15 feet in length. One stood at one end and the other at the other end. They played for ages heading a small rubber ball between them.

Mrs Elliott wasn't his aunt but his oldest sister Elizabeth, or Lizzie. Jimmy Elliott was his 'nephew', but not a blood relative, as Lizzie adopted him and his sister. Nevertheless, the two Jimmys were close all their lives and Jimmy Elliott was to be McGrory's best man at his second wedding in 1946. Herman Schoning and Margaret Gruer, the parents of that particular bride, Barbara, would marry in London in 1911 and emigrate to Canada.

The end of the first decade of the new century was also the beginning of a new professional age in football and the start of the first great Celtic phase. The team now drew crowds of 25,000 to Parkhead and Willie Maley, their former player, was devoting more of his time to being Celtic's first full-time secretary-manager rather than to his flourishing business in the Gallowgate as Hatter, Hosier and Glover – which sounds like a half-back line in itself. In 1904, Maley was 36 years old and had given up playing to take full responsibility for team selection, but what he was really doing was creating a lifetime's job for himself.

Backed by directors Kelly and Dunbar, also ex-players, he had discontinued the Celtic policy of buying success through the purchase of experienced names and had slowly developed a whole team of youngsters from junior level. In this way, he was to eventually create the first truly great Celtic team. Even today, their names ring like a nostalgic welkin for an unforgettable epoch in Celtic's rise as a football club. Older Celtic supporters still recite this team like a rosary: Adams; McNair and Dodds; Young, Loney and Hay; Bennett, McMenemy, Quinn, Somers and Hamilton.

Their exploits were sufficient to win six League Championships in a row from 1905 until 1910 – three Scottish Cups, five Glasgow Cups and two Charity Cups – an incredible feat for the times. This then was the team that developed in tandem with the boy McGrory. Up till then, he had never seen Celtic play, but he grew up 'Celtic-minded', as he himself called it. There wasn't a Catholic boy in Glasgow who wasn't. Centre-forward Jimmy Quinn, from Croy, became everyone's hero for his legendary exploits like scoring the first hat-trick in a cup final and, even though young McGrory had never seen him in action, Quinn had the same exuberant, physical approach that McGrory was later to relish. Both enjoyed a Wayne Rooney-like build, not tall but strongly built with thick neck and massive shoulders, slim hips, fast legs, and a tireless stamina. They could run all day and would harass the opposition right up to the final whistle. Not that they couldn't play a bit, too. McGrory at this time played at outside-right for St Roch's School, but, as he said years later, it had always been his ambition 'to wear the famous green and white and lead the attack'.

The great Celtic run coincided with his primary school days at the new St Roch's parish school. This had been established in 1907 alongside the new Catholic church on Garngadhill, only five minutes from the latest McGrory home, now up a close at the corner of Rosemount Street and Garngadhill. The new mission was set up to cater for the expanding Catholic population. This had grown so much that the less pious dubbed the district Nazareth. ('Can there any good thing come out of Nazareth?' John 1:46.)

The ten-year-old McGrory would have known there was a war on by seeing for himself the forest of new wooden coffins that grew up in front of Cowieson's factory at the top of Charles Street ready to be sent to France. And, coming back from the Front, the wounded in

28

their Red Cross ambulances were rushed past the same street on their way to Ruchill Hospital. Ambulances always meant there had been a big battle somewhere. But it wasn't only the soldiers who were casualties. For the first time in history, the civilian population was in danger. Zeppelins, the German cigar-shaped dirigibles, floated over the Channel and dropped bombs on towns and cities as far north as Edinburgh. Garngaders were told to close their blinds at night in case they attracted bombs from these strange, lethal balloons in the sky.

One civilian who died at this time, but not from enemy action, was George Green, the Englishman who brought the carnival wagons to Vinegar Hill in the East End and stayed to give motion pictures to Glasgow. He died at his East End showground in 1915 at the age of 54, but the family had not yet come into the McGrory story, although the house then bought for George's widow, Craigie Hall, a mansion near Bellahouston Park, was one that McGrory was later to know well. Historically speaking, the Scots don't revere the English much, and both distrust the Irish, but now, suddenly, with this new kind of warfare they realised they were all in it together.

This was shown when Zeppelins bombed the English town of Whitby, on the Yorkshire coast, with some loss of life. Parkhead honoured their memory by calling the new street created alongside Parkhead railway station, Whitby Street. This is the station that was later to be called Parkhead Stadium due to its proximity to Celtic Park. Regrettably, the station is no longer in use. Given the new road rearrangements currently planned for that area, it might even come into use again to serve the new Celtic stadium, but it has been filled in and grassed over like so much of old Parkhead. Such is progress.

In 1916, soldiers in uniform were not only seen in the street but on the terracing at football matches – and also on the pitch. One such was Trooper Joe Cassidy, then on leave from the Lovat Scouts (Scottish Horse). Handsome Joe was a crowd-pleaser, and his heading technique pre-dated McGrory by a decade. He was centre-forward when, on Saturday, 15 April 1916, Celtic played two matches in one day. At 3.15 p.m. they beat Raith Rovers at Celtic Park 6–0, then they travelled to Motherwell where, that evening, they won 3–1. Twelve-year-old Jimmy would have read all about it.

Sadly, in the same year, on 21 August, his mother, Kate, died – a victim to her woman's lot in the tenement. Wives were the workhorses of the family, on call all day long to the needs of their husband and children, in conditions that made such unrelenting,

29

hard, physical work almost unendurable. The constant stress gave little time for rest or relaxation, except perhaps on a pew at Mass on a Sunday morning. Small wonder their bodies gave out in their middle years. Medals weren't given to tenement mothers but they had their own kind of valour.

The two older McGrory sisters, who were not yet married, were able to take care of the household and their widower father and things carried on much as before. The younger boys still at home carried on much as usual, with Jimmy giving all his time to playing football anywhere and at any time. With the war still in progress most of Britain's young men were in France being slaughtered mindlessly. One survivor was Hughie McGrory, who had been travelling home on leave from the trenches unaware that Mrs McGrory had died. He arrived at his home expecting his mother to meet him at the door. Instead, he had to be taken to see her grave. He never really recovered from the shock.

Hughie had never been the most outgoing of the brothers but now he retreated even further within himself and became a silent presence in the home. Like so many young men of that era, he had seen horrors at the Front and was glad to have survived, yet the unexpected death of his mother almost broke him. He never married. Much later, when Hughie faced hard times, Jimmy, by that time a big football star, took care of him and his sister and her family at their large flat in Bellgrove Street, Dennistoun. Jimmy, the youngest child, took Hughie's place as the oldest son, and virtual head of the family. He did so without any protest. He would have thought it expected of him.

The November Armistice of 1918 was greeted with relief by a weary country. The two-minute gesture of silence was initiated for the war dead and life tried to get back to normal. People flocked to football matches. The legendary Celtic team of pre-war was a casualty to natural causes and only McNair, Young and McMenemy remained of that elite squad. As if to compensate for the retiral of the immortal Quinn, another terracing God appeared in the fragile person of Patsy Gallacher from Donegal, although Clydebank-reared. He was actually christened 'Gallagher' in the Irish form but the brass nameplate on their tenement flat was mistakenly etched out as 'Gallacher', and rather than pay for a new nameplate, the Gallaghers decided to go with it – which was why Patsy Gallagher became Patsy Gallacher. So be it.

Patsy Gallacher was, arguably, the greatest footballer, in the finest sense of that term, that Celtic ever produced. 'The Mighty Atom', as he was called, became the elusive dynamo of a whole new Celtic team. He was to prove a football mentor to the tyro McGrory in the coming years, but 1918 saw the arrival of another Irishman in his life – one who was no frail figure by any means, but a stout, well-set-up Cork man with a cherubic face and a splendid temper – Father Edward Lawton.

Later a Very Reverend Canon of the Church, and Justice of the Peace in the City of Glasgow, Canon Lawton was aptly titled, for his personality was as explosive as any artillery and he kept it trained on his patch of the Garngad for nearly 20 years. Like every second priest in Glasgow, he was Irish, and it showed in his enjoyment of a fight. He was to hold such sway in the district that his parish became more like his own fiefdom; a militant little kingdom on its own which he ruled, not with a rod of iron, but with a stout shillelagh. He had no hesitation in using it to rouse his congregation to Mass on a Sunday (did he keep it under his vestments?) or to deal with rowdies after closing time on a Saturday night.

Indeed, the police were known to call on him when a gang-fight was brewing and he would come storming out of the Chapel House, eyes blazing, stick held high and wade into the mêlée laying about him on Catholic or Protestant, Billy or Dan, whoever it was who had the temerity to disturb the peace of his mean streets. He dealt with the frequent gang brawls to such effect that the hard men soon gave him a very wide berth and tried to conduct their tribal scuffles well out of reach of that famous blackthorn stick. There was a fight a night at the height of the season (around 12 July every year) when it was said that the No. 21 tram was the only thing that could go into the Garngad and return with its top deck still attached.

What Canon Lawton is most famous for, however, was the founding of the first parish Boys' Guild, which he had originally instituted at St Patrick's, Anderston, in 1914 before going on to serve at Duntocher. He came to St Roch's in 1918 and one of the first things he did was to form a Boys' Guild football team. This is important to our story because the St Roch's Boys' Guild football team was the first organised team the 14-year-old Jimmy McGrory had ever played in.

Interestingly, it was as a Boys' Guild player that he saw Celtic Park for the first time when he played for a Glasgow Boys' Guild Select against an Edinburgh Boys' Guild Select in 1919. Oddly enough, he still didn't own a proper pair of football boots. He played, as he had always played, in his sannies (sandshoes) in summer and in a pair of old working boots during the winter, so a borrowed pair of football boots was quickly found for him. They were far too big, and he did not shine on that occasion – his first ever game at Celtic Park. As he said, 'I didn't exactly set Parkhead on fire.' What he did though was to ignite a small spark and, although he didn't know it, Celtic had him watched from then on.

Two years later, on 7 June 1921, he was again at Celtic Park before a crowd of 4,000 in the Inter-Parish Cup final. This time he had his own boots. You can be sure that the same Father Lawton would have made certain that young Jimmy would have his own boots by this time – size six. No doubt a special collection would have been taken up one Sunday at St Roch's. The boots must have fitted because young James, playing at inside-left, scored a goal in St Roch's 2–0 victory over St Michael's, Parkhead. The Celtic interest in McGrory grew.

Meantime, in 1921, Herman Schoning had died in Canada and Mrs Schoning decided to bring her children, Barbara and her sister and two brothers, back to Britain. They settled in Braemar in Aberdeenshire and young Barbara went to the local primary school just when Jimmy McGrory had left school and was looking for a job.

The only one who made him an offer was Father Lawton and that was to become hamper-boy for his newly formed St Roch's junior football team, made up of the best of his old Boys' Guild players. At the end of its first season, the 16-year-old hamper-boy got only the occasional game at outside-right. He didn't really mind where he played, just as long as he got a game.

St Roch's Juniors had a remarkable start as a junior club. They had some fine local players. At the end of the first season, their captain, and the scorer of their first goal, John Carragher, signed for Bury and began a long career in football that took him to Southampton and then to Norwich City. Carragher's sister, Maggie, kept the fruit shop at 45 Rosemount Street, so the family were well known to the McGrorys. Bury also asked Jimmy to play a trial for them, no doubt recommended by Carragher, but he was probably too young to take it all in. Remember, that train trip south would have been his first ever journey out of Glasgow, his first time away from the Garngad, so it would have been pretty traumatic. He had never been in an English house or heard English voices. There were few of them ever heard in Garngad. So he didn't sign for Bury, nor did he for Dumbarton, for whom he also played a trial. It was then, in his second season with St Roch's, that Celtic made their first move for him. In an interview given to the *Celtic View* on 10 September 1969, Jimmy remembered:

> One day while I was watching a match at Garngad the parish priest called me aside and said someone was waiting to see me at the chapel house. When I got there I found that Celtic wanted me to sign provisional forms. I forgot all about my reservations. I signed on the spot and I didn't even ask what the wages were.

They were £2 a week on the provisional form, which was more than his father earned in the steelworks. The 'reservations' he mentioned were due to the fact that he was then considered as an inside-right and Celtic already had an inside-right – a certain Patsy Gallacher – and even his understudy was a great player, Johnny McKay, who later went on to Blackburn Rovers. McGrory thought McKay '*nearly as good as Patsy*'. The centre-forward position was also out as Joe Cassidy, not long back from the battlefields with a military medal for bravery, was also everyone's hero on the football field, having scored *twelve* goals in a Celtic reserve match. McGrory wondered:

> What possible chance did an unknown youngster have of wearing the coveted green-and-white jersey with giants like these around? But, believe me, when I *was* asked to sign – the fee was £20, the same as it is today [1969] – I jumped at the chance . . . once I had got over my surprise. All the same, I didn't tell my family for several weeks. I knew they would give me a roasting for my 'cheek'. And they did.

There was no chance of his getting too big for his size six boots but there is no doubt that his signing-on fee must have landed like an Irish sweepstake win on the McGrory table. If anything was roasted that night it was the fatted calf. Fortunately, signing for Celtic was never really a matter of any considered decision on his part – he was meant for Celtic from birth. He had signed on provisional forms for £2 a week, which, for a boy who could only earn 18 shillings as a tea-boy in the Blochairn steelworks, was a distinct improvement. In the post-Great War world, working-class boys had to take what they could get, and Jimmy McGrory knew he was lucky to get Celtic.

They were just as lucky to get him, for other teams had begun to show interest. Third Lanark was one and even Rangers made an enquiry for him. It seems that their scout, a Mr Young ('an awful nice man', McGrory remembered), had asked if Jimmy would meet him on the corner after the game but when Jimmy made it clear that he had provisionally signed for Celtic, Mr Young, according to an *Evening Times* article of 2 December 1976, merely said – 'Ah well, just run on, son. We'll no' be botherin' ye.' Funnily enough, McGrory's St Roch's teammate, Rollo, who was also wanted by Celtic, signed for Rangers. So Mr Young's time wasn't entirely wasted.

Meantime, Jimmy was still playing for St Roch's, who were enjoying a good run with three trophies already won – the *Evening Citizen* Cup, the Victory Cup, and something called the Consolation Cup. Now, at the end of their second season, they had won the League Championship and faced the Buffs, otherwise known as Kilwinning Rangers, in the final of the Scottish Junior Cup at Firhill Park, Maryhill, the home of Partick Thistle, on 20 May 1922. They won 2–1 because, as 'Waverley' in the *Daily Record and Mail* noted, St Roch's 'were the slightly better combined and more methodical lot . . . every man jack of them pulled their weight'. The St Roch's team that day was: Steel; Clark and Brodie; Mooney, Swan and Stafford; Milne, McGrory, Barton, Rollo and Hilley. This Hilley was Cornelius, or Con, a brother of Hugh, who had gone on to St Anthony's Juniors and went from there to Celtic. Con later played for Raith Rovers and Third Lanark among others and ended up with Derry City in Ireland.

It was Con Hilley who crossed for McGrory to head the winner and give St Roch's the Blue Riband of Scottish junior football in only the third year of their existence. Celebrations in the dressing-room were suddenly cut short by Father Lawton's announcement that the cup was being withheld because Kilwinning had protested to the SFA that St Roch's had fielded an ineligible player, Miller, at left-back. He had been signed only on the Tuesday before but the letter informing the SFA of his registration hadn't reached their offices till the Thursday – a day late according to the rules. On 26 May, the appeal was upheld 'by a big majority'.

St Roch's wanted to appeal against the appeal but the boys themselves were sure that if they could beat Kilwinning once, they could beat them twice. This Irish logic finally convinced Father Lawton, who accepted the SFA ruling 'under protest'. In the meantime, the problem was how to placate the St Roch's supporters who had thought their team had won the Cup, but Father Lawton was on to that in his typical, unswerving way. He jumped in a taxi and hurried to the presbytery, where he retrieved the Inter-Parish Cup, won by his Boys' Guild team in the previous year. Returning in the taxi with the cup, he had the team show it off from the supporters' brake as it toured through Garngad that evening. To the cheering parish, one cup was much the same as another and honour was saved. If it was by a lie, then it was a green-and-white one – and if a sin in the technical sense, it was only the venial one of substitution. Father Lawton was quite unrepentant about the deception. In his eyes, the greater good was done to the greater number. Nobody argued. No one ever argued with Father Lawton.

The only problem now was that St Roch's had to win the replay, which was fixed for 3 June 1922, again at Firhill. Fortunately they did – and by the same score, 2–1. So justice was done and Father Lawton survived what might have been a tricky ecclesiastical situation. The game itself, watched by a party of Celtic players just back from a Continental tour, was a near thing. Kilwinning scored first through McLean after half an hour but only minutes later, McGrory, described by 'Waverley' as 'the best forward afield', equalised. This sparked a second-half revival by St Roch's, which resulted in wave after wave of attacks ending with Rollo netting the winner. Father Lawton had been vindicated and a lot of blushes had been spared around Millburn Street.

A week later, on 10 June 1922, they were playing in another final, this time at Cathkin, where they met Cambuslang Rangers in the Glasgow Junior Charity Cup. The Rangers won 1–0 and held out thanks to their goalkeeper, Brotherston, who was brilliant yet was never heard of again. However, 'Man in the Know' in his Celtic page in the *Glasgow Observer*, headed his column:

CELTS OF THE FUTURE:
Celtic got busy at the conclusion of last Saturday's Junior Charity Cup Final at Cathkin and signed Jas [*sic*] McGrory, the clever and penetrative inside-right of St Roch's. The Garngad team has bulked largely in the public eye. Practically, they have been playing a match daily and so we have seen a great deal of their players. Well, the more one saw of McGrory the better one liked him. He has all the attributes which go to the making of the typical player – personal cleverness, a gift for combination and fine shooting power. The newest and youngest of the many Celtic Macs scored

> some fine goals for St Roch's in recent critical ties. He 'makes'
> the game for his mates in the McMenemy manner, but when
> occasion arises he can go through on his own like a veritable
> Gallagher [*sic*] . . .

Word had obviously got out that wee James was a hot property and
the football scouts were gathering. Fulham were only one of several
clubs on the trail and Third Lanark were still interested, but Celtic
then made their move. It was an important event for both parties, as
events were to prove, but it was certainly a red-letter day for Jimmy
McGrory when he finally got his call-up to Celtic Park. More than
fifty years later, McGrory told Gerald McNee how it all happened:

> Near the end of the season, we were playing against
> Cambuslang Rangers at Millburn Park, Garngad, and I hurt
> my knee. After the match, I was visited in the dressing-room
> by the Celtic director, Mr James Kelly and Mr Willie Maley,
> the manager. After asking about the injury, they told me to
> report to Celtic Park – if I was fit. If I was fit? If necessary, I
> would have crawled the whole way. I reported all right. And
> thus I became a fully fledged Celt.

Jimmy, in this recollection, may have confused Millburn Park with
Cathkin Park, for there is no question his career-making day was
Saturday, 10 June 1922, when, in the Third Lanark pavilion, he
signed a full professional contract for Celtic for £5 a week. He didn't
know it then but he had also signed away the rest of his life.

TWO

The Green Road to Glasgow

> As late as 1948, at Sarah Keenan's shop in Garngad Road,
> you could buy 2 lbs of soda crystals, a ball of steel wool,
> black lead, two cakes of pipe clay, a bar of McGowan's
> toffee and half-an-ounce of Gallahar's Irish snuff – all for
> less than half-a-crown. I got to keep the change.
>
> Alfred Forbes Smith, the Garngad poet, 1997

In the summer of 2004, your writer stood on what was left of Millburn Street in the Royston area that used to be Garngad and read the notice on the big board overlooking what was once the Brickfields. It said, in large painted letters:

ROYSTON HILL TRAFFIC CALMING PROJECT
A Strathclyde–European Partnership
by the European Community
European Regional Development Fund
A Western Scotland Objective 1997–99

It was a daunting proclamation by any standards and its triumphant officialese spoke of how a brave new world is intended for an area that still looks derelict despite some forlorn landscaping and the new-town bloodlessness of it all. Here once breathed a living, tumbling community out on the streets with each other, leaning out of windows to chat, falling out of doorways to play, and staggering out

37

of pubs to fight – or be sick. Now at the height of the day there was hardly a person to be seen. There was a Sabbath silence hanging over the spick and span Lego brick houses to my right, where one man was washing his car watched by his dog.

It was hard to believe that Millburn Park had once stood here and that people had crowded in to watch St Roch's in their heyday. It was here, too, on this very patch of ground that 'the shows' came every summer. It was the pre-cinema entertainment for the ordinary man and woman in the city; fairground amusements that were as old as cities themselves. By the time of McGrory's youth, the shows hadn't changed all that much. He was only one of the many growing up in the old Garngad who remembered the lights and the noise at the Brickies when the shows came there, and remembered them well. They even got to know the tanned faces of people in the exotic caravans who presented their shows around the country. The Brickies in the Garngad was just another of their annual dates. It was always the same travelling families. Typical of these were the Greens with their sideshows and amusements. The Greens were to make their permanent home in Glasgow and become an important part of the future McGrory story. The difference was that these Greens weren't Scots or Irish, but English – and old Catholic English at that.

The family came from Lancashire. George Green, born in Preston in 1861, was apprenticed to a watchmaker, but when his cabinet-maker father came into the possession of a travelling fairground carousel in payment of a bad debt, George decided to take it over. He soon built it up into a series of travelling shows which he got on the road just when Celtic were getting started in Glasgow. By the time the football club was established in the East End of the city, George had married Ann Jane Bradley from Preston. They already had a young family when they, too, came to the East End of Glasgow during 1893, and pitched camp at Vinegar Hill near the old Gallowgate Barracks.

From here, the crowds now flocking to the new Celtic Park could be heard cheering on their hero of that time, Dan Doyle, the full-back with the 'Greek God' good looks. The original Celtic Park was adjacent to Barr's Mineral Water Works who made Scotland's other national drink, Irn-Bru ('Made from Girders'). Coincidentally, George Green also dabbled in mineral waters himself for a time. It was one of his diversions while resting from the road. Indeed, when his daughter, Veronica, was born at the showground on 15 March

1899, her birth certificate gave her father's profession as 'Mineral Water Manufacturer'.

His next project, however, was to prove more rewarding and it was this that helped lay the base for the family's ultimate good fortune. Not that the Greens were exactly penniless. There was no taking in of pots and pans to mend or the selling of home-made clothes pegs. They were by no means tinkers. They were aristocrats of the road with wagons that were like land-bound yachts inside, with wonderful woodwork and shining brass. He wasn't the son of a master cabinet-maker for nothing. By working hard and long and travelling far they had made a good living from 'the shows' and their adventurous attitude to living reflected this. George was always on the lookout for novelties that would attract customers and for this reason he kept his eyes on passing fads and fashions.

Roller-skating had been all the rage but now the very latest sensation was Thomas Edison's North American cinematograph for the showing of silent moving pictures. This was no more than a rudimentary flicker but it was enough to intrigue audiences into parting with good money in order to watch it. The projector itself was further developed in London by William Friese-Green and in 1896 George Green went there to find out what this newfangled cinema business was all about. He bought a film projector from Friese-Green himself and, returning to Glasgow, he showed the first moving pictures in a special mobile cinematographic booth he had commissioned to be built on the winter rest site at Vinegar Hill. Measuring approximately 50 feet by 50 feet, 'The Theatre Unique', as Green called his new attraction, was soon packing in 500 customers a time to see the brief 'flicks' (because they flickered) at a penny a head.

By this time, another son, Joseph Leo, had been born in the Gallowgate but nothing more was heard of him, so it is assumed that he died early. Since George Frederick (Fred), the next son, was born in Selby, Yorkshire, the family was obviously still on the move. His father, however, moved back to the Gallowgate permanently, devoting his time and his even more considerable energies into promoting the new 'movies', so called because they moved. In 1901, now well settled in Glasgow, yet another son, Herbert Joseph (Bert) was added to the growing family, but by then the proud father was making more than £20 a day from his Gallowgate cinema booth. By Edwardian standards, the Greens were really 'in the money'.

Meanwhile, the regular arrival of Green offspring continued with four daughters in succession: Mary Frances, Margaret Doris, Veronica Josephine and Marion Gertrude, making it eleven children in all – a Green team indeed. There was no doubting George Green's extraordinary vitality, or Ann Jane's equivalent stamina. A large family was not uncommon in the age they lived in. In the main, it was due to economic necessity as much as any natural biological inclination. It was also an attempt to counterbalance the incidence of infant deaths in the big cities. So far, all the Greens were alive and well and living in Glasgow – and it would be one of the Green girls, Veronica (Nona), who would, in due course, provide a further link in the McGrory chain of events.

In 1908, George made another big decision and left the road. He sold off his many travelling shows, keeping only the splendid domestic wagons as living quarters and began to adapt a more permanent building for his picture screenings. This became the first 'cinema' in Dennistoun, the rather upmarket East End purlieu, south-west of Garngad. The new premises were in an old 1,000-seater theatre in Whitevale Street, so he called it the Whitevale Moving Picture House. By coincidence, Helen Maley, Willie Maley's wife since 1896, lived for a time at 38 Whitevale Street with her two sons, Charlie and William Junior – which was slightly odd, as their father elected to live in Partick, a longish tramcar-ride away to the west. If the Maleys' domestic situation was eccentric, the same could not be said about George Green. Just as his family continued to burgeon happily, so his family business went from strength to strength.

He now initiated what he called the Picturedrome, created from the shells of the old skating rinks expressly for the showing of moving pictures. The finished buildings were deliberately made extraordinary and over the years they were to grow even more so, with towers and canopies and pillars and anything else that would attract attention. These places were extremely colourful and comfortable within, boasting electric lights, thick carpets, padded seats and art nouveau decor. It was the height of luxury for many Glaswegians and a real escapist experience. The first of ten of these 'picturedromes' or 'cinemas', as they came to be called, was built in the Gorbals but soon there were to be 24 of them set up around Glasgow and before long the Greens were confirmed as magnates of a new entertainment enterprise.

On their father's death in 1915, his sons Fred and Bert had quickly moved in to take over and it was they, with the help of their mother and four young sisters, who, at the peak of exciting cinema expansion, laid the seeds of the later Green cinema empire in Glasgow and its extension into Europe. Being a big man, Fred thought big. In 1917, he sensed the need for news from the war fronts and founded the Scottish Moving Picture Newsreel, which flourished until 1922 when it became the British Moving Picture News with offices in Glasgow and London. They also operated Green's Film Service, which not only built cinemas but also sold every kind of film equipment needed to run them. As a result, they were recognised as Scotland's most successful film proprietors and renters and ready to go as far as they dare to stay in the forefront. By this time, Fred was in his prime, in his mid-30s and married to an Englishwoman, 'Bunchy' Paterson. They had no children. His young sister, Veronica Josephine, was by now a mature young lady of 23 and unmarried.

Jimmy McGrory was 18 years old in 1922 and not at all mature. Since Celtic did not have a reserve team, he still continued to play for St Roch's, while trying to get used to the idea of being a professional footballer. Models he had to aspire to in 1922–23 were Charlie Buchan of Arsenal and John White of Hearts, who each got 30 goals in that season. Jimmy's total for his inaugural year with Celtic was a princely *one*. Admittedly, his first game with the senior team, at inside-right, wasn't until 20 January 1923 but even then it was in a 1–0 League defeat by Third Lanark at Cathkin. The Celtic team on that wet debut day for our hero was Shaw; Hilley and W. McStay; Gilchrist, Cringan and J. McStay; McAtee, McGrory, Cassidy, McInally and McLean. Late in the game, he was switched with centre-forward Joe Cassidy, but with little effect and Celtic ended scoreless. The first newspaper reports didn't flatter the new boy. Even the very pro-Celtic *Glasgow Observer*, out every Saturday with a page of Celtic news and views, said in its issue of 27 January 1923:

> He is a squat, sturdy, pushful youth, but like his colleagues, who wanted to make the ball do things, he found the treacherous, tricky surface a handicap, and was a trifle slow in executing his manoeuvres, a fatal defect against League defenders who adopt the almost universal style of tackling which threatens to demolish the foolish youth who waits for the arrival of the thunderbolt . . . McGrory showed much dash and not a little cleverness but he mixed the two badly. Experience will no doubt teach him that a little more finesse goes a long way in first-class football.

He played in the next three games, a Scottish Cup tie against Hurlford United, a goalless draw in a League game against Hibs at Parkhead and another League fixture game with Kilmarnock at Rugby Park on 3 February in which Celtic again lost (4–3), but at least this match was notable for McGrory's first ever goal for the club. This was described in detail by 'Quarrybrae' in the following Monday's *Daily Record and Mail*:

> After McGrory had failed to turn in a smart cross from Connolly, McAtee got going. He middled a fine ball. McLean was in two minds what to do with it, but by a tricky touch, he put McGrory in possession, who whipped the ball first-time into the net.

It was the first of the 522 League and Cup goals for Celtic in the 501 matches over the 15 seasons that lay ahead of him. They would all bear the mark of the very first encounter, that is, being alert to a sudden opportunity close in, such as a rebound, a deflected shot from a colleague or a sudden flick that put the ball in his path. It showed he already had the instincts of the natural striker; that is, of being on the spot for the least chance. Alan Shearer of Newcastle is possibly the only modern player who resembles McGrory in this aspect of the centre-forward game.

The *Glasgow Observer* issue for 23 February commented: 'McGrory improved on his Cathkin work. He is quite a paying proposition.' It should be noted, however, that he was playing in a struggling team, and, as he had foreseen himself, Patsy Gallacher's shoes were hard to fill. The famous Celtic goalmouth, once dubbed the 'Holy City' because of its invulnerability, was now proving very vulnerable and the rest of the team was suffering. Eight games in a row without a win, and third place in the League was not the usual Celtic pattern. Changes had to be made and one of the first was that young McGrory was transferred to the less-demanding Clydebank for a spell.

This practice of farming out young players was common, especially as Celtic, who, to their shame, had no reserve team at that time, ostensibly because of a sufficient pool of first-team players, but really it was because of the extra cost. It was not to be the last instance of short-sighted economies on their part. McGrory accepted the decision with his usual phlegmatism, assuming his superiors knew best and so, on 7 August 1923, he was transferred to

Clydebank for the season then starting. What he was not so phlegmatic about, presumably, although he said nothing, of course, was that his weekly wage of £5 was cut to £4, which was all the Clydebank directors could afford. He was never to rise all that much above this modest figure, for he never earned more than £8 as his basic wage for the rest of his 14 playing seasons with Celtic.

One must bear in mind that Jimmy was brought up at a time when a working man with a family was lucky if he brought back £1 for a six-day week. Wives and children had usually to find some kind of paying work to make ends meet. As a consequence, their standard of living was basic and their diet meagre to say the least. Small wonder that sickness was rife. For a young man to be offered £5 to kick a ball about was to offer him a fortune and a way out of the working-class treadmill. The other alternatives were boxing or crime, which, in many ways, were much the same thing. Football was a happy option.

Jimmy McGrory always considered he was lucky to be paid to play and this determined his basic attitude to professional football. Willie Maley said of him at this time: 'I wasn't struck so much by his ball play as by his adaptability, his versatility, and by his tremendous enthusiasm and virility.' Nevertheless, he farmed him out to Clydebank. Jimmy might have been relieved to go. Celtic weren't having a good run in those early '20s. To Maley, it seemed that the spirit had gone out of the side, and he was finding it hard to make the transition from the great side of before the war to this uncertain team of after it. A kind of lassitude settled on the players, as if just being in the Celtic team was enough. Yet there couldn't have been much wrong with a team that included Patsy Gallacher, although there was no denying they weren't getting the results. On 4 November 1922, the *Glasgow Observer*'s man commented on an 'Old Firm' encounter, won 3–1 by Rangers at Parkhead:

> I have to report that for a Rangers v. Celtic meeting, it was very quiet – almost dull. There was a slight ripple when Andy [McAtee] got his nose bled and resented it. But only Hilley and Gallacher could show the 'pep' that inspired every mother's son of the Ibrox band. An old Celtic supporter in my vicinity declared it was the worst Celtic team he had ever seen take the field against Rangers.

Johnny McKay had been transferred to Blackburn Rovers, a great mistake as many thought, and his later cap for Scotland proved. His place at inside-right in the new season was taken by another St Anthony product, Jim Cairney (no relation). He had a run at inside-left, but was freed at the end of the season and went off to play for the Boston Irish where he impressed their manager, the ex-Ranger, Tommy Muirhead. Many young boys came and went at Celtic Park and the better ones had to bide their time. That time would come, but not yet. Meanwhile, if it weren't exactly a black period for Celtic, it was decidedly grey.

Yet such are the ways of football that the same squad went on to win their tenth Scottish Cup in 1923 by beating a Hibernian side managed by Willie Maley's young brother, Alec. It was a dull, defensive final with 80,000 bored spectators watching the Hampden grass grow. The game was decided by the Hibernian goalkeeper's error. Harper, a Scottish international, completely missed a simple downfield punt from Celtic's McFarlane and Joe Cassidy nodded the ball into the empty net. The win didn't improve things at Celtic Park and the next season was even worse. There were squabbles in the dressing-room, arguments with the directors and mediocrity on the field. Jimmy McGrory wasn't missing much.

Even though he was playing for Clydebank, he still trained at Celtic Park, walking most mornings with his pal, Hughie Hilley from Garngad. They would come down from Garngadhill, across the old canal bridge into Alexandra Parade and down through Dennistoun to Duke Street and from there down to the Gallowgate and along to Camlachie, past the showground at Vinegar Hill and along past the wall of Janefield Cemetery to 'Paradise'. During this daily peregrination, many of Garngad's unemployed stood with their hands open for a coin, especially when young Jimmy McGrory was passing. Hugh Hilley confirmed that Jimmy never refused to give a handout, however small. So much so that his big sister, Lizzie, checked his pocket every morning and removed the shillings, florins and half-crowns in case he gave them away too. She knew, as he did, that a poor man would just as much appreciate a penny or two but sixpence counted as a grand gesture. So Jimmy McGrory had his following right from the start of his career, and most of them stood at street corners.

One man came out of his close every day just to bow to Jimmy as he passed. He never said anything or asked for a handout – just a silent bow as he passed. Jimmy found it very embarrassing. He didn't think he had done anything yet to deserve such a show of admiration. But then he was never to understand the hold he had on the ordinary punter. As he grew in the game and his fame spread, the begging got so bad that he was forced to go by tram, and later by motor car. Even then the crowd would be waiting for him at the pavilion door. This is the real price of fame, but he didn't think of it as all that much to pay and if it helped some poor soul, in his eyes, it was money well spent.

The old Clydebank club was managed by former Celtic stalwart, Jimmy 'Dun' Hay. They were currently bottom of the Scottish League and not very hopeful about travelling north to meet Aberdeen in McGrory's first match for the Bankies in August 1923. Their hopes were justified but at least McGrory got their only goal in a 3–1 defeat. He also got his first hat-trick in a cup tie against Blairgowrie. He became such a favourite at Clydebank's Clydeholm Park in Yoker that Jimmy Hay expressed himself 'highly pleased with his capture' and the Clydebank chairman was heard to remark, 'I hope Celtic forget all about this laddie.'

It was Hay's idea on 29 September that year to field him at centre-forward at Motherwell. Clydebank lost 3–2, but at least McGrory got their two goals – his first from the centre-forward position. McGrory was to go on and score sixteen goals in thirty League and three Scottish Cup appearances for the Bankies, which was a good rate indeed for a youngster. But the trouble was, he couldn't forget about Celtic. Sooner or later he knew he would have to face his parent club in competition. It came about after bad weather had postponed the first date, and he lined up at Celtic Park on the first Saturday of March 1924 to play, this time at outside-left, *against* Celtic.

He had spent a miserable few days at training the week before, taking a lot of stick from the senior Celtic players and dreading that he might be lined up directly against 'The Icicle' – Alec McNair. McNair had earned this sobriquet because of his cool manner of play and his poise under any conditions. Even though he was in the veteran stage, he was still a classy player and McGrory was reluctant to pit his wits against the wily full-back. Fortunately, McNair was unable to play because of injury and John Grainger, not long signed from Vale of Leven, was to take his place. McGrory was highly relieved and took the field determined to show his old manager, Maley, what an error he had made in off-loading him to Clydebank. Not that he was the only Celtic colt in the Bankies' line-up – goalkeeper Hughes and inside-right McLaughlin were also down to face the club that 'owned' them. McGrory continued the story in an interview given to the *Celtic View* on 10 September 1969:

45

Celtic opened in great style and very soon went ahead through Willie McStay. Near the interval Jimmy [McStay] fouled me in the penalty box and Smith, who later went to Hearts, scored from the spot. Encouraged by this, we held our own until the second half. Then the ball came to me and I thought I saw my chance. I lashed the ball in, but Charlie Shaw got his hand to it and pushed it out. Running in, I seized the rebound, shot – and, to my delight, saw it go into the net. It was the winning goal.

It was the shock result of the day. Clydebank had beaten Celtic at Celtic Park. It was no surprise to anyone when he was recalled by Maley before the season was out. McGrory felt as if he were back where he belonged. He returned just in time to play on the wing against Queen's Park in the Glasgow Charity Cup semi-final on 6 May 1924 and he scored again in a 2–0 win. To his further delight, he was still in the team, although again at outside-left, when they faced Rangers four days later in the final. He was now among the big boys. Look at the quality in these two teams:

Celtic – Shaw; McNair and Hilley; J. McStay, W. McStay and McFarlane; Connolly, Gallacher, Cassidy, Thomson and McGrory

Rangers – Robb; Manderson and McCandless; Meiklejohn, Kirkwood and Muirhead; Archibald, Craig, Henderson, Cairns and Morton

Patsy Gallacher got the Celts off to a good start with a goal which was equalised by Alan Morton soon after, but then Willie McStay scored the winner in the second half. Celtic had the Cup and Jimmy McGrory had his first Celtic medal. It wasn't to be the most prestigious of his medals but it was his first – and none is greater than Charity.

Described by 'Waverley' of the *Daily Record and Mail* as 'a pocket edition of Jimmy Quinn', McGrory had certainly made his mark with the Celtic following. The next season would be his first full campaign in a Celtic jersey. He couldn't wait to get going. He had come a long way from the Brickfields. It might be said that a revival of Celtic's fortunes coincided with McGrory's return. It might only have been coincidence. Then again, it might not.

Similar good fortune was attending the Green brothers – and their sisters. In 1922, they had sent John Fairweather, the cinema architect, to the United States to catch up on the latest trends in cinema styles. In those silent days of Rudolph Valentino in *The Sheikh* and the furore over Howard Carter's discovery of Tutankhamun's tomb at Luxor in 1922, everything Arabic or Egyptian was the fashion, and cinemas reflected this in their architecture and interior decor. The Greens were determined to bring their own kind of Hollywood to Glasgow and they embarked on a building project that would give the city the largest cinema auditorium in Europe, with a dance hall on its roof. Everything in the new Green's Playhouse was to be the biggest and the best, and by careful planning and judicious use of their workforce they were to achieve these aims with style. Bruce Peter, in his *100 Years of Glasgow's Amazing Cinemas*, explained how they did this:

> The brothers were astute businessmen. Whenever possible they used the Greens' own employees to do the building work. Clowns, acrobats and showmen, usually employed elsewhere in the company, were taught plumbing, joinery and bricklaying and set to work. The scheme was so carefully budgeted that, to save on travel costs, the workers walked every day from Green's Gallowgate showground to the Renfield Street site.

George Singleton, himself a noted Glasgow cinema proprietor and owner of the famous Cosmo in Rose Street (now the Glasgow Film Theatre), was to write of the Greens:

> For private individuals to invest so heavily in such a marvellous project, way before the advent of talkies, must have taken great courage indeed. I always admired the Greens for their boldness; their Glasgow Playhouse was a most remarkable theatre.

While the Greens were at work on their temple to film and dance, Willie Maley and his directors were still trying, painstakingly, to build their new Celtic side. Joe Cassidy had been transferred to Bolton Wanderers for £5,000 allowing the vacancy at centre-forward to be filled by McGrory. He did not get off to a good start in the new season, failing to score in the first three games. In the week following the third game, his father died after being accidentally stoned to death as he sat on a park bench near his work during a break. Some boys were throwing stones and one caught Harry McGrory on the temple, causing the cerebral tumour from which he died later in hospital. He was 65 years old.

The funeral was arranged for the Saturday morning and Jimmy had not expected to play against Falkirk that afternoon but Willie Maley came to St Roch's for the Requiem Mass and, taking the bereaved boy aside, suggested that he should perhaps play that day – 'It might take your mind off things,' said the manager, 'for 90 minutes, anyway.' So Jimmy played – and scored his first goal of the season. His touch returned and he had two successive hat-tricks in a row – against Third Lanark in the Glasgow Cup and Motherwell in the League. Inexorably his goal tally rose; then, in early November, he was injured and faced a long lay-off. However, he had made his mark. The *Glasgow Observer* of 20 September 1924 reported:

> So far he has given complete satisfaction, and it begins to look as if Quinn's mantle has at long last fallen on worthy shoulders. McGrory's style is reminiscent of the great Croy man, particularly in the fearless dash with which he bores into the opposing defences.

On 1 November 1924, his cartilage went on one knee and Willie Fleming was brought in from Vale of Leven to deputise, but McGrory was back into the side in time for the Scottish Cup ties and he began again where he left off – with a hat-trick against Third Lanark. He also scored the only goal of the controversial second replay of the quarter-final against St Mirren. Peter Craigmyle was the referee, the same official who had been in charge of the Junior Cup final won by St Roch's at the second attempt three years before. Now, here he was again, once more at the centre of controversy. Jimmy explained to Bill Robertson of the *Glasgow Citizen*:

> Celtic were leading 1–0 – I had scored the goal – and there were only minutes left to play. Suddenly, one of their forwards, Gillies, was brought down on the penalty line. Immediately, the St Mirren players claimed a penalty. Referee Peter Craigmyle walked over to where Gillies had been grassed, knelt down and pointed dramatically at the spot – only inches outside the box. He then rose and awarded a free kick. As the Celtic players lined up for the 'free', the Saints were still clamouring for a penalty. Mr Craigmyle put the ball

on the ground, and waved for one of them to take the kick. Not a player moved. We stood in two lines facing each other, with everyone wondering, what now? The seconds ticked away, and still no Paisley player had made any effort to kick the ball. Finally, when I felt we could stand the tension no longer, the referee looked at his watch and whistled for full-time.

Third time lucky, Celtic were through and into the semi-final against Rangers at Hampden. More than 100,000 turned up to see Celtic win in a 5–0 rout, which surprised them as much as it did Rangers. The young Celtic side seemed to come of age in an afternoon and, responding to Gallacher's astute generalship, they completely demoralised the older Rangers. McGrory got two this time, with Adam McLean getting a double as well and Alec Thomson scoring the other. The scene was now set for the final against Dundee on 11 April 1925, which was to feature one of the greatest goals ever scored – and it wasn't scored by McGrory.

Dundee led 1–0 through Davie McLean (an ex-Celt) and in the second half Celtic pressed hard until *that goal* was scored. Accounts have now passed into legend and, like any good story, extends its credulity with every telling. What would one have given to see this again – and again – on a television repeat. Eugene MacBride supplies a graphic account in the Gallacher entry for his *An Alphabet of the Celts*:

> Celtic are a goal down with 20 minutes to go. [Paddy Connolly flighted a free kick which fell to Patsy Gallacher, who was surrounded by dark-blue Dundee shirts.] He jinked, jouked, hurdled, swerved, dribbled, jumped, fell, got up, ran on, jinked again, stumbled, jouked once more, went over his wilkies with the ball still grasped between his feet and suddenly he was over the line, him and the ball past the astonished Jock Britton, and Hampden to the last 75,000th man was rising in starry-eyed tribute to a genius in bootlaces.

The time given was the 75th minute and Patsy, still with the ball at his feet, lay entangled in the rigging, until his exultant fellow players freed him. They were all laughing, and could hardly believe it. It was the most impudent, outrageous, comical but clever goal ever attempted but it was legal – and it stood – and Celtic were level. Only a genius of a player could have even thought of attempting it and

Patsy Gallacher was, indeed, a genius. Naturally, this sparked Celtic into full action in the last ten minutes and Dundee visibly wilted, yielding a free kick with only three minutes to go. 'Jean' McFarlane sent over a lovely ball and Willie Maley remembered well what happened next, and related it to his readers in the *Weekly News* in 1936:

> McGrory [had] positioned himself with his customary adroitness. He allowed the ball to do the work, allowed it to catch his head at the exact moment. The ball flew spinning off his 'pow', and before the goalkeeper could wink, it was lodged in the far corner of the net. A goal in a thousand.

In fact, McGrory was lying flat on his stomach when he looked up and saw the ball fly past Jock Britton for the winning goal. Maley went on:

> I often think that a cast of McGrory's head should be taken and added to the collection of trophies at Celtic Park. And one day, that idea of mine will become an accomplished fact.

McGrory's goal had won the cup for Celtic but it was almost ignored in the buzz still going on all round the ground about the Gallacher goal. The match would be recalled as 'Gallacher's final' – and become another Celtic myth. The number of players he beat on his way to the net would increase in each telling. Charlie Tully, himself a myth-maker, was to embroider on it outrageously. It was Patsy's last final – and McGrory's first. What a way to start – and what a way to go. It was Gallacher's swansong, but with 30 goals to his name for the season, it was McGrory's overture.

THREE

Pipes and Plus Fours

> When Irish emigrants' children had nothing, the only
> thing they had to anchor themselves here was Celtic.
> Why should they apologise for that – and why should
> Celtic?
>
> Harry McGuigan, writer, 2002

In the late summer of 1925, Jimmy McGrory could have been fairly
described as being happy with his lot. He was 21, and free of any
responsibilities other than trying to score goals in a football match
once or twice a week. He was doing exactly what he wanted to do,
with the people he wanted to do it with, and being paid for it. His
wages were now up to £6 weekly, which was a lot better than being
a can-boy. Much as any American Negro of the age had used his
hands to box his way out of Harlem, Jimmy, as the son of people
Scots had once called, in the phrase of the time, 'white Negroes', had
kicked his way out of the Garngad chasing a football. He had no
complaints.

With his father's death the year before, he had become the main
breadwinner for the family, as his older brothers could not earn
much. Bachelor Hugh, now aged 35, worked as a general labourer.
Like Hughie, Harry, too, lived with Lizzie and moved with her
when she flitted to Dennistoun after their father died. Now 23 and
as yet unmarried, Harry 'kept bad health' as they said up the close,
and only worked sporadically. Jobs were hard to come by and

queues at the 'Broo', the local employment bureau, were long. The other McGrory sisters all married and moved away from the Garngad. Frances, the youngest, set up house at 719 Springfield Road at Springfield Toll when she married Abie Wales, a locomotive fireman from Shettleston, in 1926. Jimmy moved in with them soon after, as it was only a corner kick away from Celtic Park.

Meantime, the lack of regular wages coming into the family made the winning of bonuses a priority for the youngest McGrory. These were hard times for everybody but the young footballer did what he could for his kith and kin. He always would. It was just as well that Jimmy's shoulders were broad – he had to carry quite a load. He dreaded any injury he might get, not only because he didn't enjoy being hurt but also because not playing meant losing bonuses and these contributions were missed by the family. A match bonus could be as much as a pound for a win or ten shillings for a draw, and there were also one-off cash prizes and incentives for winning cup finals. It paid to win as much as possible. Such extra monies could amount, in some seasons, to an extra wage.

Unfortunately, these payments were at manager Maley's discretion, a cause of much contention among the more experienced players, for it seemed to physically hurt Willie Maley to part with money. Dressing-room murmurings were heard. Mr Maley wasn't used to such unrest, but times were changing. A war had happened and much of what had been called the 'lower class' had been wiped out because of the stupidity of what had been called the 'upper class'. Victorian mores had drowned in the mud of Flanders and even Edwardian certainties were more fragile in the face of real civic unrest and a poor economy.

Maley, at 55, was beginning to seem a little old-fashioned in this hard, new world, but he was not going to go down without a fight. The good Celtic years had not been lost on him and he had swapped his clothing shop for a city restaurant. The Bank, as he called it, was at 25/41 Queen Street, Glasgow C1, on the corner with Argyle Street. He ought to have called it the Piggy-Bank, because that's where all his hoarded pennies had gone. He was a man of some substance now, and not one who could be easily ignored. Nor was he easily loved. He was an out-and-out Victorian, and clung to old standards. He relied on proven values like the work ethic and the game for the game's sake – especially for Celtic's sake. To everyone at Parkhead he was the Boss, although behind his back the players called him the

Big Fella (pronounced in the Glasgow manner as one word with the emphasis on Big).

William Patrick Maley had been born in an army barracks in Northern Ireland in 1868, the son of Sergeant O'Malley of the Royal North British Fusiliers at a time when North Britain meant Scotland. Sergeant O'Malley retired to Cathcart in Glasgow with a pension and four sons who called themselves Maley, in keeping with the times. The oldest son, Charles, became a Catholic priest and the other three became football managers – Tom with Manchester City, Alec with Hibernian and Willie, of course, with Celtic. Willie Maley loved the club from the beginning and championed all it stood for. After all, he had grown up with it. As it developed into a power in Scottish football, so did he.

His Celtic pedigree was faultless and he used it unashamedly to impose his total authority on every aspect of the club. Not even the Pope had greater impunity and Maley would be the last to deny that he shared with His Holiness the same infallibility. All the Maleys were devout Roman Catholics and remained so all their lives, which is why Willie adopted his own idiosyncratic lifestyle when his marriage to Helen Pye, a nurse, foundered soon after the birth of their second son in 1900. He could not divorce her, so he maintained two houses for his family – one for his wife and the boys and one for himself.

When he later moved to Hyndland Avenue, Helen flitted with the boys from Whitevale Street in Dennistoun to St James Street South, which wasn't far from Hyndland Avenue. There was never any question of a divorce, just as there was nothing said about their living apart. It was a strange domestic situation for this most punctilious of men, a Catholic manager of a Catholic club who called himself a 'mercantile clerk' and later a 'master draper' but in reality was, to all intents and purposes, a football manager – although that occupation, in the modern sense, had yet to be defined. His domestic arrangements do suggest, however, that all his life-drive went into the continued betterment of the Celtic Football Club. His heart lay with Celtic. He was in love with the club. There was no room in it for anything else, although he never missed Mass.

He tried to impart something of this attitude to his players but, naturally, some of the more worldly and Protestant signings didn't take too kindly to this blatant evangelism. To them, football was a job, a good job in such bad times, but a job none the less. They wanted to be paid for it and not wait for any reward in Heaven. They would like it in the next pay packet. That's as far ahead as any working man can look, whatever his job. Jimmy McGrory could understand both points of view. He shared a lot of his boss's Catholic and Celtic ideals and he well understood the players' working-class priorities. Apart from Patsy Gallacher, and to a lesser extent the brilliant, if erratic, Tommy McInally, Jimmy McGrory could be said to be Maley's favourite player and was referred to warmly by him as 'one of my best boys'.

If McGrory had lost his own father, he had gained another in the person of this demanding de facto manager of Celtic, who was all things to all men in anything to do with the club. To visitors to the ground, he was the genial 'mine host', to his fellow directors he was their anchor and efficient voice to the press and to the players he was a cross between an indulgent nanny and a waspish bully. There were many people who did not like Willie Maley. As the last prominent survivor of the club's founding fathers he was a proud man. James Kelly was a director at a remove and Brother Walfrid, retired since 1906, had died at Dumfries in 1915, so the Big Fella was without rival at Celtic Park. As an athlete he had been a runner, a cyclist, a cricketer and a footballer good enough to have played for Scotland – even though he was, technically, an Irishman. As a big man, he had a lot of weight and he wasn't above throwing it around.

Yet even his worst enemy couldn't deny that whatever he did, he did it for Celtic's good. In 1914 he had even acted as linesman on one occasion, at Paisley. Crowd trouble had broken out after Johnny McMaster of Celtic was ordered off for fighting and some fans invaded the pitch. Maley helped to bundle them back into their places and had his wallet pinched. He never acted as linesman again. His wallet was an important part of the Maley armoury. And yet he could be kind. After Harry McGrory's death he asked Jimmy if he needed any financial assistance – yet it never occurred to him to offer the young player a rise in wages.

Willie Maley was a formidable personality by any yardstick, but he had a soft centre. His large front was a carapace to hide his Irish sentimentality. Like many large men, his essential character was never as strong as his physique. He had come from very little to so much. In many ways it was an admirable rise. With no great formal education or administrative background he trained himself to be an astute football executive and a forceful manager of men. Despite the sentimental streak, he could be tough on his players, especially those who didn't hold his conservative views. He was especially hard on the 'personality' players and generally they didn't last long at Parkhead. To put it bluntly, he was often little more than an egocentric dictator, even though he would have thought it a benevolent despotism.

However, he interests us here as the man who made Jimmy McGrory. Maley had already expressed his admiration for the three qualities that young McGrory possessed – 'versatility and virility but most of all, enthusiasm. And on these three qualities I resolved to bank,' he said:

> His heart was ours before he himself was offered a peg in our dressing-room. We were sure of him right from the time he was a boy. We have had more skilled men in our ranks, more of greater subtlety, but none, apart from Gallagher, was endowed so superbly with the spirit that makes much of little and generates the will to win than Jimmy McGrory.

He made a great start to the 1926–27 season, twice scoring four and twice scoring five, and by the New Year he had almost passed his previous season's League tally of thirty-five which was double seventeen total of 17 for the season before that. He was obviously improving and his contribution did much to help Celtic towards their 17th Championship at the end of that season, although he was in the losing side to St Mirren in the Scottish Cup final of 1926.

It was also the year of the General Strike, from 3 to 12 May, although the miners held on for another six months. The workers' action divided the nation. Attendances suffered, especially in away games, as supporters' money grew scarce. Celtic opened an Unemployment Gate at reduced prices but for the most part, the supporters hung around the ground till after half-time when the big gates were opened for early leavers and the penniless flooded in for the last 20 minutes. It was often the best part of the game.

What may be called McGrory's 'General Strike-rate' earned him his first Championship medal. It also brought him his first representative honour – for the Scottish League against the Irish League at Tynecastle in October 1926. He scored one of the League's five goals that day. These League Select sides were notable for his first collaboration with Bob McPhail, that fine Airdrie and Rangers inside-forward, and they were later to play together to great effect for Scotland at Hampden.

Another innocent who arrived on the Celtic scene around this time, and would soon be a Scotland player too, was a slim figure from the east called John Thomson. John was four years younger than McGrory and Jimmy was never to forget the first time he saw him play. He told the Glasgow *Evening Citizen* all about it years later:

> On February 12, 1927 we went up to Dundee where we won 2–1. I remember this match particularly, not because I scored the winner, but because Celtic had a new keeper that day – an 18-year-old from Wellesley in Fife. Yes, the immortal John Thomson. Prince of Keepers. To me, he is the greatest goalie I ever played with, a born athlete who could have made his name in any branch of sport, who was as good as all the stories about him. He was so confident. I remember in that first match he lost a goal to Cook, of Dundee. Afterwards, in the dressing-room, one of our directors [Tom Colgan] spoke to him about it. 'That's a' right, sir,' said the youngster quietly in his Fife twang. 'It'll no' happen next week.' And it didn't.

Off the field, for successful footballers, it was a time of pipes and plus fours and there are pictures of McGrory's teammates, suitably attired for leisure spells at Seamill Hydro, all puffing contentedly at their briar pipes. McGrory himself was never to be without one until the end of his life. He was also known to light up a football match on occasions, and one of the earliest was a Saturday in February 1927 when Celtic were due to play St Mirren at Love Street. At that date, his goal tally for the season stood at forty-three – only two short of the record for a season, ironically held by a St Mirren player, Duncan Walker.

> Could I break the record? I could – and I did. My mates laid on every possible thing for me, and by full-time, I had scored four goals, to pass Walker's total by two. The fans carried me off on their shoulders.

By the end of the season he had scored forty-eight in the League, nine in the Scottish Cup and two in the Glasgow Cup, giving him a total of fifty-nine – which equalled the British top scorer, Middlesbrough's George Camsell, but McGrory entered the record books for the first time as leading scorer in Scotland. He actually beat Camsell's aggregate by scoring the equaliser for the Scottish League in their 2–2 draw with the English League at Leicester, and was rewarded by being selected for the Scotland team to tour Canada. And he still had the Scottish Cup final to look forward to against East Fife, which Celtic were odds-on favourites to win. There was only the matter of a routine League fixture against Falkirk at Brockville Park to deal with – yet another chance to break his scoring record.

Instead, on that April afternoon, he broke two ribs in a 4–1 defeat. Even Celtic's one goal was scored by Alec Thomson off a Falkirk defender. It was not a happy day for McGrory. There were to be no more goals, no Cup final (which Celtic *did* win) and no Canadian trip with the SFA, which might have confirmed him as Scotland's centre-forward despite the competition from Hughie Gallacher. But it was not to be. Never mind; on Maley's recommendation he got his second Scottish Cup medal for all the goals he had scored to get Celtic to the final and he had enough bonus money to see him through the summer while his ribs mended.

According to Jim Friel of Baillieston, the St Roch authority and ex-Garngad man himself, much of McGrory's convalescence might well have taken place in Ireland with a couple of Garngad pals like Jim McAree (who became Jimmy Donaghue, the comedian) and Tom Carracher. Friel remembers his mother (who was a Carracher) telling him about the Donegal holidays that young lads went on then because travel was cheap and they stayed with their Irish relatives. McGrory would be relaxed in their company because these were men he had known all his life. He would, in fact, become godfather to Jim McAree's son. They had been boys together in the streets. They all had the same church and Boys' Guild background and their families were Irish – and mostly from Donegal – so they weren't going among strangers.

There were still plenty of McGrorys on the Rosguill Peninsula and cousins were thick on the ground around Mulroy on the way up to Fanad Head, or at Carrigart on the road towards Downings, by the banks of Lough Swilly (where he would later buy a house). He loved it there because he was back among his own, the land of his father and mother, of his very blood. It must still have stirred as he looked out at the Muckish Mountain or splashed in the waters of Mulroy Bay. He and his pals could cavort here and act daft because it didn't matter. There was always someone within a hundreds yards who was related, however distantly, to one of them at least, and keeping an Irish eye on them. Not that the Glasgow boys were any trouble. Noisy perhaps, but no trouble.

From personal experience as a Glasgow tenement boy of just such Irish holidays with pals in the late '40s, the present author feels it is likely that nothing much will have changed since McGrory's time to ours back then. We were the same town boys in the countryside – and a truly rural countryside it was. Hens went in and out of the houses; there were pigs at the back door and cows had been known to stick their heads through windows. It was not the normal scene for boys who lived up closes, but it was certainly a change.

McGrory, in those early years of his professional life, would be the only real earner of his group and, no doubt, he would put his hand in his pocket to help out the others. Getting to Ireland was no strain on his pocket. Once there, they were distributed around the cousins and each then dropped his cheap suitcase into a dark little bedroom that smelt like oatcakes before hurrying out to his mates again. They would usually meet after breakfast at the cross at Carrigart and decide what to do for the day. They would then go for a walk and enjoy the fresh air, away from the Garngad chimneys, or play Gaelic football with the local lads for fun, even if McGrory was strictly forbidden to play any kind of football between seasons under the Maley regime.

Similarly, cars and motorbikes were out. If Mr Maley had had his way his players would have been on long walks after daily Mass, a good book before tea and Rosary and Benediction at night. That wasn't the Garngad idea of a break at all. Sunday Mass somewhere, OK, with the uncles and aunties – but for the rest, it was taking each day as it came and the night as you found it – whether it was at a go-as-you-please concert in the Church Hall or a local dance in the same hall – when there would be girls.

There was never a mention of a girl in McGrory's life at this period – although after he died in 1982, Margaret Anderson, a childhood girlfriend, was reported in the Glasgow *Evening Times* of 15 December 1982, as saying: 'I should have married Jimmy. He was my best friend.' To prove it, she bought one of his international jerseys at a charity auction. His second wife and widow, Barbara McGrory, commented that Margaret had been saying that for years – but she was still her best friend. She also said that all the medals were in the bank except the one she had on round her neck – 'because it was the prettiest'. His own favourite, she said, was the first one he ever won – the Junior Cup final with St Roch's.

In a robust sort of way, Jimmy McGrory might even have been thought good-looking, though not in the sense that the slim and graceful John Thomson was thought handsome by girls. Jimmy was burly, more rugged and there was no doubt he was manly – but no girlfriend. His near-monastic devotion to football must have been an inhibiting factor; he had thought of little else since he was 14. He had lived for the game and even in the more relaxed holiday atmosphere of his youth and early manhood, one feels there would be a natural restraint in anything to do with sexual expression. The shadow of Canon Lawton loomed large even yet. It would be the same with his pals – 'No sex, please – we're Catholic.' After marriage, there was no holding them – but before it – nothing. At least that's how it was supposed to be.

Fortunately, Jimmy McGrory had more exciting things on his mind than losing his virginity. It was soon time to get back to training sessions in the woollen pullover, long shorts and scuffed sannies that was the required dress. One can't help think that this was his real world and the one where he was most himself. This is what he had to get fit for again.

He got off to a good start early in the new season by scoring in extra time during a Glasgow Cup game against Rangers, a semi-final tie replayed twice at Ibrox. It was in this match that Patsy Gallacher went on a wander, beating a trail of Rangers defenders to put the ball in the net for the last goal he was ever to score for Celtic. Celtic then went on their own kind of roller-coaster season, being beaten where they should have won and winning where they might have lost, but in the end they pipped Airdrieonians, who featured the likes of Bob McPhail and Hughie Gallacher in their line-up, for the Championship.

As these two were beginning to make their names, so was McGrory. Garngad pals like Peter Flynn and Ronnie McDonald, who would also remain lifelong friends, lived for details of his weekly exploits. Ronnie McDonald was unique in that he was half French. His Garngad father had met his mother during the First World War, and Ronnie spent the first four years of his life in Cherbourg before coming back to his father's city. *Quel change*. He always wore a French beret. It must have caused a stir among the street-corner bunnets, but they knew a good dresser when they saw one. McGrory was also clothes-conscious. There was no need here to swank or show off, but a nice suit always went down well, even though few could afford it. McGrory always knew when *not* to show it, however.

He remembered when he first joined Celtic his own early enjoyment in wearing smart clothes, although he did admit to a self-consciousness about being 'a bit of a swank', as he told Gerald McNee:

Dress was very important in those days and on a Saturday players were encouraged to appear in their best suits. At first I was terrified to walk out of the door in Garngad all dressed to kill in case people who had known me all my life thought that playing for Celtic had gone to my head. The truth was I liked clothes . . . probably because I never had the opportunity to dress well in my younger days. Plus fours in those days were only worn by the toffs . . . but I had my heart set on them and when the sales came along I managed to pick up a pair at a reasonable price – and a soft hat to go with them.

The problem now was: when would he have the courage to wear them? The first chance came when he still lived at Garngadhill. A Sunday ramble had been arranged by John McMenemy, a fellow player at Celtic Park, and son of the famous Jimmy, with people from St Columbkille's Parish in Rutherglen. The trams didn't run on a Sunday from Garngad so he would have to walk down into town. The thought frightened him to death, so he hit on a plan. 'I got up at dawn and set off through the back streets until I reached John's house above a pub on the corner of Springfield Road and London Road – a house I later bought from him.'

Most tenement flats were rented through a factor in those days, but he may have done a deal through Celtic to buy the place for his sister, as this was his registered address at this time. He did, in fact, buy Fanny a wee sweetie shop in Parson Street in Townhead – a tidy little business, but a fair distance then from Parkhead by tramcar. At any rate, it was to Springfield Road that the dapper McGrory arrived exhausted, before he even went on the ramble. Yet he had walked to Celtic Park from Garngad with Hugh Hilley every day – but not in plus fours. He returned with John McMenemy at the end of the day and waited until it was dark before walking back all the way to 256 Garngadhill. The price he had to pay for being in the fashion. Although a time was soon approaching when he would miss the old-slipper ease of his boyhood companions and be forced to step out in other, more fashionable shoes.

Other players didn't have the same scruples about clothes. Some of them, like Charlie Napier, were very snappy dressers. Patsy Gallacher wasn't above a bit of sartorial display, believing that if you have it, show it. In fact, when away at special training at Dunbar he once dressed up as a woman to fool Maley in order to get out after curfew. Tommy McInally, typically, didn't even bother with any disguise; he just sauntered out and nobody tried to stop him. Both players were laws unto themselves – Gallacher earned his status, Tommy just took it.

McInally had two stints with Celtic, one for a couple of seasons before joining Third Lanark prior to McGrory's arrival in 1922, and then again, after McGrory had joined the club, for three seasons between 1925 and 1928. After this second spell, Tommy was transferred to Sunderland.

McInally was a towering talent but he had personality problems which would be thought of today as an attention deficit hyperactivity disorder. He had to be centre stage at all times – even in the dressing-room or at tactical talks. These talks were rare, but when they did happen, they were always at risk when Tommy was present. Once, when Maley was urging the wing-halves to carry the ball forward, Tommy questioned the tactic.

'Is that no' a foul?'

'What is?' asked Maley.

'Carryin' the ba'. Use of the hauns,' replied McInally deadpan.

Another time, a complicated move was being discussed involving a pass from the defence to the wing-half, across to the opposite wing, in to the inside-forward and on to the centre-forward, who moves left and crosses for the other inside-forward to score. It was all very technical and elaborate and would have to be timed precisely but the earnest mood was punctured by Tommy, who asked simply: 'Whit's the ither team dae'in' – staunin' watchin' us?'

Even when he turned up at Maley's Bank Restaurant on match days, which was mandatory for all Celtic's first-team players, he approached the daunting owner with the bland enquiry: 'Say, Boss, am I on a bonus for this?' The man was unquenchable. The players loved his antics but they hated it when he clowned it up on the field. It was not only time-wasting but could be self-defeating. Then, just when he was at his most exasperating, he would turn on the style or use his devastating speed to score two or three goals at will before returning to his favourite role as jester. Charlie Tully had something of the same tendency 30 years later. The difference was that Charlie was brilliant in a bad team, Tommy was great among great players – or could be when he liked. The fans loved him, and Glasgow comedians would use his name warmly. Tommy Morgan, for instance, used to call out, 'Who ate the belly oot the ludger's shirt?'

and the Metropole audience would yell back, 'Tommy McInally!'

McGrory loved him. Even Maley loved him, or he wouldn't have tolerated him so long. Bill Struth, the formidable Rangers manager, had wanted to sign him, but Tommy was determined to ruin a vast talent by being dissolute with it. It was a great shame, because he was a natural, even as a schoolboy at St Mungo's. Unfortunately, his home circumstances weren't easy, and he didn't seem to have had McGrory's personal stability.

Tommy was his own worst enemy – and he eventually killed the genius that everyone knew was in him. Maley indulged him to the limit. He knew what he had on his hands, but Tommy went his own way – downhill. Latterly, he refused to train. He didn't need a manager, he needed a psychiatrist. Inevitably he hit the bottle. One has only to think of George Best's liver troubles today. Or George Connelly's psychological problems in a later Celtic. Prodigious talents – prodigally thrown away.

Jimmy McGrory had no such hang-ups. He was too simple a man – or too well adjusted. He never seemed to feel the strain of appearing in public. In his mind, he was still playing at the Brickies and whether a hundred people were watching or a hundred thousand it made little difference to him on the park. This is the mark of the true professional and of the great player, to play with total concentration, yet, at the same time, to *play* the game with all the enthusiasm of a boy. McGrory never lost his boyishness. Perhaps that's why he liked to remember one of Tommy McInally's 'acts'. After scoring one of his typically 'cheeky' goals, he would turn away and waddle upfield to the centre spot doing his Charlie Chaplin walk.

If Tommy had gone on walking he might have headed out of the ground by the Janefield Street gate, continued across the Gallowgate to the old Green's showground at Vinegar Hill, then down to Glasgow Cross, passing Mr Maley's former drapery store at 155 Gallowgate and on through the Trongate, along Argyle Street to the Central Station at Union Street. There, if he'd turned right and walked up to Renfield Street he would have seen the huge electric sign telling all of Glasgow that the brand-new 'GREEN'S PLAYHOUSE' was now in business and showing Monte Ray in *Play Safe* as the main attraction.

The cinema, theatre and ballroom complex was opened with great ceremony on Thursday, 15 September 1927 by Mrs David Mason, wife of the Lord Provost of Glasgow, in the presence of all the local dignitaries and known personalities, some of whom were from the sporting world, as Fred Green was known to be interested in football and boxing. Luxury double seats, known as the 'golden divans', were provided in the balcony for courting couples interested in other things. A total of 4,368 plush seats were available and the dance floor would accommodate 6,000 dancers – surely more than adequate for 'dance-mad' Glasgow.

In all, the brothers spared no expense and the Playhouse was a showplace from the start. A full orchestra accompanied the silent films and a troupe of dancers featured in the stage shows. The rich interior was magical in its effect. The Greens had obviously not forgotten their carnival roots. The visual impact was all. The main staircase was marble, pillars adorned the restaurant and theatrical balustrades decorated the foyer. The whole interior was ablaze in orange, primrose and gold, and carpets were everywhere. This was a film house which itself looked like a Hollywood set. Zigzag neon strips in the ceiling gave the effect of lightning and added to the enormous dramatic impact on patrons. The Greens hadn't spent all those years on the road without learning the basic Barnum lessons of catering to the public, but even they had never attempted anything on this scale before . . . and the result made Glasgow gasp.

The Playhouse was to become a Glasgow landmark, one way or another, for the next half-century and the famous golden divans were well used by courting couples. Millions of Glaswegians must have passed through the Playhouse portals in that time, including football players. After training they had nothing else to do other than playing golf in the afternoon or going to the dancing at night. Footballers were nearly always good dancers. They had the footwork, you see. McGrory wasn't known for his fancy footwork but he did go to the dancing in St Alphonsus Hall in London Road with Alec Thomson and John Thomson when Thomson was still in lodgings at 618 Gallowgate. All three were shy with girls, so it is likely they went more often to the pictures. Jack Harkness, the Hearts and Scotland goalkeeper, was one footballer who used to meet up with them for a Saturday night at Green's Playhouse. The Greens not only owned the Playhouse, they had cinemas in nearly every district of Glasgow, so the boys had plenty to choose from. By this time Glasgow had fully earned its title name as the Cinema City.

Nothing was more than a couple of stops on a tram so McGrory and his teammates would have their pick of picture houses anywhere from the city centre to Parkhead Cross. Every admission ticket sold was another brick in the Greens' property portfolio, which by now extended to residential investment on the other side of the city. From the 'mother-hen' mansion that was Craigie Hall, other real-estate chickens came home to roost nearby like 'Ashcroft', 'Glen Ard' and 'Belltrees' and the family gobbled them up. It was a big change from the wagons on the Gallowgate showground or living above the paybox at the Whitevale in Dennistoun. Another Green enclave had been established. It could be said that their caravans had come to rest.

They were a long way now from Vinegar Hill and they still had a long way to go yet. So had Jimmy McGrory in the autumn of 1927, carrying 59 goals from the season before. He could only get better. Meantime, the Green road kept a-winding – and soon their paths would cross.

FOUR

Pursuit of a Goal

No player in the world is worth £10,000.
                    Sir Charles Clegg, FA President, 1928

By the mid-'20s, Ann Jane Bradley, Mrs George Green, the matriarch of all the Greens, had moved to Craigie Hall in Dumbreck from the East End, where she had lived for nearly 25 years and had raised most of her large family. Now she was living like a dowager, a well-to-do widow with hired help, although she may have had her unmarried daughters with her. Old Mrs Green had enough children – and memories – to prevent her ever being lonely. In any case, she had the size of personality to fill the biggest house.

When she died there in 1927, around the time of the Playhouse opening, the house was temporarily unoccupied, each of the siblings having his or her own place. Fred Green and Bunchy lived at Abingdon but now that Craigie Hall was available, Fred decided that he would take it. It was a big house, but then he liked everything big – except his wives. Bunchy wasn't sure but Fred was determined, so they came up and settled into the mansion and to the appropriate style of living. Her niece, Mrs Jean Peacock, remembers how Craigie Hall was in the '20s:

> Uncle Fred made a great fuss of [us] . . . we would go down
> to the garden and all play tennis, and then we would get up a
> badminton net across the grass and we had croquet going, and

Chrissie [Martin], the housekeeper, would come down with a tray of orange drinks for us all and then we would come up here and go into the dining room and have lovely salad tea. In the library there was a lovely picture of Uncle Fred with Charlie Chaplin and another one of him standing between Chaplin and Mary Pickford. He went out to Hollywood to find out more about the film and cinema business. They say he put money into United Artists when they were starting up and that's why he had his photographs taken with Charlie Chaplin.

Perhaps if Fred Green had put the family money into the Green and White of Celtic he might have had his photograph taken with Tommy McInally – or even Jimmy McGrory. James Edward was becoming something of a celebrity himself. On the field it seemed as if he couldn't put a foot – or a head – wrong and, even though he was only halfway through the 1925–26 season, the goals kept coming – 49 in all by the end of the campaign. Trainer Eddie McGarvey had told him he couldn't jump. 'You've got flat feet,' he said, 'and people with flat feet, can't jump.' Of course, Jimmy went on to become famous for his ability in the air and for the number of goals he got with his head, but at this stage he imagined everyone knew better than he did. He just got on with things in his own way, going for everything and never giving up in a game. No ball was ever too hopeless to chase, no cross ever completely out of range. As he later explained in an interview with John Rafferty for the *Observer* on 15 August 1971, his goal-scoring was less a matter of technique and more an attitude of mind:

> My mind was set on scoring goals. I got into positions from which I could head or shoot. When the ball did come . . . I did not have to waste any time. I hit it. I see players trying to control and manoeuvre the ball when it comes to them, then looking up to see what they are going to do with it. They waste so much time.

This was the centre-forward's credo in a nutshell – to get into position where his lightning reflections can act to best effect. It's a reliance on instinct as much as basic skills. His very speed of reaction meant he missed some sitters. In 1926, 'Waverley' had commented in the *Daily Record*: 'McGrory may often miss what look like pinches, but what a lot of goals he gets.'

A lot of injuries too, but that had always been his style and no amount of professional training would change it.

Training for professional football in the '20s was hardly a scientific exercise but more a concession to general fitness as acknowledged by a token circuit, or circuits, of the running track around the pitch under the eye of the trainer, generally a former player. At one stage this was also a cycle track, which might have led to some bunching on the bends. Maley was never involved in training sessions. It was a hard enough job trying to get him to remove his Homburg hat, much less don the training gear. He was usually busy in the office writing letters or pondering the current cash situation with a view to impending transfers. He was always readier to sell than to buy. Celtic rarely bought big. They preferred to rear their players young then sell them big. This got them the name in the trade, as in the phrase of the time, 'Catholic Jews', intended then as a compliment to the traditional Jewish business acumen, but to Maley it was mere desk-work.

The Celtic players were more or less left to get on with it. Some senior men, like the peerless Patsy, were allowed to fix their own training schedule so that they could attend to their pub businesses or newsagent shops or whatever before making a cursory appearance in the afternoon, and it went without saying that characters like the idiosyncratic Tommy McInally were one-offs that did their own thing in their own time.

Young players learned their trade on the park, in the heat of the game. Lessons learned there were hard-earned and therefore not easily forgotten. Players shouted a lot more to each other in those days and the language wasn't always pretty. Apprentice players picked that up too. Jimmy McGrory remembers in his first games being yelled at to 'Hold it! Give it! Out right! Out left!' 'And all at the same time. I didn't know where I was,' he added. Yet only weeks later, it was: 'Young McGrory was leading his forwards like a veteran – showing distribution reminiscent of Jimmy Quinn.' Obviously, McGrory was a quick learner.

His physical style, too, was like the great Quinn, as was evident in a moment from a previous Scottish Cup tie against Hearts in February 1926 at a packed Tynecastle. Mounted police had had to clear spectators from the running track when Celtic won a free kick. Tommy McInally prepared to take it, and as he did, he called over young McGrory. 'As soon as I hit it,' said Tommy, 'run straight at their goalie.' Jimmy did as he was told and as McInally floated the ball into the penalty area, Jimmy charged the Hearts goalkeeper, Willie White, who had caught the ball, and bundled both into the net for a goal. A fair shoulder charge was permissible in those days, but it was McInally's know-how that made the goal. Celtic went on to win 4–0.

Managerial advice before a game, according to McGrory, turned out to be no more than 'Get out there and win. The only time we got any advice was on a Monday morning if we had lost on the Saturday. Then we got it hot and strong.' Celtic, in fact, lost their best unofficial coach when they sensationally released their star player, Patsy Gallacher, in July 1926 to save on the close-season wage bill. Patsy had been having knee trouble and Celtic thought him finished, but he went on to play in the United States and at Falkirk until he retired in 1932. McGrory remembered clearly the pre-game tactical advice given by Patsy Gallacher just as soon as Willie Maley shut the dressing-room door on his way up to take his seat in the directors' box. Patsy often put his finger on what was needed against particular opponents, especially Rangers . . . or he would joke to lift morale.

One day he took the young winger, Paddy Connolly, aside. Paddy had just succeeded Andy McAtee in the side, and because of his speed was nicknamed 'The Greyhound'. Patsy told him loudly: 'Now look, son, you're in the side because you're fast. Don't be gettin' any notions you're here for any other reason. When you get to the by-line, get that ball across for Jimmy here's head – and make sure you get the lace on your side so that it's away from his forehead. We don't want him cuttin' himself now, do we? You just go and practise that an' you'll be fine, so you will.'

This kind of banter with words more or less to that effect, spoken quietly with all of the Mighty Atom's authority, was taken very seriously. Connolly did practise, and Jimmy McGrory scored a lot of goals from his pinpoint crosses. And on days when he couldn't think of anything to say, Patsy would give the boys a song. No wonder he was so prized by the club and adored by the players. Yet due to typical Celtic, or Malavian, parsimony or short-sightedness, he was allowed to leave at the end of the season.

Willie Maley had always taken extreme pride in Celtic Park's being the venue for international matches, such as the famous Rosebery International of 1900, but the last of these had been just before Jimmy McGrory was born, in April 1904, when Scotland lost to a Steve Bloomer goal. In Maley's opinion that was too long ago and Celtic needed the prestige of a modern stadium. The Grant

Stand had served its time and was now in urgent need of repair before a possible disaster struck. Ibrox had its calamity in 1902 when a wooden stand collapsed with heavy casualties and Celtic had to take warning from such a tragic example. Fire was always a risk at football grounds. It would later destroy Celtic's first pavilion, at the western end of the ground at Janefield Street in March 1929, but by the end of the 1926–27 season the Board had been alerted to the fact that the Grant Stand would soon require attention.

In 1898, it had been the first two-tiered timbered stand ever built at a football park. A massive construction, it was the work of Ulsterman James Grant, who lost money on the project but sold it cheaply to the club in return for a directorship, which led in time to a maiden descendant of his, Felicia Grant of Toomebridge, County Antrim, becoming the largest Celtic shareholder. In her lifetime, as late as the 1960s, she was known as 'the old lady who owned Celtic'. She was also a great John Thomson fan but it is not known if she was consulted in the '20s about the rebuilding of the family stand. While negotiations were going on, someone on the Celtic Board came up with a moneymaking idea to pay for the new stand – and that was to sell Jimmy McGrory. The *Glasgow Observer*, *Catholic Herald* and *Glasgow Star* all carried the same story in August 1927:

> The football world was startled to learn last Friday that Jimmy McGrory was about to leave the Celtic. The first intimation obtained was that Celtic and Arsenal had come to terms for the transfer of the record goal-scoring centre-forward. Jimmy had already signed for next season and few expected events to take this turn. At any rate, Celtic seemed to consider the Londoners' terms satisfactory and had decided to release the player. When McGrory, however, was brought in to sign, he refused, ostensibly because his share of the transfer was not to his liking. A deadlock set in and up to the time of writing the transfer has not been completed.

If it all came as a surprise to the press and supporters, it was a positive bombshell to the player. That they should even think of disposing of a player who had scored 59 goals in the season just ended and was to score 62 in all competitions before the end of the season ahead was bad enough, but that they would imagine he would leave just for the sake of the money was insulting. Tommy McInally had been the nearest Celt to him with 19 goals but *he* was now out of favour and sometimes never even showed up for training. William 'Wuggie' Gray, the Human Siege Gun as he was called, was brought in from Maryhill Hibernian in August 1927 to replace McGrory who was confidently expected to join Arsenal. What were Celtic thinking?

As already stated, McGrory had signed up for the new season, with a rise bringing him up to £9 a week. He saw no reason to ask for more. Now here was the club he loved willing to sell him. In his eyes, this was treachery. He had a contract to honour – and honour was a meaningful word to Jimmy McGrory. His mistake was to think it was mutual. It was a gross misrepresentation to say that the transfer foundered due to the player's refusal because personal terms 'were not to his liking'. The real truth of the matter was another story altogether.

There had been many offers for McGrory in the previous two seasons – his goals saw to that – but he and Maley just laughed them off. Arsenal had come for him before but he hadn't even bothered to talk to them, so he thought no more about it and prepared for his annual holiday in his beloved Ireland. Instead, Mr Maley suddenly asked him if he'd like to go with him on a pilgrimage to Lourdes. Jimmy was flattered. It was known that the manager went regularly to the French Marian shrine as a helper to the sick, but now his own health was suffering and he wanted the company of a younger man as his escort. Tommy McInally had originally been asked, but his idiosyncratic behaviour put an end to that. One can only speculate on the havoc Tommy might have created among the devout. Pilgrims lying helpless on their stretchers might have been too much of a temptation for Tommy. Something stronger might have been added to the holy water. There would have been some unholy miracles with that prankster around. Jimmy McGrory was an altogether safer bet.

As a good Catholic, he knew he would appreciate the religious significance of the place and the prospect of its summer foreign-ness was exciting. He was still something of the innocent abroad. Here was a chance for an adventure, his first time out of Britain. He never thought of Eire as being anything more than old Ireland as he'd always known it, but this was 'abroad' and it would be a change from Lough Derg. He entrained with Maley at the Central Station and looked forward to his first visit to London with all the excitement of a boy.

It was common knowledge at Celtic Park that some players couldn't even face a three-stop tram ride with their manager. Now here was their star player off on a jaunt with the old boy when he would never be away from his side. One of the Catholic players suggested that McGrory should regard the trip as a penance. McGrory did notice that before they left the station Maley's son, William, arrived with a telegram for his father. Maley never said anything about it, so Jimmy never thought to ask. On the journey, no doubt, the older man told him about Lourdes and what he should expect to see, but first he would enjoy an overnight stay in a swanky London hotel. This was a pleasant surprise for McGrory – he hadn't expected that.

Nor did he expect to see a smartly dressed Herbert Chapman, the manager of Arsenal, with his chairman, Sir Samuel Hill Wood MP, waiting for them on the Euston platform. How did they know they were on that train? Maley had said nothing about any meeting. Was that what the telegram was about? However, the Celtic manager made the necessary introductions and the quartet adjourned to the nearby Euston Hotel for a meal. It was all very grand and quite a step up from his sister Fanny's good plain cooking, but Jimmy found his way around the cutlery without disgracing himself and treated the whole thing as part of the holiday experience. It was only when Sir Samuel and Willie Maley adjourned to the lounge leaving Jimmy with Herbert Chapman that the real reason for the meeting came out.

Chapman had been instructed to go to an amount that would be a British record for a transfer fee to secure McGrory's contract from Celtic and make him an Arsenal player. That's how keen they were to get him. It only remained for 'personal terms' to be agreed. McGrory didn't even want to talk about it. Somehow, to him, McGrory of the Arsenal didn't sound as right to him as McGrory of the Celtic, but the English manager persisted. According to Gerald McNee in *A Lifetime in Paradise*, Chapman told the young Scot: 'There's a fortune to be made here. You could do very well in London. We'd paint the town to get you.' He seemed to forget that Jimmy had never ever been in London – he'd only just got as far as Euston Station. England had no appeal for him at all and he tried to tell Chapman that.

He tried to explain that he was happy where he was. He had only ever wanted to play for Celtic and had no wish to go anywhere else. Chapman reminded him, somewhat tartly, that Arsenal wasn't 'anywhere else' – it was the best team in London, and soon it would be the best in England, and that meant the best in the world. He was serious, and he was indeed to make that happen. McGrory was seen as a vital part of the jigsaw, and Chapman played his big card to

71

tempt him – money. Realizing that he might get talked into agreeing to a transfer by the glib Englishman, and thinking to put an end to the conversation, McGrory said he would need £2,000, cash in hand, before he would even think of moving from Glasgow. He knew this was asking for the moon, and he guessed rightly. The moon wasn't for sale.

It was late when the other two returned to the table and they were both surprised that a deal had not been agreed, but Chapman told them that McGrory had wanted the equivalent of the national debt as personal terms. In that way the matter was laughed off. The Englishmen left and the Scots were allowed to go up to their rooms. They did so without exchanging a word. Next morning they caught the boat train from Victoria. It could be said that both of them had rather an uncomfortable Channel crossing. Neither could bring themselves to even mention the matter, but neither could they get it out of their heads. The Arsenal conspiracy had failed and if there had been covert collusion with it by Celtic, it had not been rewarded. Everyone had assumed that money would talk as it always did but they had reckoned without James Edward McGrory. Celtic had given him his first football chance and he saw no reason why he should not repay them for that by continuing his service on the field.

For once, big money had lost its voice, or was it that one player at least had the sense to be deaf to its appeal? Many would think McGrory stupid to turn down such a tempting professional offer, but he knew when he was well off and was happy to leave it at that. So, with his integrity intact and his thoughts free of material things, he entered into Lourdes with an appropriate peace of mind. One cannot be sure that his mentor felt the same.

The shrine at Lourdes in France has been a place of pilgrimage for Catholics since 1858, when, on Thursday, 11 February, 'a beautiful lady in white with a blue belt and holding a yellow rose' appeared to a young peasant girl, Maire Bernade Soubirous, at a grotto by the banks of the River Gave. Eventually a chapel was built on the spot and Bernadette was eventually canonised after due ecclesiastical process. Lourdes was firmly placed on the map as a place of holy pilgrimage for Catholics worldwide.

Today it is a Lourdes industry but miracles do happen, people are cured and prayers are answered, which is why ten thousand people visit the shrine every day of the year. Millions have come from all over the world and in 1928 William Maley and James Edward

McGrory were only two of many. To Jimmy's eyes it was breathtaking. There were thousands of pilgrims here and not many would have come from St Roch's, he imagined. He wondered how Canon Lawton had reacted to this Catholic commercialism. He had been to Lourdes, but all he got was the Scottish Junior Cup for St Roch's – a small miracle in itself.

Was Maley here for the same reason – looking for a football miracle perhaps? The shrine to the Virgin Mary, whom both he and McGrory believed to be the earthly Mother of God, was also a monument to the commercial opportunities available to those who cater to pilgrims of such faith. Everything possible was for sale, from holy water to statues, to prayer books and rosary beads – and all of these seemed to be in the worst of taste. The only thing in the place that was not for sale was Jimmy McGrory.

St Bernadette herself could not have been more sincere at the first Lourdes vision than Jimmy McGrory was on his first visit. Sincerity was the basis of his attitude to most things, but especially to his religion and this, as far as he was concerned, encompassed his attitude to life in general as much as to his life in football. This was the rock on which he built what philosophies he had and it would stand firm, no matter what power lay in London's Arsenal. Miracles may have happened that year at Lourdes but nothing happened to convert Jimmy McGrory into a mercenary. He returned much as he had left, a Glasgow boy with the uncomplicated faith of his fathers, knowing that it would remain so even if Mr Maley had taken him all the way to the Vatican.

If Lourdes surprised him, it was nothing to the shock he got in realising to what lengths people at the higher levels of football would go to get what they wanted. To his amazement, on the return trip from France, there, waiting to greet them off the boat train, was Herbert Chapman. Willie Maley seemed similarly taken aback to see the Arsenal manager standing there, smiling and holding out his hand. McGrory felt uneasy about having to go through the whole business again, but he said nothing and politely shook hands.

Back in the lounge of the Euston Hotel, Herbert Chapman made it immediately clear that he really wanted McGrory and had his reasons. Chapman was no fool. He had dragged Huddersfield Town from nowhere to win the English League three times in a row and now he had been hired to do the same with Arsenal and to spare no expense in doing so. Money had never been one of Arsenal's problems, although their previous chairman, Sir Henry Norris, had been banned from the game for making illegal payments to players. Now they were determined to be Britain's best, which meant seeking out the best in Ireland, Wales and Scotland and since McGrory was the best buy in Scotland in 1928, they wanted him. Whatever it took. They hadn't reckoned, however, on Garngad grit. This was something Chapman had never met before and he wasn't sure how to deal with it.

This time, there was no fancy meal, no pretence at anything other than driving through a deal. Chapman came straight to the point – the offer was now £10,000 to Celtic and a blank cheque to the player. This was unheard of. Maley couldn't believe his ears. It was all too much for him, and he had to rise and go to his room. It had only been a dozen years since Alf Common caused a sensation by moving from Sunderland to Middlesbrough for £1,000. No one surely could be worth ten times that much. Well, here was one, sitting opposite the shrewdest man in football, pitting his native honesty against big-city London smart. Chapman repeated the offer and showed Jimmy the blank cheque in his hand. His smile showed his confidence that the Scot couldn't resist such an opportunity.

McGrory remained quite impassive and explained in his soft-spoken voice that while he was flattered by the offer, he was not for sale. Chapman couldn't believe it but the player was adamant. Realising he was beaten, Chapman put away his cheque book, and rising, held out his hand to McGrory.

'Well, I must say I admire your attitude. I just wish I had players as loyal to their clubs as you are to Celtic.'

They shook hands. At that, Willie Maley returned to the table, smiling, thinking a deal had been struck, but Chapman was quick to disabuse him.

'Mr Maley, if we offered this lad the Crown Jewels and next year's output of the Royal Mint we'd still not get him. I think the deal's off.'

Maley looked at McGrory keenly. 'So you're staying?' he said.

'Yes.'

'Well, if you're determined . . .'

'I am.'

'Well, that's it.'

Maley then turned to Chapman and offered his hand. 'I'm sorry, Mr Chapman . . .' he began.

Chapman cut him off with a wave of the hand. 'And so am I, Mr Maley. Believe me, I am.'

They shook hands, then, turning to McGrory, the Arsenal

manager patted him on the shoulder saying, 'Good luck to you, James,' and briskly left the room.

What Mr Chapman could never have understood, and perhaps even Mr Maley underestimated, was that Jimmy McGrory was as much a Celtic *supporter* as player. He had green genes from the start. Football, for him, was more than a tribal rivalry ritualised in urban divisions; it was an expression of the life force as seen from tenement windows. Larger global considerations did not concern the working class. All they knew was that who you were was where you came from. This atavistic sense of identity was something Jimmy McGrory, and thousands like him in Glasgow, understood and they found its complete expression in a green-and-white jersey. It was a bloodline to a deeper reality than day-to-day existence, and it certainly wasn't something that was for sale. It was as complex and as simple as that.

Having failed to land McGrory, Herbert Chapman paid £20,000 for Bolton's David Jack and Preston's Alec James, and, later, added Charlie Buchan from Sunderland. He built a world-beating team around them just as he said he would. Had McGrory taken the Arsenal gold, he would have joined fellow Scot Alec James in London. The little Mossend ball-juggler had always had an eye for the main chance and was happy to pose in long shorts in Harrods for a fee. Oddly enough, it was in Mossend around this time that the first Jimmy McGrory Fan Club was formed, but it's doubtful if any of them would ever have travelled to London to see him had he gone there. In a final irony, when McGrory received his first pay packet of the new season he found that his wages had been cut from £9 to £8. No reason was given. Had he been penalised for his loyalty?

As a result of the Arsenal business, a kind of cloud came down between McGrory and the great sun that, for him, had been Celtic. He had been out into the world and he found that it was not good. Even though he hadn't eaten of its fruits, he felt that they had stained him. Such introspection, however, was not a normal part of the McGrory personality and he struggled to throw off the depression he felt as the season got under way. It was a very natural sense of anti-climax but all he knew was that the zest had left his game, and, as a result, he embarked on the worst period he was to have with Celtic. He hated all the new uncertainties that had suddenly gathered about the so-certain world he had known. He missed Patsy Gallacher, he missed the truant Tommy McInally and he felt he had stepped back some distance from Willie Maley.

Despite the cloud hanging over his head at the beginning of the new term, both he and Celtic had a good first half in the new 1927–28 season and this was shown by again beating Rangers, this time in the final of the Glasgow Cup when Jimmy got the first goal – a cheeky chip shot. Subtlety was not always his strongest suit but he was able, from time to time, to proffer the unexpected to good effect. His heavy feelings resulting from the Arsenal affair lifted and he was soon back at what he did best – scoring goals. However, his best performance of the season – indeed, the best performance of his career – came early in the New Year of 1928. It was 14 January and Dunfermline had come through from Fife to play Celtic at Parkhead. Let him explain in his own words:

> The Scottish First Division record for goals scored in a match was six and this was held by three players – the great R.S. McColl, Laurie Bain of Queen's Park, and Davie Brown of Dundee. Earlier in the season, McNally of Arthurlie had set a new Scottish Second Division record with eight goals in a match. Thanks to my teammates who were here, there and everywhere, laying it on for me, I equalled McNally's tally.

Finbar O'Flaherty put it a little less tersely when he reported on the match for the weekly *Glasgow Observer*, and pointed out that McGrory had really scored nine, the last being netted in the closing minutes but ruled out for offside. The report began:

> Rain fell throughout the game and conditions were depressing but McGrory lost no time in getting to work. In two minutes he smartly netted a Connolly cross and immediately and exactly repeated the feat. Soon he butted a header so forcibly that the Fife goalkeeper, although clutching the ball, couldn't hold it. For his fourth, McGrory had to elude the bodyguard which had now formed to watch him and very cleverly he steered the ball into [a] scoring position and hooked it home. Alec Thomson then went through alone and made it five.
>
> In the second half, the Celtic players visibly set themselves to give McGrory every chance to beat the record and, spoon-fed by his comrades, Jimmy enraptured the crowd with goals, five, six, seven and eight. When his seventh goal was scored and the record broken, the crowd went wild with joy and exultant cheering lasted for several minutes, while the Celtic

players surrounded their hero and warmly congratulated him
on his brilliant feat.

The scoring phenomenon did not go unrecognised on the day.
Students from Glasgow University were there in their annual Rag
Day costumes to take up the half-time collection for charity. They
stayed on for the match and as the final whistle blew they raced on
to the park to grab the centre-forward but, as 'Waverley' in the *Daily
Record* noted, 'the smiling hero, realising their object, evaded them
and disappeared amid a torrent of praise'. No doubt the students
hoped they could have held him for the usual charity ransom. They
would have got a good price for him too, but then, as Celtic had only
recently learned, all the money in the world couldn't buy Jimmy
McGrory.

FIVE

The Golden Crust

> Now come listen all you football fans, and I'll tell you all
>   a story
> Of a famous Celtic forward whose name was Jim
>   McGrory.
> He was the leader in whom Celtic put their trust
> Smiling Jim McGrory with the golden crust.
>
> <div align="right">From a poem by John Biggins of the Gallowgate,
<i>circa</i> 1928</div>

Jimmy McGrory never made any secret about his disappointment in never having played at Wembley against England. Despite his obvious goal-scoring knack, he was omitted time and time again from the full Scotland team and the reasons are not far to seek. He played for Celtic. Worse than that, his father was Irish. Even worse, he was a practising Catholic, and in some eyes this meant his first allegiance was to the Pope in Rome, and not to Scotland. This is incredible today to the point of inanity, but in Scotland at that time it was, unfortunately, only too believable.

This bias has been a factor in Scottish football politics since Celtic first began to make their presence felt, and its effect has never been more exemplified than in the scanty selection over the years of Celtic players for the Scotland team. This was made glaringly obvious in the complete disregard of Jimmy McGrory for a cap at a time when he was the leading goal-scorer in Europe and when, in the current season, he had scored a Scottish record-breaking eight in one game.

To be fair, he did not do his further cap chances any good by being involved in two losing Scottish teams. His Scotland debut on 25 February 1928 against Ireland at Firhill was spoiled by the Irish goalkeeper, Elisha Scott, who had a brilliant game. McGrory didn't score and was therefore branded a failure. On 10 March, he scored two for the Scottish League against the Football League at Ibrox, but the Englishmen scored six and McGrory fell victim to the post-match post-mortem. Consequently, he was passed over for the next full international at Wembley in favour of Airdrie's Hughie Gallacher, now of Newcastle.

It has been said that McGrory was unlucky altogether in that his career paralleled that of the mercurial Hughie, but while admitting that Gallacher at his peak was a great centre-forward, he was no greater in scoring goals than McGrory, as their respective tallies show. In their careers, Gallacher scored 387 goals in 543 League and Cup games and 22 in 19 internationals, whereas McGrory scored 538 in 534 Scottish League appearances and 12 in just 13 matches for Scotland and the Scottish League Select. Even allowing for the higher playing standard and longer season in England, McGrory's goal tally from all games in first-class football was impressive by any standards. Six full caps for Scotland was small recompense for heroic deeds on the field week after week. Yet he never got to play at Wembley – which meant, in 1928, he never got to be a Wembley Wizard.

The Scotland team on that legendary occasion in the rain at Wembley Stadium on the last Saturday in March 1928 was under-sized, under-prized and underrated but it has gone into football history for its systematic 5–1 demolition of England . . . although it should be noted that Hughie Gallacher didn't score any of them – a fact which annoyed him at the time. He complained bitterly about the poor service given to him and the selfishness of the other forwards. The mind boggles at what McGrory might have done with those wonderful centres from the wings by Alan Morton and Alex Jackson, not to mention the inside passes through the middle from Alec James, but it was not to be. Jimmy McGrory always regretted it. So did every Celtic and Scotland supporter.

In the Scottish Cup final at Hampden that year Rangers finally broke their hoodoo and beat Celtic 4–0 in front of nearly 120,000 spectators. After a scoreless first half, Rangers won a penalty when Willie McStay handled in the box. It was a crucial moment for both sides. Captain Dave Meiklejohn couldn't persuade any of his forwards to take the ball, so he had to take the penalty kick himself. He placed the ball on the spot, calmly and efficiently, took five steps back and then – bang – the ball was in the back of the net. The terraces erupted with Light Blue joy and Meiklejohn went into a daze. 'For ten minutes I was hardly conscious of where I was,' he said. 'If Celtic had attacked up the middle they might have passed me by without my seeing them.'

The penalty completely demoralised Celtic, and Rangers cantered home with three more goals in the last quarter of the game to win their first Scottish Cup since 1903. Admittedly, Celtic had a weakened defence due to the loss of Peter McGonagle at left-back through a cartilage injury and the replacement, Donoghue, was no match for Sandy Archibald, the Rangers outside-right, who had a field day. McGrory, in contrast, did not have a great day because Meiklejohn was in inspired form (he always did well against McGrory) – 'nearly good enough to be a Celt' was the opinion of Man-in-the-Know at the *Glasgow Observer*, the highest accolade he could bestow on any player. The whole Celtic team stayed on the field to clap Rangers off. It had been a most sporting contest, and theirs was a fitting gesture after a great game. If only both teams could show each other such professional courtesy today.

Rangers went on to win the League as well and thus complete their first double for a quarter-century. Celtic had to be content with the bridesmaid's place in both League and Cup and wait for next season. To add to their woes, Tommy McInally finally left for Sunderland in May 1928 and a lot of the fun went out of Celtic Park. Adam McLean, such a long and loyal servant to the club, followed him to Wearside because Celtic would not give him a second benefit, even though he was entitled to it. It was typical of manager Maley's fastidious application to the business side of football.

He was no less rigorous in his attention to his Bank Restaurant near the corner of Queen Street and Argyle Street. It was doing well even if it was not a place where the best people went. It was more the haunt of gentlemen of the ring and the turf who gathered for all the latest gossip in the sporting world and, given the status of the proprietor, football names were not unknown. Rumour had it that his players were contracted to eat at his establishment at least once a week. Not all Celtic players were so keen on these public appearances but Jimmy McGrory was. He enjoyed putting on the style occasionally and eating 'up the town' as he called it.

There was a 'Great Gatsby' element in Glasgow at that time and there were people in the West End who knew how to party. The working man kept to his pub but the well-to-do visited each other's big houses and for well-known faces around the city there was no shortage of invitations. Jimmy McGrory's face, thanks to the sports pages, was just on the edge of being well known and he was beginning to be noticed about the place. It was something that never occurred to this most unassuming of young men. All he knew was, despite his present slump, he was the roundest peg in the roundest hole, which was why he hadn't wanted to change things. He was his own man in his own city and that just suited him fine. Teammates now called him 'the golden crust', because his head had earned them so many winning bonuses, but he just grinned, slapped his bowler over it and went out to enjoy himself. The 1920s roared about his ears, and not even the bowler could keep out the noise.

Business was booming for the other Greens. If their 'flicks' had become the 'movies', the 'movies' had now become the 'talkies' – because people *talked* on the screen and the family profited. The coming of sound heralded the golden age of film that was to last until the advent of television in the 1950s. So many people wanted to hear their favourite stars speak that cinemas grew bigger and better and more outrageous. The former skating rinks became veritable palaces, ornate temples devoted to the worship of the new gods and goddesses who spoke from the screen to their worshippers in the dark. These silver deities offered a larger-than-life dream world in luxurious and ornate surroundings which drew the audiences as if to Mecca. Many cinemas were even called 'Mecca' and ordinary people were then drawn to them as if by a mirage. They needed all the dreams they could get. This was nowhere truer than in Glasgow.

Cinemas now vied with pubs for space in that rowdy, crowded city and the upsurge in ticket sales did the Green family no harm at all. As a family business they saw that it was in everyone's interest to keep the family *in* the business, and as far as ability and availability allowed, every relative and near-relative did something in relation to the company's activities. Every member of it had a specific role to play. Something of the old travelling camaraderie still remained in the workforce and when required each could still lend a hand on the ropes, as it were. Survival on the road had often been a matter of everyone's pulling together and that didn't change because they were now operating from fancy offices.

However, it was known that Fred Green liked all kinds of sport and John Farrell, a great friend from schooldays at St Joseph's in

Dumfries and a well-known amateur athlete, was his contact with the football world. Farrell, a well-respected professional man, was a frequent guest of Maley's at Celtic Park and he, in turn, would invite Fred to join him there on a Saturday. John Farrell's son, Jimmy Farrell, was the Celtic director of recent times, and it was he who told the present writer that Fred's young sister, Veronica, was also a regular in the directors' box. Tony Green, her surviving nephew and former Green executive, confirms this. Family legend has it that his Aunt Nona met Jimmy McGrory for the first time at Celtic Park.

It appears that she had been sitting in the stand with Fred during a game in the early 1928–29 season. Just before the final whistle he had taken the chance to escort his young sister from her seat in the stand in order to avoid the crush of the crowds outside the pavilion but their arrival in the main foyer under the stand coincided with the entry of the Celtic players hurrying to their dressing-room. There was a moment of confusion as the Green party collided with the green-and-white contingent and in the mêlée, the young lady was knocked to the floor, quite accidentally, by, of all people, Jimmy McGrory.

He, of course, was immediately apologetic and bent down at once to pick her up. She was quite unhurt, only flushed and embarrassed. McGrory, however, was mortified but Fred smoothed things over in his usual way and led his sister off – but not before he had invited Jimmy to visit them at Craigie Hall the next afternoon to have Sunday tea. Jimmy, still sweating from the game but more agitated by the unexpected collision, nodded his agreement then turned to join his mates in the dressing-room.

No doubt he took some stick about how girls always 'fall' for the dashing centre-forward . . . but what they didn't realise was that Jimmy might have 'fallen' himself. He was still troubled by the occurrence, realising that he might have seriously hurt the girl – and she wasn't bad-looking either. The next day, with a good suit on and the bowler in place, he reported to Craigie Hall as requested. He had never been as near to Ibrox Park on a non-match day. However, the Greens made him feel very much at home and he found that Veronica, or Nona as everyone called her, was quite charming.

According to those who knew both at this time, it wasn't love at first sight; it was more a case of liking at a second glance. The attraction was mutual, not that it became a wildly passionate affair. Both were basically undemonstrative people and they went calmly and gradually into a relationship without any evident fuss. Nona had always been delicate and had to watch her health, and the unassuming McGrory, with his innate kindness and sympathy, would have been just right for her. The Green family was surprised at this development, especially Bert, who had a soft spot for his shy sister – but he liked Jimmy. So did Fred, although it might have been as much for McGrory's sporting fame as his qualities as a man.

For his part, Jimmy was happy enough to enjoy Nona's company and the Greens' warm hospitality, although when he tried to return the favour by asking Maley for stand tickets for the Greens on two Saturdays running, the Big Fella growled, 'Don't your friends ever pay? I thought they were supposed to have money.' Jimmy got his passes but he never asked again. He also played down the prospect of any great romantic attachment. As far as he and Nona were concerned, he would wait and see how things worked out.

The Green sisters, too, apart from the youngest, Marion, were just as cautious. Jimmy McGrory, for all his football fame, seemed quite unlike the kind of men they met at tea dances, tennis parties or yachting trips off the Ayrshire coast. He had been to Seamill on the Ayrshire coast on special training with Celtic from time to time, but it is not likely he ever sailed. He didn't smoke Craven A either or speak the latest smart '20s slang. In short, he wasn't their type – but he seemed to be Nona's. They thought their reserved sister would have chosen someone more bookish, a professional man. Well, Jimmy was a professional footballer.

From then on, his social life certainly picked up. He began to receive invitations to show-business functions, civic dinners and gala nights. Despite himself he became a welcome guest at every kind of Glasgow table. Again, this could only have been through the Greens. He didn't know anyone else in this other Glasgow, still less in show business, except for the acts that used to come to Canon Lawton's Sunday-night shows for which a dinner jacket was not an option. Now, however, a black tie was mandatory and, sometimes, white tie and tails.

The Celtic players began to rib him about moving into high society but Jimmy could hardly believe it himself. This sort of thing normally happened only to Rangers players. Bill Struth, their manager (known as God's Truth to his teams – or God, for short), was very keen on having his players seen as sharp dressers and insisted on each of them wearing a smart suit and bowler on match days. Not all Rangers players enjoyed this sartorial mandate. Some of the older hands were known to wear their bunnets as usual travelling from their digs and would carry the requisite bowler in a paper bag. They would only swap their headgear when they came in sight of the players' entrance.

McGrory, on the other hand, delighted in his bowler, but he had the sense not to wear it too much around Springfield Road or Parkhead Cross. He was always to have a strong sartorial sense, without being in any way a dapper dandy. Not being a snob, he moved easily in any company for he never tried to be anything other than himself, so there was never any social strain. He did find, though, that certain types he was now beginning to meet did not always immediately understand his Garngad accent. His vocabulary, too, wasn't always up to subtle conversational niceties, but he was so plainly unostentatious that they were hardly needed. If he saw someone frown, as if not understanding, he just spoke slower – or better still, never spoke at all. He didn't mind that. He could manage his own silences.

And then it was time to get back to his first love, Celtic. As usual, the close season in 1929 saw him with another 42 goals to his name but the new season would see a lot of changes, not least of which was that work had begun on the new stand, which meant, among other things, that the players had no dressing-room facilities. For home games, they had to be bussed to Shawfield, Clyde's ground in Bridgeton, before and after each match, which was a nuisance. At any rate, it would seem that money had been found from other sources to update the stand, so they didn't need his transfer to Arsenal after all.

The Celtic team at that time appeared to be a two-man affair – Johnny Thomson in goal and Jimmy McGrory up front. The slim and graceful Thomson, although hardly more than a boy, was a phenomenal goalkeeper and was so many times the only one between Celtic and defeat. At centre-forward, McGrory, burly and bustling, was the tireless spearhead, often making goals out of nothing but ploughing something of a lone furrow up the middle. When either player was injured (and because of their similar fearless style they often were), the whole Celtic team suffered and results were poor.

Though they managed to capture the Glasgow Cup, McGrory was again out of action for a lengthy spell after receiving a bad knock during the game against the English League at Villa Park, Birmingham, in November 1928, a match noted for the brilliance of John Thomson in goal for Scotland. Despite his similar heroics for

Celtic, League results were erratic. Indeed, so depressing was the team's performances when minus McGrory that one supporter, after a typical 3–0 defeat by Partick Thistle, felt impelled to write to the *Daily Record* on 16 January 1929:

> Saturday's forward display was woeful. There is much talk of re-building the Parkhead grandstand, but I think they should build a team first. People can't be expected to pay a shilling to watch such Celtic sides.

The directors, of course, claimed that the team was in a process of transition – which is the way a bad run is always explained in football, but even McGrory felt the slump. His 42-goal tally for the season was one less than the 43 scored by Evelyn Morrison (there's a football name for you) for Falkirk, as did Dave Halliday for Sunderland, playing alongside old Celtic favourites, McInally and McLean. McGrory badly missed their service.

John Thomson, at this time, had an interest in going into business in men's clothing after football but McGrory, for his part, never made any mention of what he might do on retiring. He had almost a child's attitude to the present in that it went on for ever if you didn't think about it. 'Whit's fur ye will no' go by ye,' as they used to say in the tenements. There was still enough Garngad fatalism in him to counter any danger of over-optimism. There might be a whole world outside the pavilion but he wasn't at all curious about it. He had no ambition whatsoever outside football and his ambitions for that engulfed any ideas he might have for a 'proper job' as he called it. He was never to lose the joy he felt in playing this boy's game as a grown man. This was something he had in common with John Thomson. Their world was not in the real world. Neither of them could believe their luck. In 1929 the outside world was not a happy place to be.

Black Thursday was on 6 October 1929. It got its name from events in a small back room somewhere in the New York Stock Exchange on Wall Street when an unknown investor decided to sell his or her shares in a hurry, so much so that the injunction, 'Sell at any price', was heard. Within minutes this had translated itself into a general instruction to sell, which, quickly fanned by rumour, soon whirled itself into a panic need to 'sell at all costs'. Within the hour a frenzy swept through the building and before long pandemonium ensued as brokers tried to get rid of investors' money.

It was, in reality, only a paper storm but people refused to believe that their money was safe and a city-wide hysteria set in as banks were rushed by people who wanted to get their cash out – and quickly. The banks couldn't cope of course, and police had to be called out to prevent riots in Wall Street. It was a tragedy, all the more so because it might have been avoided had someone taken decisive action right at the start. By now, it was totally out of control and the damage to the stockbroking communities around the world spread like a deadly cancer. Nothing like this had happened on such a scale since the Great Plague. The repercussions of the usurial catastrophe were worldwide and the fall of capitalism appeared to bring everything else down with it. Easy money was no longer there for the taking. The good-time years had gone in a night, taking investors' confidence, as well as their capital, with them. The boom time was over, the bubble had burst and a great depression hung over the entire globe. As David Potter put it, 'America sneezed and the rest of the world caught a cold.'

Celtic Football Club Ltd, like Green's Picturedromes Ltd, survived the storm, for neither was dependent on outside capital. Although both were limited liability companies, they were essentially family businesses and could keep themselves to themselves, so to speak. They were thus able to weather any outside financial downturn. Shops and factories could close down, investment capital disappear, but both the football club and the cinema empire survived, due to their ability to offer an amenity people craved even more in depressed times – escapism. The Greens did it with motion pictures, Celtic with football matches. Audiences were still hungry for both.

Money might have been tight but something could always be squeezed for the pictures or the match. You paid your shilling and you took your place on the terraces. Millions did so all over Britain despite the fact that for the next decade every second or third man would be unemployed and unable to pay his bob at the gate. Thousands fled to the countries of the Empire to make a new start, but the majority remained to stick it out just as they had in the trenches not so long before. Anyway, season would follow season, and there was always the game on Saturday.

During the last season of the '20s, what might be called the Celtic 'Grant Stand' had been refitted to suit the times, but, on the field, Rangers surged ahead to win all four major honours in Scottish football (winning the Charity Cup on the toss of a coin) and so laid the ghost of Celtic's 'Grand Slam' of 1908. Rangers, assisted by a seasoned reserve side, seemed unassailable. As the late John Rafferty so wisely pointed out in his *One Hundred Years of Scottish Football*:

> Bill Struth, in his years as Rangers' manager, not only set out to make Rangers the best team in the land but always to think that they were. They were the best dressed. They had the best facilities. They were the best paid and the best treated. He instilled in them a tremendous conceit, which eventually developed an arrogance in themselves and a sense of inferiority in most of the others. It was reckoned that Rangers' reputation could usually be depended upon as worth a goal start.

This was at the root of Rangers' supposed invincibility that presented them as the Roundheads of Scottish football, backed by the bastions of big business and, therefore, of the Establishment. Celtic, by contrast, were a people's team from the wrong side of the tracks, immured in the East End and rooted in their Irish past. Their natural style was cavalier and spontaneous, and therefore liable to be more volatile than consistent. When in transition, as in 1929, they could also be very bad and in the season now ending they won nothing. However, they opened the new stand with some pride and couldn't wait to show it off in the new season beginning in 1930, reassured that things could only get better.

They did. They beat Rangers 2–1 in the Glasgow Cup final on 11 October 1930 – a day when, before the kick-off, both teams and their supporters observed a minute's silence for the passengers and crew of Britain's R101 airship which, six days earlier, had gone down in a fireball over France after hitting a hillside. McGrory continued to be plagued by injuries and their continuing effect caused him to miss the first six matches of the new season. As a result, the team performance suffered. When he returned, they picked up at once and his 36 League goals in 29 matches allowed them to threaten Rangers seriously for the Championship, but with the faltering of this challenge, only the Scottish Cup now remained as a prize to be won in the season. A new young team, featuring players like Peter Scarff and Charlie Napier, was growing up around him and, suddenly, the next game was the Cup final. And what a game it was to be at Hampden on Saturday, 11 April 1931.

Celtic and Motherwell drew 104,803 spectators to the match – the largest crowd ever to watch a Motherwell side until that time. The Lanarkshire town went wild with delight about just getting to the final and those who weren't able to travel through to Glasgow for the match gathered outside the windows of the *Motherwell Times* to get the telegraphed news as it happened, or they listened at home to the post-match report on the wireless as it was relayed by the BBC. Some might even have waited for the pigeons to arrive with the final score strapped to one leg. The local team had never been lower than third over the last few seasons in Scotland, and no team deserved more to win something. Their manager, 'Sailor' Hunter, was a popular figure and he had worked wonders with the Steelmen on a minimal budget. Motherwell was everyone's favourite.

Celtic had come through their doldrums of the previous season and now were able to field the best team they'd had since the heady days of 1908, and would not have again until 1937. McGrory would score forty-seven goals in thirty-eight games that season, but this was still three less than the current top scorer in Britain, Joe Bambrick of Northern Ireland's Glentoran, who had fifty. Notwithstanding, Jimmy was to remember this Celtic team as the best he had ever played in. It was: John Thomson; Cook and McGonagle; Wilson, McStay and Geatons; Bertie Thomson, Alec Thomson, McGrory, Scarff and Napier. There were three Thomsons in the team but none was related. There were also three Fifers – John and Alec Thomson and big Chic Geatons. Peter Wilson brought a touch of class to wing-half play, Peter Scarff was improving with every game and Charlie 'Happy Feet' Napier on the left-wing played with a cheeky panache.

The elegant Motherwell team was successful in the League largely due to its international goalkeeper, Alan McClory, a solid defence and the famous left-wing partnership of George Stevenson and Bobby Ferrier (nicknamed The Rolls and Royce of football, such was their class). At centre-forward was the McGrory-style Willie McFadyen, who was to pip the same McGrory for the Scottish League's highest scorer in a season record only a few years later. The inside-right was John McMenemy, who had been transferred from Celtic the previous season for £1,000. McMenemy was McGrory's closest friend in football – but they both had to forget being mates for the afternoon.

McMenemy showed his commitment early when he scored for Motherwell after twenty minutes, his shot being deflected past Thomson by McStay's outstretched leg, just as their first had gone in off him when George Stevenson had shot hard after six minutes. A touch lucky perhaps, but fully deserved on play and Motherwell went in at the interval in the lead.

It was all one-way traffic in the second half and those in the stand could hear McGrory's voice exhorting his mates to even greater efforts, but the Hampden clock showed that the minutes were ticking away. Then, with only seven of them to go, Craig handled outside the box and gave away a free kick. The Motherwell players lined up to face another Napier thunderbolt but, noticing McGrory had crept up on the other side, Charlie calmly lobbed the ball over the defensive wall, taking Motherwell by surprise – but not McGrory. He stretched out a foot and touched it into the net off the post. As the Celtic players hurried to congratulate him he pushed them off and, hurrying into the net, retrieved the ball and ran with it up to the centre spot, pointing to the clock on the main stand as he did so.

By this time, the Glasgow sports editions were in the presses with reports of a Motherwell victory and the pigeons were being got ready to fly, but they reckoned without the joker of the Celtic pack, outside-right, Bertie Thomson. With two minutes to go, and Peter Craigmyle checking his referee's watch, John Thomson cleared a ball straight to Bertie, who scampered up the right wing and Motherwell got ready for yet another cross into the goalmouth. Bertie said later that he only intended to play out time at the corner flag so that he could grab the match ball, but then he heard Jimmy McStay bellowing from the centre of the park, 'Get it across, man!' The perky winger immediately doubled back and lobbed over a high ball with his left foot. The change surprised Alan Craig, the centre-half, who, bothered as usual by McGrory, hesitated before jumping to clear, shouting, 'Let it come.' As he did, another voice called out 'It's yours, Alan.' Craig may have thought this meant the other Alan in goal, but whatever the reason, he mistimed his jump and the ball spun off the side of his head into the net. Referee Peter Craigmyle immediately blew for a goal and for the end of the game.

Poor Craig lay face down, pummelling the turf with both hands. McGrory was the first to pat him on the shoulder in sympathy. There was not a man there that day who wasn't sorry for Alan Craig. He had to be helped to his feet by Peter Craigmyle. 'I've done it, I've done it,' the unfortunate player kept saying, the tears flowing unashamedly.

In Motherwell, people walked away slowly from the newspaper's windows and the edition with the wrong result was hurriedly recalled from the shops. Poor Craig; he was never to forget his worst moment. Jim Hossack, the author and journalist, tells of how, in

1988, he went to meet big Alan, now shrunk into an iron bed in the Paisley geriatric hospital. The former Motherwell, Chelsea and Scotland player had had a long professional career but he could never get that last-minute mishap out of his mind. He told Jim that he went straight home to Paisley after the game and spent the night sitting alone on a bench in the park. Hossack went on:

> To sit in a hospital ward while an old man grips your hand and, fighting back the tears, recalls a personal nightmare which happened well over half a century earlier, was a very moving experience. One fleeting moment had blighted his entire life. He had denied his mates a coveted Cup medal [and] Big Alan took that sense of personal guilt to his grave.

The Celtic players had a very different reaction, naturally, and enjoyed a very different Saturday night. They still had to replay in midweek but they knew that they'd win. After such a last-gasp draw, it was meant to be. They won 4–2 after a 5 p.m. kick-off, floodlights not being available back then. McGrory and Bertie Thomson shared the goals between them and Murdoch and Stevenson scored for the luckless Motherwell. The stage was then set for a proper celebration.

So, on that Wednesday evening, the party went on well into the night at the Bank Restaurant. Thirty policemen tried to control a crowd of almost a thousand who jammed Queen Street in a bid to get a glimpse of their heroes inside. Had they all been able to see through the windows they would have seen Bertie Thomson cavorting with the Cup, now wrapped in green, and Charlie Napier chatting up the waitresses, all bedecked in green rosettes. And, presiding over everything, the proprietor, William Maley Esq., beaming. Bertie Thomson got very drunk, as he usually did, but Maley, for once, let him have his moment. He had played for it. Jimmy McStay sat with the quieter Thomson, Alec, and young Peter Scarff, talking over the game yet again and so proud of his 'team of triers'.

John Thomson sat at another table and with him was a young lady who seemed a little out of place among all the green-and-white jollity. Margaret Finlay, however, carried her own sense of assurance and seemed quite at ease. Johnny Thomson took every chance to introduce her as people kept coming up to their table. He said she was his 'girlfriend' – nothing more. She was not his fiancée, there was no ring, but there was no mistaking the pride he had in her, and she in him. In the Glasgow phrase, they were 'going together' and generally that meant they were going in the same direction – towards the altar. It was thought by friends that they might name the day when he returned from Celtic's American tour in the summer.

Theirs was definitely a football 'match'. Her father had taken her to Celtic Park from their home in Uddingston, when he was invited to sit in the directors' box. She saw John Thomson's first game at Parkhead against Kilmarnock when he made his wondrous save against 'Peerie' Cunningham, whose pivot shot swerving on the volley was lethal, but Johnny somehow saw its deflection and, twisting in mid-air and with the tips of his fingers, turned the shot round the post. The Celtic players agreed that it was the greatest save they had ever seen. Margaret met him afterwards and saw him on every occasion she could after that. Now here she was with him at the Cup final celebration. They left early and Johnny had to fight his way through the crowd still standing outside in the street. He had to catch a train at Queen Street for Cardenden in Fife. Had he but known, these same Celtic supporters would have carried him there on their shoulders.

It's not known whether or not Nona Green was with Jimmy at the Bank party on that April evening in 1931 . . . or whether he had been influenced by John Thomson's 'engagement', or if it were merely that love was in the Glasgow air, but not long afterwards, Miss Veronica Green of Craigie Hall, Dumbreck, accepted his proposal that she become Mrs James E. McGrory.

SIX

Yankee Doodle Celtic

> It is rush and rattle, bang and bustle all the way and all
> the time. Everybody seems to be in a deuce of a hurry. It
> is too strenuous. The pace is absolutely killing. All the
> same it is a wonderful city. The sights are arresting. The
> buildings are marvellous. Wealth parades. But there is
> another side to the picture. There are the poor. There are
> slums.
>
> Unidentified Celtic player to the *Daily Record*, 28 June 1931

On Wednesday, 13 May 1931, the TSS *Caledonia*, a steamship of the
Anchor Line, under the command of Captain Alexander Collie,
stood berthed at Yorkhill Quay, Partick, in the port of Glasgow,
waiting to take on board a 23-strong Celtic party bound for New
York and their first tour of the United States and Canada. A crowd
estimated to be well over a thousand Celtic supporters waited to
cheer them off. It was almost as if they had gathered to watch a game
on the quayside. The Celtic party, as given in the Glasgow *Evening
Times* of 14 May 1931, consisted of directors Tom White (chairman),
James Kelly, James McKillop and Tom Colgan, manager Willie
Maley and his Scottish Cup final team plus full-back John Morrison,
half-backs Bobby Whitelaw and Dennis Currie, and forwards Hugh
Smith, Joe McGhee and Willie Hughes. Thomson was the only
goalkeeper. Trainer Will Quinn completed the party, making a grand
total of 23 Celtic souls in all.

It is difficult to appreciate at this distance in time the full emotional impact that this tour had on both sides of the Atlantic. Celtic had been trying to get 'across the pond' every year since 1891 but something always turned up at the end of each season to prevent it happening. Now, at last, the dream had come true, not only for the club but also for its vast support in America. For Celtic, this wasn't a tour abroad for the Glasgow side; it was a family homecoming. This would explain the extraordinary welcome they were to have wherever they went in the United States. It was the difference between exiles and emigrants. Many of those American supporters were Irishmen who had gone to America to avoid being arrested as rebels. They were real exiles, because they couldn't go back. The emigrants, on the other hand, had fled the Great Hunger or poor economic conditions in Ireland or Scotland and were looking for jobs and the chance to better themselves. Once they had made their money, many of them went back on the first boat to strut their stuff before the home folks.

Now, Brother Walfrid's Celtic, the team of their fathers, were on their way to the New World – and with the Scottish Cup on show. If a thousand-plus supporters waved them off from Yorkhill Quay with their green-and-white banners raised high above their heads, singing 'Will Ye No Come Back Again?', similar crowds stood on both sides of the Clyde and cheered them all the way to Greenock. It was, indeed, a royal progress down river to the Tail o' the Bank. And all this for a football club. But 'this is no ordinary club' as Billy McNeill was later to say. After making a port of call at Belfast, the *Caledonia* turned into the open seas and pointed her bows towards New York.

Jimmy McGrory, not previously known for his literary efforts, kept a diary of the trip. This was collated by Pat Woods, a much-respected Celtic historian, from a typescript that was privately bound for the McGrory family. It is with their permission that the following extracts are quoted. The literary standard of the entries or the quality of comment will not challenge Samuel Pepys or John Evelyn, but as Pat Woods says: 'This is Jimmy McGrory's own account and it vividly conveys the atmosphere of the tour, containing, too, some interesting observations on life in America at this time.'

Was the diary kept at the request of Nona? There must have been *some* talk of the impending wedding between their families, as later events will show, and it is hard to believe that Canon Lawton had not been brought into things – although no record exists of any such discussions before he sailed. One can well understand McGrory's excitement – going off on his first trip on an ocean liner and in the company of his closest friends. This was certainly bigger than crossing to Larne or going 'doon the watter' at the Glasgow Fair, yet he makes no mention at all of shipboard life on the voyage out.

This despite the fact that one of the big events on the voyage was a very formal concert given in the main dining room commencing at 9 p.m. on Tuesday, 19 May under the auspices of Captain Collie and the chairmanship of Tom White. The show featured the ship's orchestra led by Mr T. Wilson and the first item on the elegantly printed programme was our own Mr J. McGrory singing 'The Old Bog Road'. Also featured was Mr A. Thomson, who sang 'Afton Water', followed in Part Two by Mr R. Thomson, who gave the company 'The Sangs My Mither Used to Sing'. Mr T. White obliged with 'Ballymoney' and the team contribution to the entertainment concluded with the song, 'A Farewell', from Mr W. Maley. There must have been rehearsals for all this, yet no mention is made of it. Nor of Mr T. Hendry's banjulele selections, or of 'Where My Caravan Has Rested' sung by Miss N. Innes, or that a collection was taken up at the end by Misses M. McLean and I. MacMillan. Whoever these people might be, they certainly weren't worth mention by diarist McGrory.

Nor did he say how Bertie Thomson's increasing fondness for the bottle was contained or what their training routines were on board, or with whom he shared his cabin, although it's likely to have been Chic Geatons or Jimmy McStay. What we do know, however, is that his first impression of New York's Manhattan skyline, seen nine days later, was not all that he had hoped for:

> Going up the Hudson, I was very disappointed with my first sight of New York's famous buildings. I thought they were very ugly, but later on – when I got used to them – they didn't seem quite so bad.

This is choice comment from a man brought up on the banks of the Monkland Canal, and no mention was made of the newly completed Empire State Building opened just a few weeks earlier. The New York welcome exactly echoed the Glasgow send-off with milling crowds on the docks, yet there was not a sprig of heather nor a kilt in sight to greet a party of Scotsmen from Scotland. The truth was that they were there to welcome an Irish club to America with green-and-white banners to prove it, yet photographs taken on board the *Caledonia* before the departure clearly show the team in tartan Tam o' Shanters and plaid socks under the plus fours. They looked more like a Scottish concert party than a football team. However, there was little tartan or sprigs of heather displayed on Long Island as they disembarked – and if there were kilts, they were worn discreetly. It was Hibernian, in the fullest sense of the word.

This Irish/Scottish ambivalence has hung around Celtic since its foundation, but in New York in the early summer of 1931 there was no doubt whatever that tartan had no place at the feast. This was underlined in the very songs they sang as they waited for the team to disembark. As Jimmy himself commented, 'The only thing they didn't sing was "Faith of Our Fathers".' He continues:

> We went in a charabanc to the Knights of St Columbus Club, Brooklyn, a Catholic Club for men only and our headquarters for the trip. It was a 10-storey building and every room had its own shower bath, which was very useful and refreshing in the hot weather. On the third floor they had a beautiful swimming pool with all sorts of gadgets to make it more enjoyable. The boys took full advantage of this great treat. It had its own bar where drinks could be had in exchange for tickets previously bought at the office. Incidentally, breakfast was served at this bar, which reeked of stale beer and stale tobacco smoke. It certainly didn't whet your appetite.

This was the time of Prohibition in America but McGrory saw that all it amounted to was 'an excuse for bootleggers to make money'. He didn't mention that those bootleggers who weren't Italian were generally Irish:

> My bedroom was on the fifth floor. [It] had a marvellous view. Below us was a 'circus' into which eleven highways converged. It was a wonderful sight to see eleven steady streams of traffic controlled only by lights. They looked like swarms of bees going into one big hive.

Traffic lights were the latest thing. They were part of what was called by the planners 'traffic rationalisation', which saw the banning of horses and carts and the introduction of 'no waiting' in certain areas. The Celtic players were to get to know all about American traffic, for a lot of their time was spent 'on the road'. Their first match was against the Pennsylvania All-Stars in Philadelphia on Saturday, 23 May. As Jimmy explains, the team bus took the party . . .

> Through the Holland Tunnel under the Hudson river to New Jersey, Newark, Kearny, Elizabeth, New Brunswick and Trenton, then over the Delaware river to the outskirts of Philadelphia. Outside the city we were met and escorted by speed cops along Philadelphia's famous Boulevard. We had a police escort all the way. They stopped all other traffic and cleared the way for us as though we were royalty. We were met by the mayor, Mr McKay, and entertained to lunch. After the lunch we drove to the ground and could hardly get in for the crowds. The grounds here are not like our own – everybody gets a seat and there would be about 20,000 spectators.

Celtic won 6–1, McGrory getting a brace with the two outfield Thomsons, Charlie Napier and Peter Scarff, getting the others. This was not bad for a game right after lunch, never mind an Atlantic crossing. What McGrory objected to, however, was that every time a goal was scored, '20 or 30 frenzied spectators rushed on to the field and, in spite of the referee, insisted on kissing the scorer. It was terrible.' One wonders how they reacted to kissing Bertie Thomson. A sweaty footballer in the middle of a game is not an obvious Adonis. The diary goes on:

> We were all very sorry to leave Philadelphia. I made two very good friends [there] – Mr McGrath, a brother of my old schoolmaster, and a Mr Quirk. I'd liked to have spent more time with [them]. With only a stop at a roadhouse for coffee and sandwiches we arrived back in Brooklyn and went straight to our rooms to prepare for the dance. Ten o'clock we were in the dance hall midst an unexpected din. Everybody seemed to be drunk and letting the world know about it. We went up to the platform to be introduced. Mr White tried first, and then Mr Maley, but the crowd just wanted the players – and that was impossible. None of us would have taken a fortune to try and speak to that crowd. We spent the rest of the night signing autographs and we were glad to go back to our beds as we had to play a match the next day.

TOP LEFT: This rare photograph shows Irish Marist Brother Walfrid (Andrew Kerins) at the end of his life. He was the man, while serving in the East End of Glasgow, who had the first idea of Celtic FC, the club that gave us Jimmy McGrory. (By courtesy of I.D. McNamara, USA)

TOP RIGHT: 'Do you recognise him? This is a photograph of Jimmy McGrory taken before he had even learned how to kick a tuppenny ba'.' Wager, the cameraman, didn't know his subject of 20-odd years ago was destined to become world-famous in the sport.

ABOVE: Canon Edward Lawton with the Prince of Wales at St Roch's, Garngad, in 1933. It was not true that he tried to sign the Prince for St Roch's Juniors, but he did set young McGrory on the football road.
(By courtesy of A.F. Smith, Glasgow)

TOP LEFT: The young McGrory, whose heart was set on Celtic. (From the James McGrory collection)

TOP RIGHT: Clydebank's clever new trio: (from left) Devon, Murphy and McGrory.

RIGHT: James McGrory: Scotland's record goal-scorer, 1926–27.

THE BEST.

JAMES McGRORY
Scotland's Record Goal-scorer, 1926-27.

ABOVE: Early teammates: (from left) Charlie Geatons, William ('Peter') McGonagle, McGrory and John Thomson. (By courtesy of Gerald McNee)

BELOW: Two by plus fours: (from left) McGrory, John Thomson, Peter McGonagle and Jimmy McStay. (By courtesy of Gerald McNee)

ABOVE: Pipe dreams while training at Seamill: Adam McLean, Eddie McGarvie (trainer) and Jimmy McStay. Was this where McGrory picked up the habit? (By courtesy of Gerald McNee)

BELOW: Showing off the Scottish Cup to comedian Dave Willis (right) with captain Jimmy McStay (with the Cup) and manager Willie Maley. (From the James McGrory collection)

LEFT: McGrory with Bowler: was it all going to his head? (From the James McGrory collection)

BELOW: His first car: taking delivery of his Morris Oxford at Celtic Park.
(From the James McGrory collection)

ABOVE: A taste of the good life with the Greens and friends.
(From the James McGrory collection)

BELOW: Mr and Mrs James McGrory witness the wedding of Bert
Green to Marjorie in 1935. (From the James McGrory collection)

ABOVE: McGrory scores Celtic's first goal in the first match
of the 1931 Scottish Cup final against Motherwell.
(By courtesy of Gerald McNee)

BELOW: Meeting Prime Minister Ramsay MacDonald with the
Scotland team, 1933. (From the James McGrory collection)

ABOVE: The 353rd world-record-breaking goal scored against
Aberdeen on 21 December 1935, with typical flying header.
(By courtesy of Gerald McNee)

BELOW: Celtic Football Club, Scottish Cup winners, 1937: (top row,
from left) Geatons, Hogg, Kennnary, Morrison, Bucham, Paterson;
(bottom row) W. Maley (manager/secretary), Delaney, McGrory,
Lyon, Craw, Murphy, J. McMenenny (trainer).

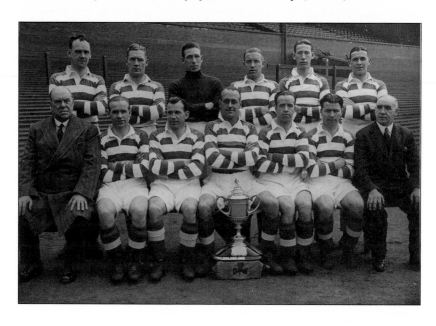

On Sunday, 24 May, they played the New York Giants on their baseball ground and possibly the Scottish players were confused by the 'diamond' baseball markings on the field. Despite this, Charlie Napier scored after 20 minutes but then the hosts replied by scoring twice before the interval. In the second half the Celts fought back as they had done so recently against Motherwell and, two minutes from time, McGrory equalised – 'from a beautiful pass from Alex Thomson'. With only minutes left, he snatched the winner with a typically opportunist effort. The final whistle blew before the Giants had time to re-centre. He said later: 'It was a wonderful finish to a wonderful game. I was carried off the field on the shoulders of the spectators. Everybody seemed to want souvenirs, because I was left with half my shirt.'

Thirty thousand people attended at a dollar a time for the cheapest seats, so it looked as if the tour would pay its way. Next day the players of both teams attended a baseball game on the same ground but the Celtic players were not too taken with it. 'None of the boys felt like taking the game up,' wrote McGrory:

> On Tuesday we just lazed about in Prospect Park in Brooklyn. I never saw so many squirrels . . . so tame, they just ate out of your hand. Wednesday we left at 4 p.m. for Boston. We travelled by paddle steamer up the Hudson where we had a wonderful view of the Empire State Building, America's pride and the biggest in the world and also the famous 'Statue of Liberty', which is 170 feet high. Arrived Fall River 8 a.m. next morning. After breakfast went to Fall River Football Club to put in some practice. It was so hot we had only short pants on. Some of the lads suffered from sunburn after it. In the afternoon we drove to Newport and saw the yacht that beat Sir Thomas Lipton's [in the America's Cup]. Left Fall River at 10.30 p.m. and arrived in Boston at 12.30 a.m.

This was the professional footballer as amateur tourist and already the pace of sightseeing and the incessant hospitality, not to mention the sapping heat, were beginning to tell. A day was spent at Revere Beach, where 'millions of people were in their bathing suits'. The sight of so much flesh did not impress him, but seeing his first game played under floodlights that night did. Some of the players were keen to try it out themselves – but not that night. They were under orders for an early bed. They had a game coming up against the New York Yankees at Boston on the Saturday and they wanted to be ready for it.

The match was played on 30 May in tropical conditions on a bone-hard pitch before 8,000 spectators and resulted in their first defeat by 4–3. They were down 3–0 in the first 20 minutes but drew level after the interval. Gonzales did a McGrory by completing his hat-trick in the last minute and claiming victory for the Yankees. McGrory said afterwards it was the worst game John Thomson ever had for Celtic. It was not like the Fife boy, and it was very unlike McGrory to comment disparagingly on any player. So John Thomson must have been off form that day, but then he had set himself his own exceptional standard and no one can keep to the highest level all the time – even Homer nods. It may have been a simple matter of sunstroke. Some of the others were so dehydrated they couldn't walk after the game. They were hardly recovered by the next day when they had to meet Fall River, where they lost again, this time 1–0, on a ground like concrete. The result was severe blisters all round. McGrory blamed the dreadful conditions entirely: 'I'm sure if we got both these teams together we would take five or six goals from them.' However, he was impressed by the Fall River's goalkeeper, Joe Kennaway, who held out single-handedly against a determined Celtic forward line much in the manner of their own John Thomson, who, unfortunately, was still rather shaky and misjudged Watson's lob to give Fall River the only goal of the game and their goalkeeper a heroic clean sheet. McGrory was to meet Kennaway again, and before very long.

Everyone was glad to get on the paddle steamer again and get back to Brooklyn for four days of nothing but gaping at New York, New York. Well rested and blisters healed, they were eager to make amends in their next game against Pawtucket Rangers at Providence Cycledrome, Pawtucket, Rhode Island, on 6 June. McGrory is typically blunt about the encounter:

> I want to forget this. This was easily the worst place we had been to yet; the worst crowd [in a behavioural sense, there were 20,000 present] and we lost 3–1. Chic Napier got our goal. We didn't mind being beaten, if we'd been treated fairly [but] the game was played on a field that was no bigger than a boys' pitch on Glasgow Green. The referee was hopeless

and again the heat had a big say. Near the close of the game, Kennedy of Pawtucket kicked our right-back, Willie Cook, deliberately and that started a riot. The spectators invaded the field and fighting was their aim. Luckily no one was badly hurt. [We] managed to get to the dressing-room safely.

The following day they were due to play Brooklyn Wanderers at Ebbet's Field and, after three defeats in a row, the team was beginning to feel a little anxious. They needn't have worried. They thrashed the Wanderers 5–0 with McGrory scoring two and Scarff and the two Thomsons getting the others. According to McGrory, Peter Scarff had a wonderful game out of position at left-half. Unfortunately for Jimmy himself, he sustained a fractured jaw and was knocked out in a collision with the goalkeeper, Jimmy McGuire, as he punched a clearance. McGuire was an American-Scot with a Celtic connection, but this didn't help McGrory. He woke up that night in the Swedish Hospital in Brooklyn, where he had had his jaw rewired. This meant that he couldn't attend the presentation and dance held in his honour that same night at the Pride of Erin Ballroom on Bedford and Atlantic, where, as the poster had it, the Jimmy McGrory Brake Club were to honour him as 'the world's most famous soccer player'. Tom Maley, Willie's brother, who had sailed out to join the party at Willie's insistence, accepted the testimonial on McGrory's behalf. As a former schoolteacher, he could be relied upon to be fluent, and Jimmy got his gold wristlet watch suitably inscribed. The Yanks saw McGrory as the Pele of his day and he was treated accordingly. It was all part of the transatlantic experience and he loved it all, as his diary shows. He was never to lose his love of Americans.

> 10 June
> Received at the City Hall, New York, by the Mayor, Jimmy Walker. He donated a cup to be played for against Hakoah, the Austrian-Jewish team at a later date. Spent the rest of the day at the Club.

While at the Club, did he take time out to write to a certain young lady at Craigie Hall, Rowan Road, Dumbreck, Glasgow? He may have had a broken jaw but he never speaks of her in his diaries. This is odd, considering that they were engaged to be married.

11 June
Leave from Grand Central Station 10 a.m. – arrive Montreal
10 p.m. Pipe band leads us to the Queen's Hotel. Next
morning a tour round the city. Received by French Mayor, M.
Houde. [See] the harbour, the Church of Notre Dame and St
Joseph's Oratory on Mount Royal. Meet Brother André.
Thousands come every year to see him and be cured. A
wonderful old man of 88 years. In the evening entertained to
dinner by the Knights of Columbus.

What a wonderful experience for these young men of football to be
given these opportunities of seeing people and places that would be
so much beyond their normal expectation. It cannot have done them
anything but good in terms of maturation, although Peter Wilson still
considered a walk round any Woolworth's in Glasgow as the height
of aesthetic stimulation. Peter was known to have spent a whole
afternoon just wandering around the counters. Well, here he was at
the heart of Woolworth's country but there is no record of his ever
visiting the original. What would he have made of Macy's? Or any
shop on Fifth Avenue?

13 June
We played Carsteel at the Baseball Stadium and won by 7–0.
After the game, we just strolled about the town. Others went
somewhere to dance and Charlie Napier won a very nice prize
for waltzing. We left Montreal at 10 p.m. and arrived in New
York at 8 a.m. next morning.

14 June
We played Hakoah All Stars for the cup donated by Mayor
Walker at the Polo Grounds, New York, and it ended in a 1–1
draw. Hakoah were even rougher than Pawtucket – Charlie
Napier and Peter Scarff being ordered off for fighting with a
Hakoah player – and Alec Thomson got a bad knock. Crowd
was about 30,000. Celtic supporters after the game went
down Broadway in their cars singing and shouting 'Good Old
Celtic'. People must have thought they were mad.

Which they were, of course. Mad about Celtic. It's a condition
which, when caught young, is hard to cure. In certain Glaswegians,
it is congenital and often runs in families.

15 June
Left Pennsylvania Station, New York, the largest in the world, for Chicago. Nothing outstanding about the scenery, although we passed Sing Sing Prison.

16 June
Arrived Chicago 9.30 a.m.

17 June
We played the Chicago Bricklayers at Wrigley's Field, beating them 6–3. Tour of the city. Saw Soldier's Field where Dempsey fought Carpentier for the Heavyweight Championship of the World. Drove along by the shores of Lake Michigan. I spoke on the radio to apologise to the citizens of Chicago for not turning out for the game because of my broken jaw. Visited friend of Mr Maley's.

21 June
Left Chicago for Detroit 10 a.m.

On 24 June, they toured the Ford Motor works in Detroit despite the irony that the players were forbidden to drive cars at home. The Detroit game on 25 June was against the Michigan All-Stars and was the first he played in following his injury but he came through it unscathed. It was also his first game, and Celtic's, under floodlights. It never troubled him, nor the team, for they won 5–0, although he neglects to say whether he got among the goals again. No doubt he did but what would matter to him was that they won. While in Detroit, he took the chance to visit an old Celtic supporter, a Mr Martin, who hadn't seen Celtic for years, and no doubt he made Mr Martin's day. Jimmy McGrory was good at this kind of personal, one-to-one contact, wherever he was in the world. The Celtic party then left for Toronto at 11.45 p.m., crossing by ferry to Windsor, Ontario.

25 June
Broke journey at Niagara. Visited the famous Falls. All the boys dressed in oilskins to walk underneath [them] – a wonderful sensation. Board little steamer, the *Chipewa* to sail up the river that opens on to Lake Ontario. Arrive at Toronto around 8.30 p.m.

27 June

Play Toronto Ulster at Toronto Stadium, winning 3–1. Got a great reception. I played against the son of that great Celt, Peter Somers . . . scored twice. We liked playing in Canada. More like Scotland. Left Toronto at 9 p.m. for New York.

28 June

Arrived New York 10.30 a.m. Most of the team went to Mass at 11.30 a.m. After wash-up and lunch went straight to Yankee Stadium to play the New York Yankees team who beat us 4–3 in Boston. This was a very important game, a game we had to win. We played our best game of the tour and beat them 4–1. Great scenes afterwards. I was presented with a box of cigars and inside a request for a photograph. I sent the photograph. After the match, some of us went to the Brooklyn Paramount Picture House, and others went off to play in a floodlit match at Baltimore against Baltimore Canton, which they won 4–1. I think we had a better time than they did.

29 June

A farewell dance was held for us at the Brooklyn Columbus club. Most of our time was spent signing autographs.

It was all over. It was time to pack the suitcases and cram in all the souvenirs. All in all, it had been a most successful trip. They had played thirteen games, won nine with one draw, scored forty-eight goals and conceded eighteen. McGrory had broken his jaw this time instead of records but, wired up, he was as strong as ever.

He had to be. His direct, full-blooded style was to take its toll throughout his career. Black eyes and bloodied noses were commonplace for him, teeth were vulnerable and now his chin. This might have been because so many of his goals were scored with his head. It was estimated that nearly two-thirds of them were headers, but what few realised was the power that was behind these bullets to the goal. 'Jaymak', who saw McGrory at his prime, was to write an article, 'Giants of Scottish Sport', for the *Evening Times* of 7 May 1955, where he said of McGrory:

> His scoring headers gave a goalkeeper as much chance as a full-blooded shot. When it came to corners, McGrory, as I saw it, always stood well out to see the ball all the way as it

left the kicker's foot. He positioned himself [so that] he was able, if need be, to run in and meet it, putting the full force of his body behind his header – so often with the best results.

And sometimes with a broken jaw.

Meantime, the touring team of 1931 had done much more than play football. They had given hope and pleasure to thousands who thought they would never know such emotions again. They had fulfilled dreams and left a lot of people happier for their having been there. That is the kind of reward that can be lost among the trammel of statistics. They had touched hearts and fed souls. They were the missionaries that Maley had always wanted Celtic to be. They could go home full of memories, contented and fulfilled.

They boarded the RMS *Transylvania* under Captain Bone on the first day of July. The same crowds gathered to see them off and many had to be forcibly put ashore before they sailed. It was heart-rending to see so many who wanted to go home with them. Celtic had obviously touched a nerve and there was a lot of homesickness around on the wharf that day. Eventually, the autographs were signed yet again, the cameras clicked until their spools were empty and then the *Transylvania* weighed anchor and set off up the Hudson River towards the Atlantic.

Tom Maley was on the homeward trip with the team this time and he proved himself a better sailor than his brother. He had also been useful on the tour in addressing civic bodies and meetings of the American Football Association and now he became the unofficial Master of Ceremonies for most of the social activities on board. Their fellow travellers were the Students Travel Union, whom he describes as 'a jolly lot' and they vied with the players in the nightly sing-songs. There is no evidence on this occasion of a formal concert but Tom also enlisted the help of Chief Steward Alexander, setting up film shows and in seeing that Bertie Thomson was refused alcohol for the duration of the trip.

Poor Bertie had once again gone beyond the mark on the voyage and was placed on the wagon for his own good as much as for the comfort of the other passengers. This was such a pity, for Bertie on form was great value, both on and off the park. He was a McInally without Tommy's likeable élan, but he was a good singer and great fun at a party. Unfortunately, the drink was beginning to bite and gradually it pulled him down so that his fitness suffered and his game declined. Now, on the ship going home, Bertie was bored. Not even the sing-songs, which he had liked to lead, could cheer him up.

Tom Maley arranged things like visits to the ship's engine rooms and to the telegraph cabins, where the players could send wireless messages home to Scotland – and perhaps even receive them. This last thought occurs because events in the latter part of this voyage could only have been accomplished given some degree of planning and forethought on the part of the ship's officers and other parties involved. If the tour so far reads like something out of 'Roy of the Rovers' – Irish Rovers perhaps – then this next section is like a scenario for one of the romantic films then being made in Hollywood for the huddled masses of the world, cocooned in their cinemas.

Jimmy McGrory's final entry in his tour diary is dated 10 July 1931 and reads:

> The ship arrived off Moville, County Donegal, Eire. I disembarked on the Custom's Officer's boat, and that morning, around 8.30 a.m., I started off on a life-long journey. I got married.

It was all in that laconic last sentence, but what was the real story behind those three little words? The Glasgow *Daily Record and Mail* carried the story the next day:

> A motorboat went out from Moville to take McGrory off the liner. His bride, Miss Veronica (Nona) Green had travelled to Moville from Glasgow a few days previously. She is the daughter of the late Mr George Green and Mrs Green of Glasgow. The family were proprietors of 13 picture houses, including picture theatres in Europe. The Nuptial Mass, in St Michael's Church, Moville, on Friday, July 10th 1931, was celebrated by the Reverend J.A. Shields, Falcarragh. The best man was Mr A.T. Mullan, Glasgow and the bridesmaid was Nona's sister, Marion.

After the ceremony the group travelled to Londonderry and proceeded later to Lough Derg, the famous Irish resort for pilgrims. Generally speaking, Catholics went to Lough Derg to do St Patrick's Walk over the stones on their knees, which doesn't suggest the ideal honeymoon activity, but they seemed to have made an amenable foursome all the same because Marion Green later married Tony Mullan. Contemporary reports had it that Moville itself went *en fête* for this wedding of the famous footballer to a cinema heiress, but very little noise was made of the event back home – which was just the way the young couple wanted it.

The *Glasgow Observer* of 18 July 1931, which might have been relied on to trumpet the doings of one of her favourite sons, said very little about it. Its comment was almost terse in its brevity: 'Jimmy McGrory left the *Transylvania* at Moville and was married at St Michael's Church to Miss Veronica Green of Glasgow. The Reverend Father Shields, Falcarragh, performed the ceremony.' Such is the tone of this report, one would think he had married a Protestant. Since a Nuptial Mass was celebrated, one must assume she was not, as this ceremony is only available when both parties involved are Christians in the Roman Catholic rite.

This brings up again the matter of arrangements that would have had to have been made long in advance for such an event to have taken place when it did – and how it did. The early-morning disembarkation to a waiting motorboat could not have been a spontaneous happening. Who spoke to whom about what – and when? Somebody must have worked it all out and it certainly wasn't Jimmy McGrory. He had been out of the country since 13 May. Of course, he could have worked it all out with Nona beforehand, but somehow that doesn't sound like Jimmy. Forward planning of this order of intricacy would not have been his forte. One can feel the work of the Greens in this. Their organisational skills and web of contacts – not to mention money – would have been vital.

Canon Lawton would have made a great Garngad production of the wedding, which was the last thing this diffident couple wanted. Several thousand Celtic fans would have turned up at the reception. Donegal was McGrory's favourite holiday patch so Moville would have been a natural choice of Irish location, but after that there were so many other practical and legal matters to be seen to. For instance, the marriage banns would have to have been called for three Sundays running – or posted publicly in the church for eight days. One of the parties had to reside in the parish; if not, the Bishop's approval would be required, which would mean another meeting, letter or telephone call. The priest would have to be arranged and a date booked. All these things take time and effort. Who did it all?

Even more important, whose influence did it take for an ocean liner to be persuaded to make an unscheduled stop after an Atlantic crossing to let one passenger off in a Customs boat before breakfast. The whole saga may have a charming romantic ring but there were logistics involved here and someone had to deal with Anchor Line and Captain Bone or with Mr Llewelyn Davies at their office in Glasgow. To navigate several thousand tonnes of ship between Inishowen Head and Magilligan Point was a maritime manoeuvre of some asking even if it did not have to enter into Lough Foyle and the little harbour at Moville. Lying off in deeper waters was still a big undertaking and only a big man could have considered it – Fred Green.

He would have done it all on the grand scale and with some style and taste. After all, it was a family matter; a Green was being married. Nona was no giddy young girl, marrying on a whim. She was 32 years old and knew what she wanted. He was 27 and trusted her completely. So, it was all arranged. To some extent, theirs was more of a subsidised elopement, rather than a conventional wedding, but it was hardly Gretna Green – more like Glasgow Green perhaps. It was carried through in a way that would have pleased a very private couple. It is assumed that Nona had got what she wanted.

SEVEN

Mansion Polish

> When society requires to be rebuilt,
> there is no use attempting to rebuild it
> on the old plan.
> John Stuart Mill, *Dissertations and Discussions*, 1859

For the new season beginning in August 1931, Jonny Connor joined Celtic on trial from St Roch's Juniors as a possible understudy to McGrory. This was hardly a good career option given McGrory's normal durability, but it did illustrate the parallels in their beginnings. Only ten years before, McGrory had been signed from the very same club and after the very same Boys' Guild start. Connor was just as 'Celtic-daft' as Jimmy was and used to do an early-morning roll delivery around the Garngad just to earn the sixpence that got him in at the Boys' Gate at Celtic Park. He developed into a good two-footed player with 'a very useful head near goal'. His professional career, however, only serves to underline how unique McGrory's was.

Both were good footballers; the difference was that McGrory was star material and Connor was just another pro. After only seven first-team appearances in two seasons at Parkhead (none at centre-forward), Jonny was deposed as a McGrory deputy by the arrival of John Crum from Ashfield Juniors and transferred to Airdrie in 1934. After that, he seemed to go all round the football houses from Airdrie to Plymouth Argyle, Swansea Town, Queen of the South, Albion

Rovers, Alloa and St Johnstone until he ended up in 1948 back where he started, in the Garngad playing for the local British Railways Works team and acting as St Roch's match secretary. He had come full circle, but on the way he had scored a lot of goals and pleased his many masters. What is to be borne in mind is that his was the normal pattern for a footballer's life. He goes at first where his heart is then follows wherever his feet take him and it's more or less an up-and-down journey over a dozen years at most if he's lucky. At the end of it all he'll kick a ball for anybody, but nobody asks him. This is why McGrory's story is distinctive.

He was a one-club man from the start and the only way he went in his playing days with them was up until, in the phase now being considered, his status within the club was sacrosanct and with its supporters, near iconic. Yet what was also typical was that he remained a good friend to Connor all his life and they never lost touch. Neither ever forgot his Boys' Guild and St Roch's roots and both men took pains not to lose touch. They would each grow old with few regrets – except that Connor may have wished he had come to Celtic at any other time than between Jimmy McGrory and Johnny Crum.

Speaking of these tenement boys (Crum was a Maryhill man) allows mention of the fact that McGrory now moved into what might have been considered a whole tenement by all three of them, when he took up his first marital residence at 23 Miller Road, Ayr. 'Greenways' was a solid, stone, detached, four-bedroom villa in a douce Ayrshire town and stood four-square to a sober street that obviously had money. Streets wear their prosperity in the same way people do. Perhaps it is politely understated, but they want you to know they're doing well all the same. On the other hand, people who live in poor streets can't hide their poverty so to hell with appearances. Well, the boy from the poor street was now set down among the well-to-do and he had to make some adjustments.

Greenways is now part of the Elms Court Hotel next door, but one can still see what a fine home it must have been. The spacious upstairs rooms and generous bay windows on the ground floor indicate a comfortable lifestyle and there would have been plenty of room for the newlyweds to entertain in the Greens' style, as established by Fred at Craigie Hall. It soon became party time at Greenways as McGrory was introduced by his wife to mansion-style living. As a famous young couple they were in constant demand socially. At the beginning Jimmy may have needed a little bit of polishing and, as a Garngad boy, he would have understood that 'Mansion Polish' was more than a brand of furniture cleaner. Many a poor stick of tenement furniture had a weekend shine put upon it by a Glasgow housewife using the same. It didn't guarantee to improve the quality of the furniture but it certainly gave it a sparkle.

The metaphor is apt for McGrory. He could be said to be quality furniture; he just required a bit of polish. Some sources have said that he was given elocution lessons by Nona at Miller Road. This is unlikely, as she had neither the training nor had he the aptitude to turn himself inside out for the sake of any drawing-room acceptance. Robert Burns had the same trouble when he first went to Edinburgh, but then it's not thought that McGrory knew much about Scotland's National Bard either, even though he was now living in the poet's home town – 'Auld Ayr, wham ne'er a town surpasses for honest men an' bonie lasses', as Tam o' Shanter put it. McGrory was almost sinfully honest, and added to that he was street-smart from boyhood. The particular lass he had not long married might have given him a few wifely tips about basic grammar in order to get round any tricky conversational corners, but Jimmy would have picked up a few things along the way.

He was not entirely without sophistication. He had survived the Euston Hotel with Maley and already caught a glimpse of the Glasgow good life with the Greens over the past couple of years – but he was from the tenements and tenement boys are not trained for table talk. They know street-corner chat but small talk is not their forte and big talk is just bragging. They are also encumbered with the impediment of the glottal stop, which is why so few Glaswegians became public orators. On the other hand many have 'the patter' or 'the crack' (the Irish *craic*) – that natural ability to swim with words at high speed – for instance, Billy Connolly. Jimmy McGrory, plain man, did not have the patter. The last thing that could be said of him was that he was glib. McInally had this gift, so had Napier and Bertie Thomson to a lesser extent, but Jimmy was your quiet man. He let other qualities do the talking for him. Nona would have no need to kick him under the table during dinner with friends. In any case, he had been kicked enough in his career and there wasn't a week when he wasn't nursing something sore from the Saturday before.

Because of his open nature and warm personality, and also his growing reputation, famous entertainers of the day, like comedian Dave Willis, were glad to have their photograph taken with him. He had his own trading name, Jimmy McGrory of the Celtic, and that opened doors enough, although most of them were ecclesiastical. Unlike Willie Maley, who had pretensions to a clerical dignity, Jimmy had a total lack of pomposity. What you saw was what you got. Nona was more concerned about what you *heard*. She would have known that snap judgements were often made on the strength of a vowel misplacement or a personal assessment arrived at merely on the strength of a past participle lost.

This is by no means to assert that married life became a centre for further education but it could be said that Nona was good for Jimmy in a lot of respects. She also introduced him to the telephone as a private amenity. It went with the house. Jimmy was delighted with it, but couldn't think of anyone he could ring from Ayr 2322. Anyway, none of his friends had a phone.

His family, however, were near at hand in the person of his adopted niece, Kathleen Elliott, who served as the McGrory's housekeeper, even though, in her time, various little ornaments and knick-knacks went missing from the house. However, the finger of blame could not necessarily be pointed at Kathleen as, Jimmy being Jimmy, he was known to give away small items, like medals or engraved drinking glasses, to guests as mementos of their visit.

Speaking of glasses, Veronica Dunlop, writing from an address in Ayr in 2004, told the author that her mother was Janet McCartney, and that she, too, worked at 23 Miller Road. Veronica, who says she was named after the first Mrs McGrory, also mentioned that she has in her family a whisky glass with an illustration of Jimmy McGrory engraved on it. There were only four made but she has no idea where the other three went.

Greenways was part of the Greens' property portfolio in Ayr. Another was the Playhouse Cinema in Boswell Park off the Sandgate. Even though she was brought up in the cinema business Nona took little responsibility for the picture house, which did not have a great local reputation. In any case, Nona preferred to stay at home and attend to her slipstitch embroidery even though she now needed glasses to work on it. Jimmy might have put in a few nights at front of house but it is unlikely. He was happy enough to sit and listen to the wireless, and wait for the phone to ring.

A more important aspect of his becoming a worthy citizen of Ayr was the fact that it necessitated the purchase of his first car. As already mentioned, there was an embargo on cars for footballers and Maley strictly enforced the rule. This is all the more ironic when around today's new stadiums the parking lot resembles the Earls

Court Motor Show with the number of flash cars parked by the players. Most of these cars cost more than the average house, yet McGrory was only allowed to drive his Austin 16 (a black saloon, registration number CS8 511) because his house was too far away to be accessible by tram. Public transport was thought the thing for football players. The private car was out as far as Maley was concerned. He wrote personally to McGrory:

> Dear J,
> The Board have decided that no player will be allowed to use a private motor car during the playing season. They feel that the risks of the road are too great and in addition they are of the opinion that it is not helpful to a man's physical condition as a football player. They quite appreciate your personal position and are quite willing to rely on your promise not to use your car except in exceptional cases and that you will not take other players in your car at any time. I feel sure you will understand the position and loyally accept it.
> Yours always,
> W. Maley.

One can understand the club's need to protect their investment. The same restrictions still apply to actors in films and today jockeys and acrobats find it hard to get reasonable car insurance. However, the docile McGrory complied with the club's edict, leaving his new car in the garage behind the house and taking the train up to Glasgow from Ayr Station on match days.

Mrs Mable Houston of Irvine remembers an anecdote from that time:

> My mother often told the story of how he [Jimmy McGrory] would come to my grandmother's [Isabella McGrotty's] house with a few of the other players on a Saturday morning before the match – no luxury hotels or flash cars in those days – to meet up with my grandmother's lodger, John McFadden, who was a friend [of McGrory's] and wrote a sports report for a Sunday paper. After a spot of lunch, they would set out for wherever the game was being played [and] Jimmy McGrory's parting remark was always – 'I'll score a goal for you Granny,' to which she would reply, 'Mind your head, son.'

This rings so true – both of the man and the time. We can see, even from more than 70 years on, a real perspective on the game as it was played by carefree young men who never gave it a thought as an onerous duty to be performed for public appraisal. They genuinely *played* football. Well, Granny McGrotty got a lot of goals from her lunch guest – and he, no doubt, got lots of plates of lentil soup.

Celtic resumed training in July 1931 feeling that it was going to be a good year. The team had found a great spirit on the American tour and the younger players had matured at a bound. Charlie Napier, now 20 years old, was getting more and more confident and Peter Scarff was headed for great things in the game according to those who knew their football. These two were held to be the young lions in the side, the pride of Celtic, so to speak, yet Scarff, at 23, was a year older than John Thomson, who was already established as a senior player and Scotland's first-choice goalkeeper. McGrory himself was only five years older, so it was a young team that was being assembled at Parkhead. Their cohesiveness was quickly appreciated as they were unbeaten in the first seven games of the 1931–32 season, their attractive play being described by one journalist as 'the pure wine of soccer'.

All eyes, therefore, were on their first meeting, which was at Ibrox on Saturday, 5 September 1931 and 80,000 congregated on the slopes on a still, windless afternoon to witness this vital encounter, which kicked off at 3.15 p.m. Celtic fielded their touring team with John Thomson in goal, Cook and McGonagle at full-back, Wilson, McStay and Geatons across the middle and the forward line was the well-tried two other Thomsons, McGrory, Scarff and Napier. Rangers played Jerry Dawson in goal for his debut game, Gray and McAuley at full-back, Meiklejohn, Simpson and Brown at half-back and their forward line was Fleming, Marshall, English, McPhail and Morton.

With so much depending on it, the players on both sides were less concerned about being clever and more about not trying to make a mistake. As a consequence it seemed as if the match were heading for a dull, scoreless draw. At the interval, only the statisticians could have been satisfied by a point apiece but then, five minutes after the restart, something occurred that took the event out of the match reports and into the history books. It not only shook Celtic but most of Lowland Scotland as well, and it all happened so quickly.

John Thomson had made a long clearance to Bertie Thomson on Celtic's right wing but the move broke down and Davie Meiklejohn, the Rangers right-half and captain, came out with the ball and passed it on to Jimmy Fleming on his right. Fleming beat off a tackle by Geatons before releasing it quickly inside to the young centre-forward, Sam English, who had evaded Jimmy McStay well upfield and was advancing to the right-hand corner of the Celtic penalty box. Thomson, in the Celtic goal at the Copeland Road end, was made to come out but hesitated for a moment on the six-yard line as English pushed the ball ahead of him. Then, as he saw the centre-forward prepare to shoot, he dived full length, knee-high from the ground. There was a crack of bone as his head collided with knee as English followed through with his shot and the ball went harmlessly past Thomson's left-hand goalpost. He had made the save but seemed to know little about it. As he lay on the ground, English stumbled over him and also fell holding his knee. Thomson was lying as he had fallen, one hand outstretched, the other on his cloth cap, which had been pushed to the back of his head. His hand fell to the ground as blood spurted from his right temple on to the grass.

His brother Jim, sitting in the stand, remembered: 'I knew at once it was serious from the way his hand fell slowly.' Meanwhile, Sam English was being helped to his feet by colleagues, but Thomson lay ominously still. The Celtic players were round their young teammate immediately and Jimmy McStay, the captain that day, signalled frantically to the stand, although Will Quinn, the Celtic trainer was already running on to the park. It was 4.15 p.m. – exactly an hour since kick-off.

'Doc' Marshall, the Rangers inside-right was a medical student at the time and he saw at once the seriousness of the injury. He suggested to his colleagues that they stand respectfully apart but one of them made a crude remark and was immediately rebuked by Alan Morton. The Celtic players were in a daze and Willie Maley was already with them, trying to hold them together. The Rangers supporters behind the goal, who couldn't see how grave the situation was, began to grow impatient at the long delay and started to jeer and catcall, suspecting that Thomson was feigning injury to save time. Davie Meiklejohn immediately went to the running track in front of them and raised both hands, like a priest making an incantation.

As he held his hands high the noise gradually faded and Meiklejohn returned to the field, his head bowed. The Rangers end immediately became quiet, sensing something unusual was happening. Their silence spread round the ground until, by the time the ambulance men were carrying the unconscious Thomson past the main stand, his head swathed in bandages already red with his blood, a complete hush, far deeper than any formal or two minutes observance, had come down on 80,000 people. It was eerie. All that could be heard was the hard breathing of the hurrying stretcher party. Suddenly the silence was broken by a woman's scream, which rang out from the stand as Thomson was hurried into the tunnel and out of sight.

It took a while for the referee, W.G. Holeburn of Govanhill, to get the game restarted. Both managers were now on the field, Bill Struth counselling his players and Willie Maley trying to organise another goalkeeper. Peter McGonagle was the normal substitute but Maley needed him more in defence, so Chic Geatons pulled on the spare goalkeeper's orange jersey which had been brought out. Eventually Mr Holeburn blew to continue the match. It restarted with a Celtic goalkick. Since Thomson had diverted the ball past his post, it should have been a corner kick to Rangers, but nobody was at all interested in such details. Spectators at the Celtic end were already streaming away and the players on both sides didn't seem to have the heart for it. The atmosphere was quite unnatural and a game of football was the last thing on anyone's mind. The echoes of the female scream seemed to hang in the air and were only dispelled when the referee blew to end the game, the players walking sadly towards the tunnel. Sam English walked off with his head bowed and apparently broke down in the Rangers dressing-room. He was sent home at once with Hamilton, the other Rangers goalkeeper, as his escort. Jerry Dawson was also in a state of shock. It had been his first game in the Rangers goal. Nobody knew what to say but they all knew the first act of a tragedy had just been played out.

Meanwhile, Jim Thomson had come down from the stand and seen his brother put into the 1928 Austin ambulance in front of the main door. Mr Struth brought a young girl to the door of the Celtic dressing-room and said that she was asking to see John. She had been sitting with Jim Thomson in the stand and followed him down but had gone to the Rangers dressing-room by mistake. It was Margaret Finlay, his 19-year-old girlfriend. It was she who had screamed.

There was pandemonium at the Victoria Infirmary. Thomson had been admitted to Ward A. Word had got out about the incident and there were scenes of confusion both outside and inside the hospital as people clamoured for news of the young goalkeeper. After an initial examination, which diagnosed a depressed fracture of the skull, an operation was immediately carried out to relieve the pressure on the brain but at 5 p.m. he suffered a convulsion and the odds were shortening all the time on any kind of recovery. He was moved to Ward 5 and only certain visitors were allowed to wait in the ward waiting room. These were Jim Thomson and Margaret Finlay, Willie Maley, director Tom Colgan, Jimmy McStay, Peter Wilson, who was close to John, and Jim Maguire, a young Celtic player with whom Thomson shared digs in Queen's Park. He and John had just bought a half-share each in a car and were learning to drive. Jimmy must have learned fast for it was he who drove John's parents back to Fife later that night. Rangers manager, Bill Struth, had sent a car for them. John and Jean Thomson, with their other son Bill, arrived at the bedside at 9.20 p.m. John Thomson Junior died five minutes later. It was as if he'd been waiting for them.

The switchboard at the hospital jammed and all six Glasgow newspapers were flooded with calls – but it was the kind of news that needed no wires. Soon the whole city knew and the death numbed everyone. All of Lowland Scotland seemed to go into a state of shock. Bob McPhail of Rangers learned the news from the front window of the *Sunday Mail* office in Hope Street on his way home from a dinner at Rombach's Restaurant. He had played in the game and knew John Thomson well from their international appearances. He couldn't take it in and burst into tears on the pavement. Jimmy McGrory, too, remembers that awful night, when the telephone rang at Greenways:

> I was living in Ayr at the time and motored home. I can hardly remember driving. I was in such a daze and when I got home I just didn't know where I was as I waited for news. I was just married . . . and I sat with my wife all evening wondering if the phone would ever ring. Then I decided to phone the Victoria Infirmary itself but the switchboard was jammed with calls. Jimmy McStay phoned me about 10 p.m. to tell me, broken-voiced, that John was dead – 'He died half an hour ago'. That's all he said and put the phone down, obviously too choked to say any more. I was dazed. I could have died myself. Never in a hundred years did I think he would die – only 22. I went through to the living room and said to my wife, 'He's dead.' 'God rest his soul,' she said.
>
> I remember we sat there in disbelief.

How often McGrory had been reminded to 'keep the heid' and now here was a dear young friend dead from a head wound. Did Granny

115

McGrotty's injunction, 'Mind your head, son', return to him from the Gallowgate? He'd never thought of football as a danger sport, even though a handful of players had died on the field over the years. Countless numbers have been seriously injured, and there are those who succumb to sudden illness at the very height of their careers and in their prime.

One such was to be John Thomson's teammate, Peter Scarff, who coughed up blood after one game against Leith Athletic in December 1931, only months after John's death, and exactly two years later he was dead from tuberculosis at twenty-five years of age. He was buried at Kilbarchan with all the Celtic players present. Peter was always the quiet one and his was a quiet end.

The same cannot be said of John Thomson's interment. On Wednesday, 9 September 1931 he was laid to rest at Bowhill Cemetery, near Cardenden, among a sea of grief-stricken faces crowded into every spare inch of that tiny graveyard. Almost everyone carried a wreath and, in a nearby railway siding, a whole train, packed with floral tributes sent from all over Scotland, waited silently, not knowing what to do with them all.

Working men took the Wednesday off to pay tribute. Twenty thousand people swamped Queen Street Station and its surrounds in Glasgow to see his coffin entrained for Fife. Two special trains were added to take supporters to the funeral. The long road from Parkhead to Bowhill, covering, as it does, the broad Lowland waistband of Scotland, was a veritable rosary of salute. Knots of people stood at every crossing watching those ordinary men in cloth caps, just like the goalkeeper's, some still in working boots, walking all the way from Glasgow to see their hero buried in a wall-side grave in a remote mining village.

Tents were pitched on the crags above the cemetery to accommodate the thousands who poured into the village all that day. An aeroplane, not a common sight in 1931, landed in the Daisy Field bringing newspaper reporters who had to write about that sensational, sad day. From all parts of Scotland mourners came, anxious to pay homage to the Prince of Goalkeepers, a future king who had not yet properly begun his reign. Scottish football had found its first martyr.

His teammates came through the crowd in the graveyard carrying the coffin. McGrory and Jimmy McStay were at the front followed by Alec Thomson, Willie Cook, Peter Wilson and Charlie Napier. Every other Celtic player walked at either side of them as escort.

Many were near to tears, as they let their clubmate down gently into the earth. Only a few days before, he had run out on to the field beside them, full of the same youth. It was so hard to accept. It still is.

Even today, nearly 75 years later, flowers and scarves and football caps still appear at the base of the tombstone on the anniversary of his death along with cards and greetings from people who could never have seen Thomson play. When David MacLellan's play, *The Celtic Story*, with music by Dave Anderson, was presented by the Wild Cat Company at the Pavilion Theatre, Glasgow, in 1988, the John Thomson funeral was re-enacted. As the 'coffin' was carried across the stage by the actors, the whole audience rose spontaneously and stood in silence to watch it pass.

The following Saturday, 12 September 1931, a grim-looking Jimmy McStay led out an equally sombre Celtic side wearing black armbands to face Queen's Park in a League match. McGrory walked out after Alec Thomson and before Charlie Napier looking as if he were going into battle. Recent signing from Cowdenbeath, John Falconer, a known Rangers supporter, had the unenviable task of taking over in goal. Both teams observed a two-minute silence before the game and a bugler sounded the 'Last Post'. In the unreal atmosphere the crowd was, naturally, subdued. The players went through the motions for 90 minutes and the game ended, fittingly, in a 2–2 draw. Everyone was glad to get home again.

Quite understandably, the heart went out of the Celtic team in the weeks that followed and the fight went out of them for the Championship. McGrory scored his respectable tally of thirty goals, which included three in the Cup games, despite a two-month lay-off after a knee injury at Motherwell, but he never got near Ulsterman Fred Roberts of Glentoran, who got fifty-five by May 1932. Willie McFadyen of Motherwell got 52 that year, which helped his club reach a record-breaking 119 goals in the season and landed them their first League Championship. 'Sailor' Hunter's side also knocked Celtic out of the Scottish Cup in the third round. At least Motherwell's Championship win stymied Rangers' attempt at six-in-a-row and that helped salvage some Celtic pride. The Ibrox side, however, beat Kilmarnock 3–1 in the Cup final at the second attempt and everybody went into the close season with a sigh of relief, trusting that the dark clouds would soon lift.

Tom Greig's meticulous research for his book on John Thomson, *My Search for Celtic's John*, discovered that John Thomson's girlfriend,

Margaret Armour Finlay, had married an Army officer and in 1946 retired with him to Oakville, Ontario. When John Thomson's name happened to be mentioned on a local radio programme, she mentioned quite casually to her daughter, 'You know, I was once engaged to him.' It was the only time she had ever mentioned him in all the years. Margaret died of a stroke in 1980.

It was also to Canada that Willie Maley had looked to try and find some light in the shadows surrounding the club. He remembered the young Montreal-born goalkeeper who had held out against McGrory and friends at Fall River, and cabled him an offer to join up at Parkhead. James (but always called Joe) Kennaway arrived in Glasgow with his new wife, Loretta, on 29 October 1931 and signed the next day. He played his first game the day after – and was injured. He was back by 21 November for the match against Hearts at Tynecastle and, before long, Celtic knew they had found Thomson's replacement. Joe's happy demeanour and confident North American grin were the first chinks of light in a dark year and a cheering portent of brighter times to come – not only for him but for Celtic and, therefore, for Jimmy McGrory. It was time for him not only to lift his head again – but use it.

EIGHT

The Human Torpedo

> Supporting Celtic has never been simply about 90-minute football matches. It's not so much a religion, more a way of life.
>
> Ian Jack, author and journalist, 2003

It was a proposal by the Scottish Football Association that was responsible for the international change in the offside law in 1925 when it was amended to rule that two instead of three opponents must stand between the player and the opponent's goal. To offset the advantage gained by forwards, the centre half-back was used as a deep-lying centre full-back or 'stopper'. Bob Gillespie of Queen's Park was the first such player in Scotland, but his example was soon followed by Rangers, who developed their team formations based on the new system to such effect that it gave them the most effective defence in the country. Celtic, on the other hand, still considered attack the best form of defence and kept the old team formation with the centre-forward as spearhead. This meant an even greater reliance on McGrory.

Small wonder he was injured so often. But he was tough and determined and no ball put through in his direction wasn't worth chasing. Every cross coming in from either wing he regarded as his – a dangerous assumption at times – but because of his extraordinary heading ability, his courage often paid off. This projectile action earned him the nickname, 'The Human Torpedo'. It was only one of

119

the many sobriquets McGrory earned. 'The Golden Crust' had been an acknowledgement of how valuable were his many scoring headers, although the dressing-room label for him was 'The Mermaid' because 'he had nae feet', although McGrory could beat his man when he had to. Very often, he made his chances out of nothing, but what more might he have done had he received in his career the service his finishing talents deserved? As long as he was playing, the team had a chance and the supporters had hope. That's why they loved him.

The words 'effort and commitment' have become commonplace in the football jargon of today and they often serve to cover a lack of the finer skills in a player, but in McGrory's case, they meant exactly what they said. Nor was it kept just for the big occasion. As early as April 1926, he had played in a benefit game for Hibernian's veteran wing-half, Peter Kerr, and put himself about to such effect that he scored two fine goals, even though it was only a friendly and there were less than 2,000 people watching. It was all a question of attitude. At whatever level, a game called for one's best. Jimmy McGrory never gave anything less.

McGrory's 22 goals in 25 League matches had managed to keep Celtic in a respectable fourth place in the Championship behind Motherwell and Hearts, but he still had a further contribution to make before the season was out. He was to play for Scotland against England at Hampden and would be involved in inventing another piece of Scottish football folklore . . . the phenomenon known as the Hampden Roar.

The match was played on April Fool's Day 1933 and the Scottish team was notable for the presence of three Celts, Peter Wilson, Jimmy McGrory and Peter McGonagle, whose Scotland debut it was. When one considers the skill and high reputations of these players, their paltry collection of caps is scandalous but for once, McGrory was preferred to Gallacher, Wilson to Meiklejohn and McGonagle to Nibloe of Kilmarnock and all three were determined to make the most of it. Another point of interest in the fixture was that Bob Gillespie of Queen's Park, already mentioned above, was captain – the last time an amateur would lead out a Scottish team.

McGrory got off to the best possible start with a goal in five minutes. Bob McPhail sent winger Douglas 'Dally' Duncan away down the left flank. As Dally's cross came over, McGrory, arms spread, threw himself at the ball and it sped past Hibbs into the

English net. This set the crowd roaring – even more so when Arnold missed a sitter with only the Scottish goalkeeper, 'Jakey' Jackson, to beat, but England did equalise through centre-forward Hunt's brilliant shot through a ruck of players that went in at the near post. For the first half-hour of the second half, with the sun and the wind at their backs, England were on top but then the crowd took a hand – or rather, they found their voice. With only eight minutes to go, McGrory took a through ball from the tall Ranger McPhail, rounded Cooper, the full-back, and blasted the winner past the advancing Hibbs. Had Hampden's terraces been roofed then, the noise this caused would have lifted it off. The two Scots did a war dance in the penalty area while all of Hampden roared about them. Bob McPhail was to write in his autobiography:

> If I knew nothing about the 'Hampden Roar' before that moment, I certainly felt the full force of it right there and then – the noise from the crowd of 134,710 (which was then a record) must have broken every window within a mile radius. If it frightened the life out of the English players, I can assure you it damned well scared me. It was a waste of time shouting at each other in the closing minutes, because none of us on that field could hear a thing. We simply floated towards the final whistle on a vast tidal wave of noise.

McGrory and McPhail were to play together at international level nine times and became good friends as well as a powerful attacking tandem. It says much for both that they remained modest and unassuming in later life despite the fact that, between them, they had instigated the Hampden Roar. From then on it was seen as being worth an extra goal to Scotland.

'What a wonderful goal that was,' said Hibbs, the English goalkeeper, to McGrory as they left the field. It was a very sporting comment and an honest appraisal of a fellow professional's skill, but neither player could have been aware of the very real danger many of that immense crowd were in. A letter to the *People's Journal* signed by 'Disgusted of Dundee' explained the conditions. He wrote:

> I was literally swept off my feet during the alarming swaying and surging which followed McGrory's second goal. A man in front of me fell in a faint. Men shouted frantically for the crowd to get back. It was impossible. The seething mass

swayed down on us. The man was actually trampled on
before he was finally extracted by the police.

This very real risk of congestion obviously did not exist in the seated
stands. Apparently, when that celebrated goal was scored, a Scotland
fan rose up from his seat in the stand and, with both hands upraised,
uttered the one word 'McGlorious!' That one word said it all and set
the seal on the player's place in football annals.

After such heady excitement, it was back to ordinary football
business again and for Celtic it was the Scottish Cup. Even given
their erratic form they had stuttered and stumbled their way to yet
another final on 15 April. Once again, Motherwell were the team to
beat. More than 100,000 fans turned up at Hampden to see yet
another epic but what they got was a grim struggle between two well-
matched sides where defences were on top most of the time.
Motherwell now had two internationals at full-back, Crapnell of
Scotland and Ellis of Wales, and Celtic fielded at right-back nineteen-
year-old Bobby Hogg, who had been the youngest professional in the
country when he was signed up two years earlier. McGrory was less
of a threat in this game due to the effect of having lost his two front
teeth within a couple of minutes of the start. He explains how:

> Alec Thomson sent a beautiful pass right through the middle
> of the Motherwell defence between the full-backs, Crapnell
> and Ellis. I raced after the ball as Alan McClory left his line.
> Crapnell tried to block me and brought me down. I would
> swear to this day it was inside the box. As I fell I went face
> first into the keeper's knee. When I got back to my feet, I
> discovered that two of my teeth had been knocked out – clean
> as a whistle. There was no bleeding at all. At the time, I was
> so intent on claiming a penalty, it didn't bother me.

He was dazed, but within a few minutes of the restart, McGrory
showed his match-winning quality by quickly latching on to a
rebound from Crapnell's back and whipping the ball into the net.
Altogether, the game cost him his front teeth, a cut lip, a staved
thumb, a wrenched knee and a swollen ankle – but he would be the
first to say it was worth it for yet another Cup-winner's medal. What
did Nona think when he arrived home that night with bits of him
missing and the rest of him bruised black and blue? This was the
price he paid weekly for his wholeheartedness, but that was how he

played the game. 'He didn't play for Celtic, he played as if he *was* Celtic,' as Hugh Hilley, an old friend and one of his earliest Celtic colleagues, was later to say.

Not that Jimmy didn't have his bugbears – like Meiklejohn of Rangers or McAllister of Partick Thistle. 'Meek' was anything but when he played against McGrory. Like the qualified engineer he was, he read the game like a ground plan and methodically built up an extremely strong and versatile defence. You never noticed him until he was needed, always the mark of a clever player. McGrory had the utmost respect for him. Jimmy McAllister was a labourer by comparison, but he put in a good shift nonetheless. He had no plan other than to stay close to Jimmy McGrory at all times. This was an early instance of 'man-marking'. It was simple but effective, as McGrory never scored against him. He later told Gerry McNee:

> Jimmy McAllister stuck closer to me than my own jersey. The story went that even at half-time he came and sat beside me in the dressing-room. I remember one time during a match with Thistle I had to go to the touch-line for treatment, only to find the bold Mac was hovering close by. It was then a voice shouted out from the terracing – 'Hey, McAllister! Stop winchin' McGrory. Did naebody tell ye he wis merrit?'

Nobody had to remind Jimmy McGrory he was married. Domestic life in the mansion was extremely comfortable, and local friends were made. He and Nona were now in their third year of marriage but, so far, there was no hint of a child. Nona was on the wrong side of 30. If the couple had childbearing in mind, it had to be an option exercised sooner rather than later.

While on the subject of things personal and domestic, the summer of 1933 is noteworthy for containing something of a McGrory mystery. While researching this book, I visited McGrory's son, James McGrory, at his home in Glasgow. He could not have been more hospitable or cooperative. Among the many items he showed me relating to his father was a page of Celtic notepaper dated 1 June 1933. This was a receipt signed by 'W. Maley' over two penny-halfpenny stamps stating that the Celtic Football Club had 'received from James McGrory, Miller Rd, Ayr, the sum of eight hundred pounds stg as a loan to this club at interest from date of five per cent per annum'.

What did this mean? It seems a very odd amount to be the cause of a legal document. What did Celtic want £800 for? It could hardly have been easy for a player earning £8 a week, even allowing for bonuses, to have given a loan of any kind to a limited liability company with shareholders, some of whom possibly carried as much as that in their wallets. It's a McGrory enigma which still baffles the family. It is also one of which the present Celtic management seems to have no record – and no interest, regarding it as 'before our time'.

James McGrory said his mother, Barbara, the second Mrs McGrory, had always fretted about this strange loan arrangement although she would never say why. At this distance, it is hard to know anything about it, except that a single sheet of paper attests to the fact that money changed hands – and that Maley's were the hands that received it. But who gave it? That's the question. One can only assume that once again it was the Green connection that made it possible. This connection was very close. Jimmy even received letters and telegrams addressed to him c/o 'Green's Playhouse, Glasgow'. Cinema-going was more popular than ever. *King Kong* was the latest blockbuster, featuring the very Empire State Building Jimmy had so much looked forward to seeing.

Jimmy McGrory was the kind of sportsman that typified the '30s, the age of the new dancing sensations Fred Astaire and Ginger Rogers. He was to football what Henry Cotton was to golf, Fred Perry to tennis and Benny Lynch to boxing. Just say their names and you see the centre-partings in the Brylcreem'd hair. Faces from the time suggest a sort of racy innocence already touched by decadence. Such was the hunger of the era – people were hungry for distraction, any kind of distraction. Anything was better than reality, which was why entertainment boomed.

Matters off the pitch didn't engross Jimmy McGrory. As always, his first priority was Celtic, even more so as he was now their most senior player. Mr Maley had, by this time, turned a blind eye to the increasing frequency of Jimmy's motor trips between Ayr and Parkhead, although he still went by train on match days. Another increasing frequency was the match time lost through injury. He was either becoming more prone to knocks or else he was an easier target for opposing defences. Centre-halves were beginning to realise that if you put McGrory off his game you put Celtic off theirs, so he spent a lot of time on the touch-line getting bumps and bruises attended to by the latest trainer, Jack Qusklay. Very often, McGrory was played when clearly unfit and often he had to come off before half-time. This must have hurt McGrory. If ever there was a proud Celt, or one more determined in his play, that player was McGrory. The truth was, however, that he was suffering like the rest of the side from that uncertainty and low morale that are always the signs of a team in transition. With McGrory suffering a slump, this was giving other high-scorers a chance.

In January 1934, Jimmy Fleming of Rangers hit nine goals in a Scottish Cup tie with Blairgowrie, admittedly not the highest class of opposition. It was a question at the time if Celtic would have provided a superior challenge. More and more youngsters were being bloodied with every game, some used only once and discarded. Rangers' supremacy was unquestioned. In addition, St Mirren managed to put Celtic out of the Scottish Cup. It was not a happy time for the green and whites. McGrory, one of the few survivors of the great team of 1931, was essential to any transitional scheme but the aggregation of niggling injuries naturally affected his goal-scoring and he only managed 17 League goals by the spring of 1934, when, on 2 April, he broke his fibula in a game against Clyde, which meant he was out for the rest of the season.

The *Sunday Mail* of 7 October 1934 was only one of the many Glasgow voices raised against the situation at Celtic Park. It commented: 'Matters seem to be drifting too long out Parkhead way. There seems to be no room for optimism judging by the opening months of the season. A weak Celts team is a misfortune for football.' Despite this indifferent start they ended up in third spot behind Motherwell and Hearts in the Championship race . . . but you get no medals in football for coming in third.

However, 1934 was the year that entitled McGrory to a testimonial match – a matter of some previous contention among some of Celtic's finest players down the years – but there was no hesitation in granting McGrory his. Rangers provided the opposition at Celtic Park on 27 August 1934 and they fielded a strong eleven. McGrory himself didn't play because he was still recovering from the effects of the fibula injury received the previous season. Celtic fielded some of their younger players like Clancy and Dunn but they made no great impression and Rangers won the game in a canter, 4–0. The attendance, too, 8,000 at two shillings a head in all parts, was smaller than might have been expected for a proven crowd-pleaser like McGrory, but then these were hard times, although the turnstile was the one sure way the supporters could register their impatience with the club directors. There was no question, however, of their warm admiration for one of their most popular players.

The contrast between that 1934 occasion and Henrik Larsson's 'Farewell Fiesta' against Seville at Celtic Park in May 2004 is marked. Henrik played out his Celtic career in front of 60,000 adoring fans, which would net him an estimated £1 million. The difference between this amount and the small gate drawn by McGrory's own testimonial in 1934 is obvious. When questioned at the time about the lowish turnout for him, he would only comment, with a shrug and characteristic grace, 'It's all in the game.' It doesn't seem the same game somehow when a man, already a football millionaire, is rewarded still further while a faithful and valuable club servant like McGrory is rewarded with a relative pittance, but then he didn't play in affluent times, and that's the difference. Nor was the player's status reflected then in his wage packet. Celtic were always to maintain that no player is bigger than the club, but it must be said that Jimmy McGrory came pretty close. Again, the comparisons are there with the modern Henrik Larsson. Another case of the icon outsizing the temple.

Even with McGrory's lean – for him – goal tally of 19 in all, Celtic managed to finish runners-up to Rangers in the League. Despite some gloomy results, they were inching nearer and nearer to that top spot with each season. McGrory's determination to play to the final whistle gave Aberdeen a fright at Pittodrie when his late goal just failed to prevent a two-goal defeat. The opposition was always on edge while he was on the field, but one man doesn't make a team. In an attempt to improve playing standards, Celtic brought back the old, wily 'Napoleon', Jimmy McMenemy, to coach the promising Celtic colts. By the end of the season 'Nap' had become trainer for the senior team, and McGrory had managed 21 goals in a very broken term. As always, there was next season – and what a season it was to be.

In 1935–36, players like Willie Buchan and George Paterson, and, more importantly, Jimmy Delaney, began to feature more regularly. The last, particularly, added zest to a great side in the making. A further recruit was captain Willie Lyon, an Englishman from Birkenhead who played as an amateur for Queen's Park. Lyon, described by Willie Maley as 'Celtic's Bayard' (*le chevalier sans peur et sans reproche*) was to become a great Celtic example and have enormous influence on the young team which had grown up around McGrory. As a leader on the field, Willie Lyon, like the later Billy McNeill, was natural 'officer material'. Lyon was to rise from private to major in the Second World War and be awarded the Military

Cross for gallantry in Tunisia. He showed the same battlefield qualities on the football field. He and McGrory now served as the lynchpins in the emerging Celtic team which was destined for great things.

The most improved player in the team was McGrory himself. He was possibly in the finest form of his career because he was playing in a good side again and revelling in the service he got. The burden of a result no longer fell on his shoulders. Jimmy Delaney, a young gazelle on the right wing, was sending over crosses in the manner of Paddy Connolly, matched by equally effective service from Frank Murphy on the left. Malcolm MacDonald showed the silky touches of a master footballer at inside-right and Johnny Crum was just as effective when called in as replacement. Buchan and big John Divers were also available. A formidable half-back line had developed in Geatons, Lyon and Paterson, backed up by the rearguard duo of Hogg and McGonagle with John Morrison as an alternative for the latter. If you add Joe Kennaway in goal, you had a football squad of real quality.

It was a new-look team with an old-look Celtic style, and McGrory thrived on it. In the final phase of a great career, when he might have been contemplating an honourable retirement, he was about to have his best ever season for Celtic. A remarkable Indian summer spread its effulgence over his winter-time efforts. It seemed he could do no wrong. The player himself remembered every goal of it:

> When we trotted out onto the pitch at Parkhead against Dunfermline on 16 September 1935 my personal tally stood at 348 goals. Celtic won 5–3 and I had a hat-trick bringing my total to 351 goals – a Celtic and Scotland record. Now I was only one goal behind the world record set by Steve Bloomer and on 19 October two more counters (against Airdrie in a 4–0 win) saw me as the new champion. But not for long. ['Waverley' in the Glasgow *Daily Record*] found out that Hugh Ferguson had netted 362 times during his career with Motherwell, Cardiff City and Dundee.
>
> Christmas came early for me that year, for the goals kept coming and on 21 December, we met Aberdeen and, once again, I was lucky to score three goals – my seventh hat-trick of the season [actually his fourth] – which brought my tally to 364 and put the issue beyond doubt. I specially remember the third goal that day. There was a half-cross, half-shot from

Jimmy Delaney on the right. I threw myself at it and although
I thought I might be yards short, got my head to it . . . I got
all my goals by being in the right place at the right time.

Jim Rodger of the *Daily Mirror* has a slightly different memory of that
great football moment. In the CSA's programme printed for
McGrory's retiral in January 1979, he wrote his version of that goal:

As a football-daft boy in short pants, I stood on the bitterly
cold terracing at Parkhead to watch Celtic play Aberdeen.
Within seven minutes [McGrory] was on equal terms with
Ferguson's [record]. He charged at a Morrison free kick,
keeper Smith of Aberdeen left his goal and Jimmy crashed it
in. Then came the goal I say was his greatest; the one indelibly
printed on my mind. Frank Murphy sent over a cross and he
was the first to admit it was not one of his best. It seemed
impossible to get to for any mortal . . . except the immortal
McGrory. In a throwback to a trapeze act, McGrory, a human
torpedo in the air, body at full stretch and parallel with the
bone-hard ground, headed the ball into the net. There was a
silence as though a giant blanket had been thrown over
Parkhead. Then came a roar of acclaim to greet a goal that has
never been surpassed. [It was] the impossible made possible
by a genius.

It is interesting to note that Rodger says the cross came from the left,
whereas McGrory remembers it as coming from the right. Whatever
the case, one can compare this famous goal with a similar
photograph of Henrik Larsson, taken during the European
Championship finals of 2004. Henrik threw himself in the identical
McGrory manner at a cross from the wing to score the first of his two
goals for Sweden against Bulgaria. The comparison does not go
amiss as McGrory at his peak excited the same reaction with the fans
as Larsson, although this adoration was shown in a less secular
manner more appropriate to the era.

Where present-day supporters might bellow 'It's a Grand Old
Team To Play For' with Glen Daly gusto or, lately, wail the traditional
'Fields of Athenry' or the ubiquitous 'You'll Never Walk Alone', the
anthem of Celtic fans in the 1930s was invariably a hymn, 'Hail,
Glorious St Patrick', lustily rendered in parody from the open-air
slopes. Even the 'Parkhead Catholics' – those who never went to

Mass on a Sunday but never missed a match at Celtic Park on a Saturday – all knew the tune, if not the new words:

> Oh, Jimmy McGrory,
> The Prince of Garngad,
> The best centre-forward,
> The Celts ever had,
> Oh, see him rise high in the goalmouth to score
> Oh, Jimmy McGrory
> Just gie us one more
> Oh, send for McGrory (x 3)
> Tae gie us one more.

Or words to that effect. But let the man speak for himself:

> Despite the fact that I was reaching the twilight of my career it seemed my scoring was getting better and better and I scored my eighth hat-trick [actually his sixth] – a very special one – against Motherwell on 14 March. I scored three goals in three minutes. Each time the centre was taken we got possession and I scored. It was quite incredible.

What was even more remarkable was that in the penultimate game of the season against Ayr United at Somerset Park in Ayr, he scored yet another hat-trick taking his season's total to 50 in the League – only two short of Willie McFadyen's Scottish goal record for a season. Celtic were awarded a penalty, and despite having a knee injury, Willie Lyon insisted that McGrory take the kick himself in order to get nearer to that record League total. He did so, and, in his own words, 'almost hit the corner flag with it'. He had never been lucky with penalties. He'd only ever taken three in his whole career, and missed two of them. It is hard to think of one of the world's great goal-scorers being left out of a modern penalty shoot-out, but with his reputation for missing them, he would have to be.

The knee injury sustained at Ayr kept him out of the team for the final game at Firhill against Partick Thistle, which Celtic won 4–3, with Willie Fagan, his deputy, getting two and Willie Lyon illustrating how to take a penalty. Had McGrory played and scored a hat-trick he would have beaten the McFadyen record by one. So the season ended with his having scored 50 goals in 32 League games thus becoming, for that season, the leading goal-scorer in Britain.

Despite this impressive national status, he was overlooked yet again by the Scottish selectors for the game against England at Wembley. Instead, the powers that be, and that really means secretary George Graham, chose the relatively little-known Dave McCulloch, a Hamilton man who plied his trade in England with Brentford after his apprentice years at Hearts. He did not have a good game and 'appeared often out of position and never once got his head to a crossed ball'. Could one imagine that being said about McGrory? Ironically, his Celtic stand-in, Johnny Crum, was chosen as outside-right for Scotland, and when he was felled in the penalty area by Eddie Hapgood, the English full-back, it led to the famous penalty-kick incident involving the young Tommy Walker.

At this stage, England were leading through a George Camsell goal but a draw would give Scotland the Home Championship. When the 19-year-old Walker came to place the ball on the spot, the wind rolled it away as he stepped back. He came forward to re-place it but again, as he stepped back, the same thing happened. Once more he re-placed the ball and, in the tension that arose, he seemed to be the most calm. He showed this as he stepped forward for the third time and shot powerfully into the net past Sagar's right hand for the Championship. Scotland had found another hero. What a pity its old hero, McGrory, hadn't been selected to play at Wembley. It was his last chance and would have capped a fantastic year for him. But it was not to be. It was fortunate, in a sense, that he wasn't playing. He might have been asked to take that penalty.

High scoring seemed to be the name of the game in 1935. 'Bunny' Bell scored nine in the English Third Division for Tranmere Rovers against Oldham and Joe Payne, a stop-gap centre-forward on the day, scored ten for another Third Division side, Luton, in a record-breaking 12–0 victory over Bristol Rovers. However, Britain's leading scorer for 1935, Ted Drake of Arsenal, netted seven against Aston Villa in December of the same year. The nagging thought persists of how McGrory, Britain's leading scorer of 1936, might have fitted in with that well-oiled Arsenal machine all set to power its way to a sixth League title in seven years.

This, however, wasn't a priority for McGrory at that time. He had other preoccupations. In the McGrory papers held by his son is Public Notice No. 153, dated 18 April 1936, in the name of James McGrory of 23 Miller Road, Ayr, and addressed to the Irish Revenue Commission. It was an application for a transfer of residence. Whether this was relating to the McGrory house at Downings in

Rosguill, or the first stage of a planned move to Ireland is uncertain, but it does indicate that, however private and discreet, he did have a life outside Celtic Park. He had always loved Ireland, he and Nona had been married there, and it was said that he had even played in scratch holiday matches against the Mulroy Stars on the Lea Field at Rosguill, so it is not too fanciful to think that he might one day have wanted to live there permanently.

Meanwhile, in the winding down of his playing career, another Scottish Cup final loomed. This time it was against the Cup favourites, Aberdeen, who were runners-up to Rangers in the League, two points above Celtic. Saturday, 24 April 1937 was a final occasion in the literal sense for McGrory. It would be his sixth and last Scottish Cup final. It was a big occasion in more ways than one for this April game turned out to be a landmark, not only for McGrory but for the national game in Scotland. It drew the largest attendance ever for a match between two club sides up till that time – 147,365. This figure doesn't include the more than 20,000 that were said to have been locked out and remained milling around outside the gates throughout the game following the match by the roars of the crowd. They would have heard from two huge roars and one slightly lesser one that Celtic won by 2–1 with goals from Crum and Buchan. McGrory didn't score but he earned his medal with a deft slip to Buchan, which left the inside-forward free to run in and shoot the winner.

Football still mattered in 1937, despite the ominous sight of Hitler's shadow growing bigger every day over the map of Europe. Not that football fans seemed to care. Only the week before, the world record attendance figure had been broken at Hampden when 149,547 paid to see Scotland beat England 3–1. Frank O'Donnell, the ex-Celt, was at centre-forward and scored a goal and McGrory's pal, Bob McPhail, got the other two.

However, only six days after their momentous and historic Cup final victory, Celtic and McGrory suffered a huge embarrassment. On 30 April 1937, in a meaningless, final League fixture of the season at Fir Park, Motherwell, the great Cup-winning side was demolished 8–0. It was, and still is, the heaviest defeat ever sustained by the club and was the worst game McGrory ever played in Celtic colours. No doubt a natural reaction had set in among the players after the previous weekend's highs. It must have been difficult for the very same team to adjust from Hampden on the Saturday to Fir Park on the following Friday evening and it didn't help that they played half the match with Buchan in goal in place of the injured Kennaway, but

Celtic knew from previous experience how good Motherwell could be, and the Steelmen certainly showed it that night.

Stewart, their centre-forward, got six and Jimmy McGrory got none. The game simply ran away from Celtic and, afterwards, they slunk shamefacedly on to the overnight train carrying them to the FA Cup final at Wembley, where they were to watch Sunderland beat Preston North End 3–1. It was supposed to be a treat for the players for winning the Scottish Cup, but judging from Maley's grim expression, it was a long day's train journey into night. 'Yes,' McGrory was to say, 'I was never so humiliated in my life.'

He recovered sufficiently to get another goal and another medal three weeks later when Celtic, fielding two reserves, beat Queen's Park 4–3 in the Charity Cup final, so it was a season of trophies – and 28 goals in all – for their veteran centre-forward. When he came to sign for season 1937–38, he knew in his battered bones that this would be his last, although manager Maley was convinced Jimmy had a lot more goals in him yet. After all, big scoring by centre-forwards was a feature of the age. However, McGrory knew better than anyone that time was running out for him as a player, even though, on 25 September, his scoring header from a Frank Murphy cross at Pittodrie was of such class that it drew applause from the Aberdeen players. On 6 October, another headed bullet against Sunderland, again from a Murphy cross, brought a roar of acclaim from Roker Park. He was still 'doing the business', obviously.

In the new season, he got six goals in eleven games but, even so, he realised that he wasn't getting to balls that only a year before would have been his. The small warning signals that every player gets towards the end were coming to him each week now, but he hoped, at least, to get through to the Jubilee season. It was another goal for him to aim for. Unfortunately, Jimmy didn't make it. His final game was a League match against Queen's Park at Parkhead, on 16 October 1937, when he was injured yet again but not before scoring a goal in a 4–2 victory. It was his last goal for Celtic. The Queen's Park goalkeeper that day was the future Celtic chairman, Desmond White, who never forgot that last brush with the mighty McGrory:

> I moved out to take a high cross, satisfied that the Celtic forwards were too far from the action to create any mischief. How wrong I was! To my astonishment and chagrin, Jimmy appeared as from nowhere and with a flick of his head the ball

was in the net. It's no exaggeration to say that his unmatched prowess as a header of the ball brought a new dimension to this aspect of the game. Jimmy didn't just play or glance the ball with his head. He employed powerful shoulders and neck muscles to their full potential and the ball was struck and directed with an impact that lesser men could emulate only with their feet.

Jimmy McGrory would never have left his arena of dreams willingly, but he was pulled off injured, after scoring his last goal for Celtic. Everyone presumed he would be back as usual to finish the season, but it was not to be. It was time for a great gladiator of the goalmouth to put his football boots away. There is a time, and this was it.

NINE

The Kilmarnock Edition

The honest heart that's free frae a'
Intended fraud or guile,
However Fortune kick the ba'
Has ay some cause to smile.
From 'Epistle to Davie' by Robert Burns, 1786

Burns' only reference to football aptly introduces Kilmarnock FC. Founded in 1869, it is Ayrshire's senior football club and the oldest professional football club in Scotland. Formed from a union of local rugby and athletic clubs, they named their ground Rugby Park to acknowledge this. They were Scottish Cup winners in their time and have boasted some fine players, like Joe Nibloe, 'Peerie' Cunningham and Celtic's Bobby Templeton over the years, but in December 1937 the club was in a state of unrest. On the field they were not getting results and at boardroom level there were heated discussions about what action to take. At the start of the new season, shareholders were in an uproar about the secretary-manager, Hugh Spence, being made a scapegoat for the Board's failings and Mr Barr, the chairman, decided that they must do something quickly. Bob Russell, a local businessman, was a personal friend of Jimmy McGrory's. Bob had noticed that the great man was now sidelined at Parkhead and he also knew that Jimmy lived in nearby Ayr, so one night Messrs Russell and Barr called at Greenways to ask if Mr McGrory would like to become their club's secretary-manager.

No one could have been more surprised than the player himself. He had no plans about going into management. He found it hard to think of a life without Celtic and, if he ever did, he had thought that Maley might keep him on as a kind of assistant, but as long as he was playing he never gave the matter any serious consideration. Nor, it seemed, did Maley. He had thought, even at 33, he could get a year out of McGrory yet. His mere presence in the penalty area always posed a threat. He might be a little slower getting to the ball but once he got it, he knew where it was meant to go. So when McGrory told him about the Kilmarnock overture, he was not at all helpful or encouraging and only agreed when it was ensured that McGrory could not turn out for Kilmarnock as a player. Even then, McGrory was uncertain. It was only when director Tom Colgan told him to go for it, hinting that in due time there might later be a post at Celtic Park, in which case some managerial experience would be useful, that he made up his mind.

Just before Christmas 1937, he walked out of Celtic Park, symbolically leaving his jersey hanging on its peg in the dressing-room and his famous size six football boots in the care of Jimmy Gribben in the Boot Room, remarking, 'I'll never use them again.' Thankfully, they were later retrieved for the Scottish Football Museum at Hampden Park. He became Kilmarnock's first ever full-time secretary-manager, with a weekly wage of £17 10s, which was a big improvement on what he had been getting with Celtic. To celebrate, he bought a new, green Wolseley and drove it proudly to Celtic Park a few days later. This was Jimmy McGrory in his Kilmarnock Edition as a football manager.

As such, on Christmas Day 1937, he took his seat in the 'away' directors' box and received a tremendous cheer from the Celtic fans. He was touched but uneasy about the applause and, on his own admission, felt a little uncomfortable in his new seat. He was even more uncomfortable at half-time as Celtic went in leading 6–0. McGrory had to go to the visitors' dressing-room at Celtic Park, a place he had hardly seen, and try to lift a team he had only known for a few days. In the other dressing-room, Maley was telling his side: 'Don't let sentiment interfere with your play. I want the same again in this half.' Celtic went out and added another three goals – just to rub it in. It was one of the odder ways for Maley to celebrate his 50-year association with Celtic – the public humiliation of one of its legends.

Some were taken aback that his former teammates should be so merciless to a side of which he was now manager – and in his first game as such. One very angry correspondent, Father Coleman, wrote to McGrory from St Paul's Retreat in Dublin, describing the action as:

> ... one of the ugliest I have ever heard of in sport. A rubbing-it-in which was a very ungallant, uncalled-for, even dastardly act on the part of the so-called bhoys. At least that's how it appears to the man in the street.

Father Coleman spoke for many of them. McGrory himself said later he would have acted just as Maley had done had he been manager of Celtic. He understood that for Maley it was Celtic 'first and last and all the time'. So had it been for McGrory. Now he must think likewise for Kilmarnock.

They lost again in his second game as manager, this time 4–0 to Hibs, but by then McGrory had Bob Russell at his side as unofficial advisor. Their first priority was to save Kilmarnock from relegation and then pick up what they could in the Cup. On Russell's advice, McGrory brought in a couple of new players, George Reid on loan from Celtic and Felix McGrogan from Falkirk. These two made an immediate difference, and the team went into the New Year of 1938 with hope in their hearts, but with their hearts in their mouths. Against all the odds, McGrory inspired his team of mixed talents to new heights by virtue of his own enthusiasm and by Easter they had only been beaten once in a dozen games. This good run included sweet Scottish Cup victories over Celtic in the third round (2–1) at Parkhead and Rangers (4–2) in an epic semi-final at Hampden.

The Killie victory over Celtic was rather soured by Maley's boorish behaviour afterwards. He refused to shake hands with McGrory and when the latter went to the office to say farewell, Maley didn't even look up from his desk, ostensibly engrossed in paperwork. No matter his disappointment at losing out on the Scottish Cup, it was shameful bad grace on his part and McGrory had no option but to close the door on his former mentor and on Celtic. He had another job to do. This was to prepare Kilmarnock for a Cup final while still impeded by their relegation preoccupations. Perhaps because of this extra pressure they could only draw 1–1 with Second Division East Fife and in the midweek replay on 27 April they were beaten 3–2 by a goal in extra time. It was a very gallant near miss and McGrory and his team could take heart from it. East

Fife remain the only Second Division club to have won the Scottish Cup.

It would have been wonderful for McGrory to have won it after only half a season with the club but, more important to Kilmarnock, was the need to avoid relegation. Their problems were intensified by the need to complete their fixtures by 30 April, which was the rule at that time. This entailed two tough games in three days after their valiant midweek Cup final attempt – one against Morton at home on the Friday and the other against Hearts on the Saturday. They needed two points to stay up and they got them right away by beating Morton 3–0, despite having half their team on the injured list. Imbued with McGrory's never-say-die spirit, they had got their priorities right and saved their season. Altogether, Mr McGrory had not done badly at all in his first term as a manager. To have beaten the Old Firm is a feather in the cap of any manager, and to have reached a national Cup final with a team threatened throughout the season with relegation was a feat in itself. He and Bob Russell could now look forward to the new season with more than hope in their hearts.

Celtic, meanwhile, were now into their jubilee year – the official 50th year – with 18 League Championships, 15 Scottish Cups, 17 Glasgow Cups and 22 Charity Cups to show for it and with players who have gone into the football pantheon – Jimmy Quinn, Patsy Gallacher, John Thomson and Jimmy McGrory. One feels that fate ought to have allowed McGrory one more year at Parkhead if only to let him join in the celebrations as a Celt, but life is rarely that tidy. Which was a pity, for 1938 was to become an *annus mirabilis* for the Parkhead club. Maley was on the team's back all the time, reminding them that not winning the Scottish Cup the year before had cost the club about £5,000. It hurt him all the more that they'd been knocked out of the Cup again – and by Jimmy McGrory's Kilmarnock, too. Some felt there was a kind of justice in that, after Maley's ruthless approach to the Christmas Day game.

When summer came it brought with it the British Empire Exhibition in Bellahouston Park. This was also a Jubilee – a celebration of 50 years of international exhibitions in Glasgow, the first having been held in Kelvingrove Park in 1888 – a Celtic year too. A larger site was chosen at Bellahouston Park, just across the road from Nona Green McGrory's family home at Craigie Hall and only a little further from McGrory's own house in Rowan Road. The Exhibition, costing £10 million, was to celebrate the British Empire

137

and show off Glasgow and Scotland at the same time. It was opened by King George VI during a downpour on Tuesday, 3 May and all Glasgow's primary-school pupils were given a free tram ticket to go and see His Majesty in the rain. The tramcar army invaded Bellahouston Park that day and came away with their spoils – decorated drinking mugs that are still in use in many Glasgow households to this day.

An official part of the exhibition programme was a football tournament in which eight prominent British teams were invited to take part – Rangers, Celtic, Hearts and Aberdeen from Scotland and Everton, Chelsea, Sunderland and Brentford from England, the last two taking the place of Arsenal and Wolverhampton Wanderers, who declined to participate. Nevertheless, the competition had a prestige, being seen as the unofficial British club championship.

In the first round, Celtic beat Sunderland after a replay, Aberdeen beat Chelsea, Everton beat Rangers and Hearts beat Brentford. In the semi-final, Celtic beat Hearts and Everton beat Aberdeen, so it was Celtic and Everton for the final, which Celtic won by a Johnny Crum goal in extra time. One still feels McGrory ought to have been there. Such a tournament would have provided the right kind of stage for him to make his final exit. However, as with his Wembley ambition, a suitable climax was to be denied him. What cannot be denied is that Jimmy McGrory would have graced any exhibition tournament – even as a veteran.

In the distinctive, silver Exhibition Trophy, which Willie Lyon received from the Earl of Elgin at Ibrox, Celtic have a permanent scale-model memento of the impressive architectural structure created by the Exhibition's designer, architect Thomas Smith Tait. This was, in effect, a 300-ft lift shaft with observation platform and embellishments. It was immediately dubbed 'Tait's Tower' and was quickly recognised as an art deco masterpiece. To Glasgow's disgrace, it was demolished in the following summer to appease a Government defence strategy that said it would be a landmark for possible enemy bombers. In 1938, people didn't want to talk about war. It had only been 20 years since the last one, and anyway, Celtic had their Jubilee Year to see through – but first there was the Jubilee Dinner.

This was held at the Grosvenor Restaurant in Byres Road, Glasgow on Wednesday, 16 June 1938, with the chairman of the club, Mr Tom White, presiding. It was Maley's finest hour. He was at the very summit of his fame. He could not have walked taller and, like the old ham that he was, he even timed his arrival theatrically – not too late to be impolite but late enough to be noticed. Everyone who was anyone in football was there, with a good representation from the Catholic Church and the Marist Order. One can only presume that Mr and Mrs James McGrory attended.

Sir John T. Cargill proposed the toast to the club, and considering he had done the same at the Rangers dinners in 1923, he trod the expected platitudinous fence. 'I have seen many good matches between them,' was the level of his oratory. He went on to give the mandatory list of great Celts, like Patsy Gallacher, who was there, and Tommy McInally, also present, and, of course, 'poor John Thomson'. The final player mentioned was 'the great Jimmy McGrory', whom he credited with the record for goals in first-class football as 540 instead of 550, but he did get one thing correct – he reminded his audience that 'the Celtic Football Club was an Irish club, founded by an Irish religious man, Brother Walfrid, for charitable purposes in the East End of Glasgow'. The company then sang 'The Dear Little Shamrock'. One can be sure the SFA guests enjoyed that.

Chairman Tom White's task was to thank Sir John and make the presentation to Willie Maley of a cheque for 2,500 guineas – being £50 for every year given to the club. This was more than a token of respect or a mark of gratitude, it was a golden handshake, a nod to go. Even though Mr White pointed out that the name Maley was synonymous with Celtic and with football in Scotland, he also mentioned that Willie was now in his 71st year and hinted, without saying in so many words, that having reared his own players to the standard they had attained, he might now accept this handsome honorarium and live out the rest of his life secure in the reputation he so much deserved.

The Big Fella took the money but he didn't take the hint. Instead, in his speech of thanks, he took pains to 'entertain'. This was his moment and he was going to relish every second of it. He gave the audience what they wanted to hear, except the announcement of his retiral. He got his laughs and the occasional lump in the throat, but it was noticeable that in his list of Celtic greats, he made only a passing mention of McGrory among those of former players, although Mrs Arthur Murphy got a special mention as one of the oldest Celtic enthusiasts. It is not that McGrory should have had extra-special mention, but he was (and still is) their leading goal-scorer, and was (and still is) one of their longest-serving players in terms of seasons spent with the club – 15. Alec McNair served longer as a player from 1904 to 1925 consecutively but McGrory continued as manager and then as PRO until 1979, which would give him, even with time out at Clydebank during 1923, an aggregate of 49 years in all at the club – second only in service to Maley by a year. Nevertheless, the Big Fella leaned heavily on his then undisputed seniority as he spoke . . .

> . . . of the giants Celtic had brought out to do credit to their club and country. During all the years, it has been a great source of pride to me that the players who had worn our colours had never ceased in their interest in the fortunes of the old club. It is, therefore, a great pleasure for me to see so many of them present and to know that they still retained the kindly feelings they always had for me.

One can be sure that quite a few of the players exchanged glances at this. And so he went on – and ended – his voice heavy with feeling:

> No manager has been given a greater liberty than I. I am proud to say that I have never betrayed that trust. My love for Celtic has been a craze [but] there would have been no Celtic without the struggles of Brother Walfrid and John Glass. Since I took this job 50 years ago, at their invitation, the club has been my very life and I really feel that without it my existence would be empty indeed.

That was the nub – the man had nothing in his life but Celtic. He had a wife and two grown sons but he still felt empty. He ought to have been enjoying his grandchildren, but instead he preferred to worry about young footballers. Had he any degree of sensitivity at all, he would have been aware of the Board's growing uneasiness about his physical fitness. He was ill more often and his long lunchtimes at the Bank Restaurant were also noted, although much football business was done there. He had tried to sign Matt Busby on the premises and he transferred Willie Buchan to Blackpool from one of its tables. To be fair, he also gave advice to those who didn't ask for it and, less often, a handout to those who did. The truth was he had started to believe his own publicity. This comes through in his book, *The Story of the Celtic, 1888–1938*, and in the series of articles he wrote for the *Weekly News* during August 1936. He thought he *was*

Celtic and he fully expected to die in its service. A golden chance to go in glory was given to him at that dinner and he let it go. He was to realise all too soon that he had scored an own goal.

With the Exhibition Trophy on the shelf it was thought at Celtic Park that the League and Cup were surely there for the taking in 1939. Instead, they got neither. Arguably one of the best teams in Britain, they had only recently proved it and even more was expected of such an eleven. They got off to a wonderful start in the new season but fell away badly after the New Year. No one could account for the sudden slump – not even the Boss, who wrote in one of the programmes:

> One doesn't know how to explain the form of our side with all its carelessness and weaknesses so apparent to everyone but themselves. In every game it is possible to have the breaks against you, but the law of averages counts in all sports and what is lost one day comes back another day. That, of course, does not apply to clearly indolent play backed by an imaginary superiority which is, like foolish pride in one's self, a foolish sin.

One wonders if the players read this sort of thing in the dressing-room before a game. It would hardly be calculated to cheer them up. It is hard to think of Jimmy Delaney or Johnny Crum as being indolent or of the highly talented, but unassuming, Calum MacDonald as being buoyed up by any foolish pride in himself, but Maley took his managerial utterances in print as coming from above (meaning his office) and wanted them read as such. He had been so long in the job that he had taken root and now seemed immovable, but the ground around him was beginning to give way.

Maley then became seriously ill and Jimmy McMenemy took over as temporary manager. It had been rumoured that Pat Travers, a former Celtic player, was ready to come to Celtic Park from Aberdeen, where he had been manager since 1924. But no offer came from Parkhead so he went to Clyde instead in November 1937 and was to manage them until 1956. Pat might have been the saving of Celtic's season. A new broom was urgently needed. Maley had received his honorarium but the players had still not received the bonus promised them by one of the directors. When Willie Lyon brought the matter up with Maley, he was told to take it up with the director concerned. This was hardly the way to influence players and

141

win matches, but Maley seemed to be worried more about the Spanish Civil War than any dressing-room unrest.

Things didn't improve much in the following season and then, on 1 April 1939, disaster struck at Celtic Park. In the game against Arbroath, Jimmy Delaney broke his arm very badly when Arbroath's Attilio Becci trod on him in a goalmouth mêlée. The whole Celtic team seemed to feel the injury and their season went from bad to worse. Somehow, without their star player, they were never the same team.

Jimmy McGrory did not have that problem at Kilmarnock – he didn't have any stars. Nevertheless, he now saw his side of decent journeymen and keen youngsters safely installed in the middle of the League, although they went out of the Cup in the second round to Hibernian. Nevertheless, they won the Kilmarnock Charity Cup by beating Ayr United 2–1. The fact was, McGrory was beginning to build up something at Rugby Park. Even the second team won the St Vincent de Paul Trophy at Saltcoats, beating Clyde on corners after a 1–1 draw. McGrory's continued appetite for the game was infectious and his young team responded beyond their talents. What was obvious was that they were improving all the time under his control and the prospects were growing for an established mid-table team that could spring the occasional surprise.

What wasn't a surprise, however, was that war was declared against Germany on Sunday, 3 September 1939 and the Scottish League was immediately abandoned. Regional Leagues were hurriedly formed in order to limit travel in wartime conditions. National conscription was a big blow to the smaller clubs as most of their young players were called up for the armed forces and they were unable to pay the unofficial 'guest fees' demanded by star players already in the forces who were allowed to play with teams near their stations of service. In this way, Morton were able to field no less than Stanley Matthews and Tommy Lawton in their line-up in the newly formed West Regional League, Partick Thistle got Bill Shankly, Hamilton Accies got goalkeeper Frank Swift, Aberdeen got Stan Mortenson and Hibernian had Matt Busby for their East Regional League fixtures – although he had trained at Celtic Park and was known to be 'Celtic daft'.

The Parkhead club, for reasons best known to themselves, were the only side not to use guest players in wartime. Had they done so, they might have had Busby as a player at a very crucial time – who knows with what consequences. Celtic were as strained as most clubs just to keep going in the Wartime Emergency, as it was called. Petrol was rationed so travel was heavily curtailed. Clubs were limited to their geographical areas and, consequently, gates were affected and receipts were down. To compensate, players' wages were restricted to £2 a week and bonuses were abolished. It wasn't a time to make a career in football.

Willie Maley had by this time been in increasingly poor health and his condition wasn't helped when he was taxed on his ex gratia payment. He wasn't at all happy about it. He insisted the directors should pay any tax due on an ex gratia payment but they were equally adamant they should not. It was a disquieting business and it looked as if all the euphoria of the Jubilee would be squandered in a money squabble that was as distasteful as it was unnecessary. It was silly but almost inevitable, so that when results failed to come in the strange, camouflaged, blackout world of January 1940, the end drew nigh for Willie Maley. And he knew it. In a newspaper article he wrote:

> In this, my closing article for season 1939–40, my thoughts go back to August 1939 when we started off in what I imagined would be another successful season and which I did not think would be my last year in football management. Personally, I can never forget the 1939–40 season. It has been to me the end of my football career and has robbed me of the very tang of life. Football has been [in] my thoughts morning, noon, and night for all the fifty-two years I have been in it, and it has been hard to fall out of my regular ways.

It is hard not to feel sympathy for him, but he very largely brought it on himself by his obduracy in remaining in the job when the signals were so plainly set for him to go. The date given for his official departure was 1 February and he left, or was pushed out, in arctic weather and with Celtic at the bottom of the temporary League. Like Captain Oates, he should have said, 'I may be gone for some time.' In fact, he was to be away for 13 years. It's a long time to stay in the huff. Jimmy McStay, his former captain, took over as manager.

Alex Dowdells also came to the club as trainer in 1940, and he remembers the state the club was in at that time. He was sure that the seeds of its post-war difficulties were laid in wartime with its refusal to use star guests when available. He made his comments clear to Tom Campbell:

Celtic had a vintage period before I went to Parkhead in 1940, but when the war came and players' wages were cut to £2 per week many boys thought it wasn't worth playing seriously and so the standard of the team went down. But one of the biggest factors in Celtic's decline was the decision not to have guest players during the war. Guest players did a good job in maintaining a standard of play as well as bringing on a nucleus of youngsters; but not at Parkhead. Not only were the new boys not being prepared, but the standards had slumped.

It can be seen that Jimmy McStay had his work cut out. Some good young boys were signed, like Willie Miller, a goalkeeper from Maryhill Harp, John McPhail, from Strathclyde Juniors, and Bobby Evans from St Anthony's, but they were still raw and needed a guiding hand. Too much depended on the old hands like Jimmy Delaney, Bobby Hogg and Malcolm MacDonald. R.E. Kingsley ('Rex' of the *Sunday Mail*) wrote: 'It used to be a big thrill to beat Celtic; now clubs consider it an indignity if they don't. It may be dire necessity which demands the fielding of so many youngsters who should, in the ordinary way, be in the reserve side, but it's a bit sad to watch just the same.'

Manager Jimmy McGrory was not without his own problems in 1940. It may have been the 'Phoney War' but it was also 'Phoney Football' with strange arrangements and uncertain control. McGrory astutely took advantage by 'borrowing' his good friend and former teammate 'Calum' MacDonald to replace Drysdale, an injured Killie player, against Rangers in a Western Regional League match at Rugby Park on 14 May, a game Kilmarnock won 4–1 against an almost full-strength Rangers side, Willie Woodburn et al. MacDonald must have made a difference, even though he was working night shifts in a Glasgow factory at the time as part of his 'War Work'.

In the summer of 1940, however, Rugby Park was requisitioned by the army as a fuel depot. Crude diesel, oil, petrol and so on were to be stored in large, deep, rectangular holes dug out of the playing pitch and in car parks with covers to protect them from bombing. Rugby Park was used because its main stand backed on to the railway line that linked it directly to Troon and Prestwick, where the RAF had established an airfield. It was therefore a highly valuable strategic facility and could no longer serve as a football venue in the wartime Western Division.

144

Unfortunately, the servicemen who now took over had little regard for the site's important football pedigree and a lot of archival material relating to Kilmarnock FC was lost in this upheaval. McGrory himself was retained as secretary-manager during the emergency but, as his home was in Ayr, most of the club's business was dealt with by Mr James Henderson, who lived in McLelland Drive, near Rugby Park, and it was he who dealt with any day-to-day decisions as they arose. Since little happened, it wasn't worth bringing Jimmy in from Ayr. Anyway, petrol was scarce, despite the fact that Rugby Park was full of it.

McGrory didn't quite know what to do with himself. He was still officially an employee of Kilmarnock Football Club, which, at the time, didn't exist as a commercial entity, having neither ground nor players nor League status. McGrory found himself, for the first time in his life, looking for a job. A real job, that is. Nothing to do with football. He might have found himself a niche within the Greens' cinema empire but instead, thanks to sympathetic Celtic supporters, he found himself hired for 'War Work during the National Emergency' as chief storeman for ICI at their munitions factory at Hurlford in Ayrshire. It was the first 'proper' job he'd ever had and it came about only because there was a war on.

For the same reason, he also joined the Home Guard, or the Land Defence Volunteers as they were first called. These were no more than armband civilians with whatever weapons they could lay their hands on, and all Jimmy could offer, at 36, were his flat feet and a strong neck. Shooting took on a whole new meaning as he was given a rifle, a uniform, a tin hat and a number. He was Private James E. McGrory, with his National Registration given as SKSL/13/1. He was in the army now – Dad's Army – but it can be safely said he never fired a shot in anger, not even on the football park. He kept the tin hat for years afterwards.

One can only presume that he and Nona continued contentedly in their life together at Ayr as best they could in the restricted conditions of rationing and blackouts and air-raids. Everybody did then. The only problem the McGrorys might have had was they still had no children. Nona kept seeking medical advice about the problem and this eventually led to her undergoing an operation at the Redlands Nursing Home off the Great Western Road in Hillhead, Glasgow. Tragically, the operation was not a success, and Nona died as a result of complications which set in afterwards. The sad news made all the Glasgow papers at the time. The *Evening Times* of 24 April 1944, reported:

145

The death occurred early this morning following an operation of Mrs James McGrory, the wife of the former Celtic and Scotland centre-forward and now manager of Kilmarnock FC. Before her marriage Mrs McGrory was Miss Nona Green, the third daughter of the noted family of picture house proprietors. Mrs McGrory was one of the keenest Celtic admirers and her marriage to James McGrory was a romance of the football field.

Mrs McGrory went through an operation a couple of days ago. She was recovering when a relapse occurred and she died suddenly in the nursing home this morning.

Other death notices appeared in the weekly *Glasgow Observer* and the *Scottish Catholic Herald* for Friday, 28 April 1944 under the name of:

McGRORY – At a hospital in Glasgow, on 24th April 1944 following an operation, Veronica (Nona), third daughter of the late Mr and Mrs George Green, and beloved wife of James McGrory, of 23 Miller Rd, Ayr. Deeply regretted. Fortified by the rites of the Holy Catholic Church. R.I.P.

Although these notices report that Nona was the third daughter, she was actually the fifth and second youngest of the six daughters. Requiem Mass was offered for the repose of her soul at St Aloysius Church, Garnethill, Glasgow, on 26 April followed by the funeral, organised by Messrs T. and R. O'Brien of Woodside Road, to St Peter's Cemetery, Dalbeth, in the East End of Glasgow. So McGrory came back to Parkhead once again, but only to bury his wife in the vault maintained by the Green family. He and Nona had had 13 happy years together, and now she was gone in a matter of days. McGrory went back to Greenways numbed and bemused, comforted by the Greens, particularly Bert and Marjorie. McGrory always remembered that Nona's eyebrows were thin and arched. Just like a film star. Poor Nona. She was a beautiful girl, but she didn't keep well. She had everything, yet all she really wanted was a baby.

Fortunately for McGrory's state of mind, Kilmarnock returned to football in that summer of 1944 with a team of local juveniles and juniors strengthened by any senior player who happened to be on leave and available. With them, McGrory came back to reality in the

Reserve League. They still had no ground of their own and played their home games on Hurlford United's ground. Then, in April 1945, with the end of the war only a month away, the military handed back Rugby Park to Kilmarnock – and what a mess it was. However, with the help of German and Italian prisoners of war, the oil-tank pits on the pitch were refilled, new drains dug, and the ground was gradually made usable again. Kilmarnock now entered the Southern League with a new ground and a new team – but still with Jimmy McGrory in charge.

Tuesday, 8 May 1945 was VE Day and next day Celtic celebrated by beating Queen's Park in the final of the Victory-in-Europe Cup by one goal and three corner kicks to one goal and two corner kicks. The margin could not have been narrower but, no matter, it was another 'one-off' trophy on the Celtic shelf and a deserved solitary feather in Jimmy McStay's well-worn cap. Rangers had declined to take part. Celtic were just as glad. But then, in July 1945, a Glasgow newspaper ran a snippet of information saying only: 'Watch Jimmy McGrory. He will make a sensational move soon.' Jimmy himself explains what happened next:

> On a beautiful sunny day in the summer of 1945 I got a telephone call from Mr Tom White, the Celtic chairman, and father of Desmond White, asking me to meet him for a chat. I motored up to Glasgow from Ayr wondering what was going on and to my astonishment I was offered the job as manager of Celtic. I said, 'But Jimmy McStay is the manager here.' He replied simply: 'Yes, but we want you.' It was awful to think of an old teammate being put out of a job, but the Board was unanimous and I had to accept it.

Jimmy McStay hadn't been too happy about the way Celtic had treated him, although he certainly bore no grudge against his old pal, McGrory. In fact he later came to work with him as a scout, but he never forgot how he was shown the door. That day in July, as he got off the tram at Parkhead Cross after a family holiday in Ayr, he had seen the news vendors' boards carrying the news that Jimmy McGrory was returning to Celtic Park – as manager. As soon as McStay got to Celtic Park, he immediately questioned the chairman, Tom White, on the matter and was told to tender his resignation forthwith.

Jimmy McGrory took over as manager of Celtic Football Club as from 24 July 1945. It was the club he had first known as a boy of 18. Now he was a man of 41, and if life begins at 40, he was already a year late. Never mind, he was back at Celtic Park, where he belonged. No contract was signed. None was needed.

TEN

Paradise Regained

> Football is football; if that weren't the case,
> it wouldn't be the game it is.
> > Garth Crooks, footballer, in *Private Eye*, 1984

One of the hundreds of letters he received after his appointment as Celtic manager was from the wife of a friend in Leicester. Her name was Gertrude, and she had been a good friend of Nona's. She wrote:

> Nona so wanted you to have that post – and would have been so proud of you. You said in your letter you might marry again – but that you would never forget Nona. I think Nona herself would not wish you to be without good companionship for the rest of your life.

Jimmy McGrory had met Nurse Barbara Schoning when he had gone into a Glasgow nursing home for a routine hernia operation in late 1945. A friendship developed which gradually blossomed into a romance, so Jimmy and Barbara did the right thing, they set a date – Tuesday, 2 July 1946 – and the place was to be her home parish of St Andrew's, Braemar. Meantime, Jimmy arranged that his fiancée could move in with Bert and Marjorie Green at their house, Glen Ard, in Beech Avenue just along the road from Craigie Hall. The Greens were determined to remain friends with their late sister's husband while he commuted from Ayr each day to Celtic Park.

149

He had inherited something of a poisoned chalice from his old teammate, McStay. The war had seen Rangers rise as high as Celtic had declined and McGrory had no alternative but to drink the bitter cup and get on with it as best he could. Not for the first time, boardroom deficiencies had made their mark on the field and McGrory had to carry the can for the results. Still, he was stoic and applied himself as manfully in the office as he had on the park. The first player signed by him as Celtic manager was centre-half, Duncan McMillan, from Maryhill Harp on 6 September 1945 and his debut coincided with the first match won by the new boss. Unfortunately for Dunky though, he went down with stomach poisoning and lost his place to Alec Boden, from St Mary's Boys' Guild, Duntocher, never to get it back.

Then, more seriously, only eight months into McGrory's reign as manager, a real calamity: Jimmy Delaney, by now a mythical figure with the Celtic supporters, was allowed to leave in February 1946 for the sake of the extra £2 a week he had asked for. Delaney was the first man signed by Matt Busby when that Celtic-minded man took over at Manchester United. Did Delaney remember the day of Peter Scarff's funeral in December 1933, when Willie Maley threw a Celtic jersey on Peter's coffin and, as it was being lowered into the grave, Delaney had whispered to a player beside him – 'I hope they do that for me?' Delaney didn't die until 1989, by which time he had earned medals and plaudits in England, Ireland and the Highlands of Scotland but he is still remembered mainly as Delaney of the Celtic.

The 'Faithful', as the supporters were known, had shown their true colours by *supporting* the club through the bad times. Anyone can follow a winning team, but it's hard to stand up week after week for losers. For generations the football week had remained the same for millions of working-class boys between seven and seventy. They lived from Saturday to Saturday – the days between were meaningless. When your team runs on to the park, all the pent-up emotion of the week bursts out and you let out a roar as the whole wonderful circus starts up again. It was only a game, but for most people then, what else was there? This was the life. This *was* life. It wasn't history – it was hysteria.

The Celtic side in the post-war years had generally been held together by Delaney up front and Willie Miller in goal, in much the same way as McGrory and John Thomson had kept things going for the side in a similar period of transition before the first American tour in 1931. A great team emerged from that trip, but now, with the popular Delaney gone, there was little of the same hope for the post-war crop with a forward line that the supporters had christened the 'Five Sorrowful Mysteries'.

Yet, being Celtic, the same players, no doubt fortified by the rites of their fanatical support, reached the semi-final of the Victory Cup against Rangers in June 1946. After a draw, earned by the superb goalkeeping of Willie Miller, Celtic submitted to what turned out to be a shameful replay ruined by abject refereeing and made worse by draconian SFA post-match decisions that left Celtic short of three players harshly suspended. The replay team was Miller; Hogg and Mallan; Lynch, Corbett and McAuley; Sirral, Kiernan, Gallacher, Paterson and Paton. Rangers played Brown; Cox and Shaw; Watkins, Young and Symon; Waddell, Gillick, Thornton, Duncanson and Caskie. This was a strong Rangers team, brimming with hard efficiency and confidence. Celtic relied more on the power of prayer.

George Paterson complained at the interval of the referee's smelling of drink. This official, Mr M.C. Dale, had been eccentric to say the least in the first half and had ignored the heavy tactics of the Rangers defence which left Celtic down by a goal and with only seven players fit for the second half – and not a foul to show for it. Then, with 20 minutes to go, Thornton clearly 'dived' into the penalty area and Rangers were immediately awarded a penalty. Paterson and Mallan protested vigorously and were promptly ordered off. This was too much for some Celtic fans who ran on to the pitch and play was stopped. When order was restored, big George Young scored to give Rangers the Cup. Matt Lynch, to everyone's amazement, was later suspended by the SFA for a month for 'inciting his team to leave the field' when really he was telling them to stay out of it. Duncanson, the Rangers player, wrote to the SFA to uphold Lynch but, despite this sporting gesture, the 'sentence' still stood. It was par for the course as far as Celtic and the SFA were concerned.

However, Celtic had their own internal problems. A malaise seemed to hang over the club. Older players, like Crum and Divers, were moving out too fast – often reluctantly – and the youngsters were coming on just as reluctantly. The Great Exhibition forward line had gone their separate ways and their places were taken by overweights like Jackie Gallacher and Joe McLaughlin or a lumbering John McPhail, who at least could play a bit. Good footballers like Johnny Kelly and Hughie Long were let go and

McGrory was left with the sort of player that Rex of the *Sunday Mail* described as one who 'should have been sitting in the boys' chair at the barbers'.

It was almost a relief for him to shut up shop for the summer holidays and concentrate on other things, like his wedding to Barbara. This duly took place as arranged by Father Kerr in St Andrew's Catholic Church, Braemar, in the presence of the Schoning family. Barbara's sister, Jessie, was the bridesmaid and the best man was Jimmy's 'wee heidies' pal from Garngad days, Jimmy Elliott. When Barbara's family had moved to Aberdeenshire from Montreal on her father's death in 1921, she had gone to boarding school in Aberdeen before going to Glasgow to train as a nurse in 1936. Eventually, in the course of her nursing duties, she was introduced to 'the famous Jimmy McGrory' by a Catholic priest, Canon Troy, who was visiting. Barbara was impressed, even though she hardly knew who Celtic were, never mind their most famous player.

McGrory's new home was now 'Belltrees', a solid semi-detached villa at 32 Rowan Road in Dumbreck, which had been given to the new McGrorys as a wedding present by the previous owner, Marion Mullen, Nona's younger sister, who had witnessed Jimmy's first marriage in Ireland. Meantime, Greenways at 23 Miller Road in Ayr reverted to the Green family. McGrory could now get back to work.

When the new football season resumed, Celtic got off to a bad start and deteriorated fast. With one win, two draws and two defeats, the long-suffering supporters had had enough and on 4 September, after yet another defeat, this time to Third Lanark by 4–1, they congregated outside the pavilion in their thousands baying for the elderly chairman, Tom White. Significantly, they did not call for Jimmy McGrory. Instinctively, they knew the club's dire position was not his fault. It was with the ever-tight purse strings and directorial parsimony. Now the Board was raising admission prices. To watch what? A continued and embarrassing decline?

To understand their anger and frustration, one must appreciate that they were the sons and grandsons of the very men who had laid out the first Celtic playing field with their own hands and had 'followed, followed' ever since through the generations, sustained by ties to a football club that were greater than mere results. This club was in their blood and the need to support it was in their bones. Now it looked as if the shrine at which they worshipped was being allowed to become derelict. As the demonstration continued, police had to be called to control several thousand men with a justifiable grievance, who eventually dispersed when Willie Miller, their goalkeeping idol, appeared at the main door ready to go home and asked everyone else to do the same. They did, but the air was still thick with their righteous invective. This took longer to clear.

It was in this atmosphere that Celtic allowed Malcolm MacDonald, a pillar of the wartime side in every position except goal, to leave for Kilmarnock. He had years of quality still in him, but like Patsy Gallacher, he was released. It is hard to understand why. Perhaps Jimmy McGrory, his ex-teammate, was doing his old Kilmarnock friends a favour. MacDonald served them well, eventually becoming their manager, but Celtic felt his loss sorely.

Tom White died in March 1947 and director Robert Kelly was elected in his place on the casting vote of Tom's own son, Desmond, the club secretary, in preference to the older Colonel Shaughnessy, son of one the founding fathers at Parkhead, Joseph Shaughnessy. Bob Kelly, for his part, was the son of James Kelly, the first Celtic captain. When he died in February 1932, Bob took his shares and his place on the Board and the Kelly dynasty at Celtic Park was established. With such a Celtic pedigree, Bob Kelly took his place with all a young man's confidence, if not arrogance. Being a young manager, Mr McGrory naturally deferred to his chairman, Mr Kelly. This was to prove a big mistake.

Bob Kelly saw himself as 'Mr Celtic' and began to take more and more of an active interest in playing matters – especially in team selection. This was a palpable intrusion on McGrory's rights as team manager, but McGrory, never confrontational, elected to let it slide in the best interest of the club. One cannot help wonder if there might have been a change in his, and Celtic's, fortunes had Shaughnessy become chairman rather than Kelly. McGrory might have been allowed his own say – and who knows what might have been? Even in his short time at Kilmarnock, McGrory had shown he could get results.

He knew from his own experience that a good team is made from eleven good players but a great team is made from those same disparate elements somehow fusing together as one identity, almost as a choir finds its single voice. One can never guarantee that this will happen just by signing the best players (although it helps) or by signing one star and grouping players around him. The whole business of building a team is a gamble and much of a manager's skill is working on all the possible permutations. McGrory, given the time and the cash, might have shown he had that knack, but in

153

nearly 20 years of the Kelly regime he was never given the chance.

Robert Kelly was a daily communicant, which meant he went to Mass every morning before coming back to earth, as it were, by taking the tram from St Alphonsus at the Barras, along London Road to Celtic Park to be in on the start of every day at the ground. Admirable as was this devotion to a chairman's duty, it was hardly a vote of confidence in the existing manager. Kelly regarded as his life-mission the creation of an ideal Celtic rather than a working, warts-and-all 'team of triers', as Jimmy McStay had described the fine 1931 side. McGrory must have chafed at the spectre of this guardian angel with the iron hand always hovering at the tunnel. The iron hand was more than a figure of speech. As a result of a boyhood accident, Bob Kelly had a withered right arm, which had prevented his pursuing a football career himself and also may have given him that air of reserve, which grew chillier as he grew older.

Bob Kelly's rod of measurement for any player was character first and ability second which resulted in a lot of worthy, God-fearing young men being brought into a game where virtue was not always appreciated. Some of the finest players ever seen were out-and-out rogues, but all their sins were forgiven as soon as they ran on to the park. Their many faults were forever expiated by an enthralling exhibition of football skills, or better still, a wonder goal. Kelly didn't appear to understand that the dressing-room and the playing field are often two different worlds. A docile dressing-room demeanour can often mask a terror on the park. McGrory, himself, was an instance of this.

All the great players are of the same strain. They like to run free – to play, in other words. To them, tedious training was hard work. Like all gifted sportsmen they lived for the 'high' they got when they played. They couldn't be treated like clerks reporting to an office, or factory hands standing at an assembly line. Kelly never understood this and he was always uncomfortable with the personality players. This could be seen in the type of player he liked – the quiet-spoken Willie Fernie or Bertie Peacock – and the ones he disliked – the out-spoken Tommy Docherty, the gregarious Pat Crerand or the impish Bertie Auld. These young men were characters and their day would come, Mr Kelly or no.

Then the unbelievable happened. Celtic, the mighty Celtic, McGrory's Celtic, Celtic of the great deeds and legendary names, were, in 1948, for the first time in their splendid history, faced with the very real threat of relegation to the Second Division, depending

154

on how other clubs in the same situation completed their final matches. Everyone knew it had been a terrible season by Celtic's own standards but nobody expected it would get as bad as this. The fact was that on Saturday, 17 April, Celtic had to beat Dundee at Dens Park in their final League match or face the fact that they would have to rely on others to avoid the disaster of relegation. McGrory remembers what he felt like that day:

> It was with a heavy heart and a great deal of anxiety that we left Celtic Park for Dundee. On the way north I discussed the situation with our new chairman, Bob Kelly. I knew inwardly that if Celtic lost I would have to resign after only a couple of years in the managerial chair. So desperate was I that day that I decided on a positional change as the bus neared Dundee. I switched Willie Gallacher, Patsy's son, so that he would be in direct opposition to his brother, Tommy, who played wing-half for Dundee. I said to Bob Kelly, 'His own brother is bound to give him a fair game.' Well, I was never more wrong in my life. Tommy just about murdered him. The build-up to the game had been sensational copy for the newspapers, and on the way north I was beginning to believe what I was reading. I kept saying to myself, 'Imagine Celtic being relegated . . . imagine.'

Dens Park, Dundee, was packed with many hoping for the worst. McGrory was taken aback by the number of people who wanted to see Celtic relegated and was amazed to hear later from a Dundee player (probably Tommy Gallacher) that the home team were on a huge bonus for a win. Dundee didn't need the points for the Championship; Hibernian would win that. They just hoped to see Celtic humiliated and McGrory was furious that someone in Dundee was willing to pay good money to see it happen. He also wondered how Patsy Gallacher was feeling. The former Celtic idol was there that day to see his two sons play on opposite sides.

Celtic had a new man from Blackburn Rovers, Jock Weir, on the right wing in a forward line which, in addition, comprised John McPhail, Dan Lavery, Willie Gallacher and Johnny Paton. Lavery was a Gaelic footballer, born in Australia, who must have been one of Bob Kelly's inspirations. He did get a goal in the first half but it was chalked off by the referee, Mr F. Scott of Paisley, as was an effort by McPhail. Jock Weir managed to get one in that was allowed but then Dundee equalised and at the interval it looked as if the Dundee bonus was safer than Celtic's survival. Half an hour from the end, Dundee scored through McKay and Celtic hearts sank. However, sheer pressure from the desperate Celtic led to corner after corner and the effervescent Weir netted a rebound to draw level and then – a miracle. Two minutes from time, the same player scored to save Celtic and enter its Hall of Fame.

Jock Weir was an unpretentious pro who knew his own limits. In a handful of seasons at Parkhead, he earned his keep, but in this one match he achieved what many strive for throughout a whole career – immortality. And what a match. Although, as has been pointed out, relegation was only a mathematical possibility, it was a possibility and everyone associated with Celtic shuddered at the thought. However, thanks to Jock, the unthinkable had been averted and Jimmy McGrory was saved from being sacked in only his third season as manager.

The fright prompted the Celtic Board into action. McGrory was handed £20,000 and dispatched to Ireland (where else?) with orders to come back with their salvation. He did. A miracle did happen and it took the form of a jaunty forward called Charles Patrick Tully. The risk in mentioning someone like Charlie Tully in a book about McGrory is that it could soon become a book about Tully. Stories and anecdotes abound about this man and those that weren't true, he quickly invented. What is fact, however, is that his arrival at Parkhead was, in part, due to the financial difficulties being experienced at the time by his first club, that other Celtic in Belfast, who had signed him as a 14-year-old boy in 1938.

Arguably, Belfast Celtic was the most famous football club in Ireland and at the time, despite boardroom wrangles, the team was at its peak. Their chief rivals were Linfield, which drew its support from the Protestant Loyalist community, while Celtic relied more on the Catholic congregations in West Belfast. The situation was not unlike the Rangers–Celtic divide in Glasgow – only worse. On Boxing Day 1948, the two teams met at Windsor Park, Belfast, and a riot resulted when Linfield supporters invaded the pitch and a real Donnybrook ensued. The game was duly abandoned of course, but the supporters' battle continued till light stopped play.

The Irish Football Association held Linfield responsible for the outbreak and closed Windsor Park for a month but then, out of the blue, the same FA received a letter from Belfast Celtic stating simply that they were withdrawing from the Irish League with immediate effect. The Barr family ran the Belfast club much as the Kelly regime did their Glasgow counterparts, and when Bob Barr died, one of his sons wanted to take over his father's position. This was resisted by the Board, so the family withdrew their majority shares and Belfast Celtic, being bankrupt, went out of the football business. This caused a sensation. It was as if the Glasgow Celtic had suddenly resigned in Scotland.

However, one result of Belfast Celtic's abrupt disappearance was that the Glasgow Celtic benefited immediately. Hundreds of Irish Celtic fans came over by the boatload to Glasgow every Friday night and later by air every Saturday morning to support their Scottish equivalent and, of course, to see at Parkhead one of their own, your man Tully. His contract, dated 28 June 1948, gives his address as 174 Randolph Drive, Clarkston, which seems rather a prosaic location for one whom many Celtic supporters believed had come direct from Heaven.

In Tully, Parkhead gained another hero. He was Tommy McInally with a brogue. Like the latter, his antics on the field often owed more to vaudeville than football but he undeniably brightened up the skies over Celtic Park, for the sun shone bright on Charlie Tully. He impressed in his debut against Morton but in his first Old Firm game he was a sensation. He gave the future Scotland manager, Ian McColl, an afternoon to forget. Tully was the first Celtic player for years to penetrate the daunting Iron Curtain Rangers defence all on his own and, in this particular match, he trailed defenders after him like the Pied Piper of Paradise.

He could make the ball talk, as they say, but the Tully tongue also exasperated opposing players to a degree where they would gladly have murdered him. Sammy Cox almost did at Ibrox in August 1949 by viciously felling Charlie in the penalty area, but instead of being awarded a penalty, Tully was reprimanded by the SFA for 'inciting the crowd to rowdyism'. He was also in trouble after some dreadful refereeing in a Glasgow Cup tie at Parkhead, where Rangers were allowed a goal from a free kick which had been taken before the referee had signalled for play to resume. Charlie was so incensed he wanted to lead the Celtic team off in protest and the SFA came down on him once more. There were so many incidents involving him, both funny and not so funny, but, as I said, this is not a book about Charlie Tully.

In the meantime, Bob Kelly had brought the 70-year-old coach Jimmy Hogan in from his Continental accomplishments to work with the players at Parkhead. Hogan was an Englishman, a devout Lancastrian Roman Catholic with a disconcerting habit of frequently blessing himself – that is, making the sign of the cross. Whether he did so as a prayerful invocation or as a protection is not clear, but it certainly brought him results in the field of football coaching, where he achieved a considerable reputation. He may have influenced Kelly to let him take the first-team players to see Hungary give a football lesson to England at Wembley. The example must have done some good, for on 27 September 1948, Celtic beat Third Lanark 3–1 in the Glasgow Cup final to give Jimmy McGrory his first silverware as manager.

This win was taken as an omen at Celtic Park, even though they had only four players of genuine quality – Miller, Evans, McPhail and Tully – but at least this was a quartet that could provide the basis of something. McGrory certainly thought so and even Mr Kelly agreed that it was time to splash out. Middlesbrough were sounded out by McGrory about the celebrated Wilf Mannion, their inside-forward, who was an England player of world class. Celtic offered £10,000 but Middlesbrough wanted £25,000, so McGrory opted instead for wee Bobby Collins, whom he pinched from under the noses of Everton after some unnecessary legal wrangles arising from a genuine misunderstanding during the summer of 1948.

Sometime earlier, Collins had agreed to join Everton from Pollok Juniors but when he and his father entrained to Liverpool there was no one from the club to meet them, so not knowing where to go they just got on the next train back to Glasgow, where McGrory, in all innocence, signed him for Celtic on 25 April. Everton protested and the signing was declared void. McGrory was severely censured and fined £100 by the SFA, although it is hard to believe he could ever have been guilty of any duplicity in dealing with players. Both he and Collins thought Everton had lost interest, which they eventually did and wee Bobby was legally and morally free to sign for Celtic on 27 August. He was to remain at Celtic Park for the next ten years before being transferred eventually – to Everton.

All McGrory was trying to do, in difficult circumstances, was to revive the fortunes of a great club which was struggling and he didn't need to be thwarted by technical niceties. The same dilemma arose through the misdating of a provisional form when he tried to sign Pat Buckley of Bo'ness United, who, confusingly, had already signed for St Johnstone. Buckley had neglected to mention this fact to McGrory and once again the manager was in trouble with the authorities. The administrative error was as much the fault of the player as the manager. Unperturbed, Buckley eventually moved on to Aberdeen. One cannot imagine McGrory acting in anything but good faith, but for the mediocre, especially bureaucrats, things are decided not by the large intent but by the small print. All this was unfortunate, but it did show that Celtic were beginning to make an effort to lift their game, and there was no doubt that McGrory still had an eye for a player.

This was proved when, at the end of 1949, he signed a young boy from Neilston Juniors, George 'Sonny' Hunter, to take over from Willie Miller when that great goalkeeper moved on to Clyde. After one particularly magnificent performance by the young custodian in a third-round Scottish Cup tie against Hearts at Tynecastle in February 1951, McGrory said, 'he was the nearest thing in goalkeeping he had seen since John Thomson'. Sadly, Sonny Hunter was to be struck down with tuberculosis just as Peter Scarff had been and, while he made a recovery of sorts, the illness diminished his game. Celtic even sent him to Switzerland but to no avail, and a great career was stunted before it had properly begun. Hunter later dwindled down in English football largely on the reputation he had made with Celtic.

Before this, however, in May 1950, Celtic had visited Rome to play Lazio in a tempestuous game that had the placid McPhail ordered off but McGrory and the team had the compensation of an audience with the Pope. The famous joke has it that Charlie Tully even got on to the balcony with the pontiff. ('Who's that wi' Charlie?') When McGrory got back home to Glasgow, he got the sad news that Canon Lawton had died in Ireland. He was the first mentor-figure in McGrory's life and the man who got him his first pair of football boots. Another part of McGrory's beginnings went with the passing of the good Canon. However, better news was that Barbara was pregnant.

It was around this time that McGrory faced yet another threat to his job in the person of Matt Busby, whose name was seriously put forward by Desmond White and Robert Kelly's brother, David, as a possible McGrory replacement. Chairman Kelly, however, pulled rank and squashed the idea before it could gain any boardroom momentum, even though the attempt caused a rift between the two Kelly brothers which was never healed. The story illustrates two points: one, how tenuous McGrory's hold was on the managerial seat, and two, how powerful Bob Kelly was. Nobody, but nobody,

159

could brook his word. Fortunately, happier events were occurring at home.

Barbara Maria Josephine McGrory was born at St Francis' Maternity Home on 6 April 1951, a week after Charlie Tully had won the Scottish Cup semi-final for Celtic against Raith Rovers. The final brought her father into contention once again with his old Cup foes, Motherwell. The Celtic team by then read: Hunter; Fallon and Rollo; Evans, Boden and Baillie; Weir, Collins, McPhail, Peacock and Tully. It was the most talented team they had assembled for years, so hopes were high and McGrory, the family man, settled into his new status as father of one.

The final was played out at Hampden before 134,000 fans, most of them in green and white, and won by the only goal in the game scored by big John McPhail, who was having the year of his life. After only 17 appearances for the club, young Sonny Hunter had a Scottish Cup medal, and so had the Irish contingent of Tully, Peacock and Fallon. The day, however, belonged to John McPhail, who took a long through ball from Joe Baillie, rounded Andy Paton with ease and as Johnstone came out, calmly lofted the ball over his head for the winner.

It was then, as Scottish Cup holders, that Celtic left for their second tour of America just as they had done in 1931, except that they were to sail out on the luxurious *Queen Mary* from Southampton. The scenes seeing them off at Central Station were reminiscent of that 1931 farewell on Yorkhill Quay. Some things hardly change in football, and one of these is the holy zeal of Celtic supporters for their team and everyone in it. The crowds gathered for a mere sending-off of a team on tour were astonishing and the players could hardly get through the crush. It was showbiz pandemonium rather than a send-off for a football team going off on a summer tour. The crowds were so great that wee Bobby Collins might have been lost forever in somebody's coat pocket if Alec Boden hadn't kept a firm grip of him. The genial giant John McPhail was lionised but Charlie Tully was virtually deified. Police had to rescue the Irishman from the supporters' concerted need to touch him.

McGrory, apparently, kept no diary of the tour this time, or of the voyage on the luxurious *Queen Mary,* but some events stood out. They played nine games in all and won seven of them, drawing against Fulham in Toronto and losing only to the same team in Montreal in the very last match of the tour. However, the stand-out match was that with Eintracht of Germany in New York – and not for any football reasons. Celtic won 3–1 in front of, what seemed, every German in the United States and, coming off, the referee was punched by a German official. Even the piper, a Mr McGonagle, was savaged and his bagpipes burst, but when McGrory himself was suddenly attacked by an Eintracht player, Jimmy Mallan, the Celtic full-back, dealt with the assailant in a suitably Glaswegian manner, much in the way that another McGonagle had dealt with the Thistle player who had attempted to ruffle McGrory coming off the pitch at Firhill a quarter of a century before.

In the course of the tour the team picked up two trophies on the road and nearly lost one – the Scottish Cup – when it was overlooked at Toronto's Union Station. Scotland's most famous football cup had been wrapped up in brown paper at Macy's department store in New York and it had been confused with the other trophies being travelled. It was spotted by a young boy in the left luggage, and returned to a very relieved McGrory at the Celtic hotel. He could hardly have gone back to the SFA offering them two American trophies for the price of one lost Scottish Cup.

In 1951, the Festival of Britain took place. This was the brainchild of architect Sir Hugh Casson, and was held to mark the centenary of Prince Albert's first census of 1851. The Skylon became the symbol of aspiration and hope for the new Britain emerging from its post-war austerity and the Dome of Discovery arose on the South Bank of the Thames at Waterloo as a gesture of defiance against a dull age. Events to mark the occasion took place all over the country and every city vied to present itself as a bastion of culture or a mecca of entertainment. Glasgow decided to play to its strengths and its contribution was a football tournament.

This featured the Scottish First Division clubs in a series of summer ties for what was to be called the St Mungo Cup. To everyone's surprise, including their own, Celtic got through every round and found themselves facing Aberdeen in the final at Hampden on Wednesday, 1 August 1951. Aberdeen were a good side at the time and were two up just after the half-hour. Then, when Hunter had to leave the field to have a head wound bandaged, Bobby Evans took over in goal and was just as outstanding until Hunter returned. It was in this game that Tully played his notorious throw-in trick, bouncing the ball off an Aberdeen defender's back, gaining a corner and then crossing for Sean Fallon to score. The same player got another five minutes after the interval, then 'Prince' Charlie went on one of his typical, mazy runs to lay the ball on for Jimmy Walsh to net the winner.

However, when they got the St Mungo Cup home, one of the handles came off. Closer examination showed that the figure of Mungo on the top had been recently added. The cup was, in fact, a yachting cup, which explained the presence of mermaids and lifebelts. Originally it had been a trophy for a Glasgow tournament won by Provan Gas Works in 1912. Celtic just stuck the handle on again and it stands today in a proud, one-off line that stretches from the first Glasgow Exhibition Cup of 1901, the Empire Exhibition Trophy of 1938, the Victory-in-Europe Cup of 1945 and now the St Mungo Cup of 1951. It could be said of manager McGrory, quite literally, that his cups runneth over.

Of one particular cup, the St Mungo, it should be noted that a pay packet shows McGrory's wage as Celtic manager during 1951 was £14 10s a week – less £2 tax – giving him £12 10s to take home. Scant reward surely for a man who had just won a trophy made for the Provan Gas Works.

ELEVEN

Flying in the Face of the SFA

We, who admire and wish you well,
We hope you conquer in the fight,
To many hearts, if Celtic fell
'Twould bring delirious delight . . .

Lines from a poem by 'JC' published
in the *Glasgow Star*, 16 April 1915

When, on Tuesday, 4 December 1951, Jimmy McGrory, on the advice of Jimmy Gribben, a respected member of the back-room staff at Celtic Park, signed the unknown John Stein of 14 Whistleberry Crescent, Hamilton, he didn't know what he was doing. He thought he was hiring an unknown centre-half from a non-League club in Wales but in reality he was founding an institution. What was a hurried, stop-gap measure in an emergency was to have far-reaching repercussions for both club and player, for McGrory, quite unwittingly, had set in motion the creation in big Jock Stein of another Celtic icon. However, at the time, it was merely a routine event to be attended to at the desk just as another minor office chore brought to his attention would, in the same manner, have enormous ramifications and overwhelm the importance of Stein's arrival. This was the matter of the flag.

This book has made it clear that Celtic began as an Irish club, although never a strictly sectarian one. Jock Stein himself was evidence of this, being one of a long line of non-Catholics who have served Celtic both on the field and off. Nonetheless, it was never hidden that its roots were with the Irish in Glasgow and to honour them, the old Irish flag (all green with a gold harp at the centre) had always flown above the 'jungle' – the former tin-roofed enclosure opposite the main stand. This flew at one end and the Union Jack at the other, thus acknowledging the twin loyalties of the parties concerned – that is, Glasgow people of Irish extraction who were citizens/subjects of Great Britain.

This much was obvious and accepted. With the partition of Ireland in 1921 and the creation of the new Free State of Eire, the Irish authorities sent the new flag, a tricolour of green, white and orange, as a replacement and this was duly hung without any comment and flew in its place for 30 years. By this time, however, having been exposed to the industrial winds that blew around Parkhead from Beardmore's Forge complex at one end and the Dalmarnock Power Station at the other, with all sorts of small factories in between, it was getting a little air-worn and threadbare. Sometime in 1951 McGrory was asked by the Celtic Board to find a replacement for it. This ought to have been a simple administrative act involving a phone call, a letter and an invoice, but for one reason or another, Jimmy found it impossible to buy or have such a flag made anywhere in Scotland. He then decided, on his own initiative, to take direct action with Irish contacts, as he explains in *A Lifetime in Paradise*:

> I took up pen and paper and wrote to no less a person than Eamon de Valera, the then Premier of the Republic of Ireland, explaining my plight, and asking if he could provide us with a tricolour. Having been introduced to him on a couple of occasions on Irish tours, I thought I would chance my arm, although I didn't think he would remember me.

In a matter of days the new flag arrived at Celtic Park with the compliments of the Taoiseach himself. It was in position in time for the next game, which happened to be the traditional 'Ne'erday' match with Rangers, and that's when the trouble began. Indeed, 1952 couldn't have got off to a more controversial start.

Football was the least concern that day as bottles flew and tempers rose between both sets of supporters. The opposing sides in the terracing battle were mainly their respective hooligan elements ludicrously parading under 'religious' banners. The result was that eleven spectators were arrested and two of them were jailed. The Glasgow magistrates decided to take football matters into their own hands and recommend that the New Year's Day fixture be discontinued and played on another date, that drink be disallowed at such games and that they be all-ticket in future to allow for greater crowd control, and that, finally, no flags should be flown that might incite the spectators. One would have thought something with a splash of orange in it would appease any bigot. Instead, this caused an outcry in the press and the focus was stupidly placed on Celtic's new Irish flag. This aspect was blown up out of all proportion to the real cause of the fracas, which was drink and rowdyism allied to deep-set religious prejudice on both sides.

It was this last point that the SFA seized on and it provoked their deliberate malice. The SFA had never even pretended to be friends with Celtic at any time. Ironically, they had been well served in their legislative chambers by Celtic's Willie Maley and Tom White but this could not abate the almost conspiratorial attitude that grew up towards the Parkhead club after the Celtic Park disturbances. The Referee Committee (which was composed of club directors, not referees) discussed the matter and left no doubt that Celtic were to blame and, without any legal right to do so, ordered the club to remove the tricolour – 'or face the serious consequences'. This meant suspension at best, closure of the ground at worst and, at most, the loss to Scottish football of one of its greatest drawing clubs – and the loss of gate-revenue all round.

To Celtic's dismay, the SFA in full congress upheld the Referee Committee's findings and the order to Celtic was officially sanctioned. It must be understood that in the '50s, the SFA was at the pinnacle of the Scottish Establishment, which meant it was prone to masonic influence. Or rather, by one prominent member of its Order in Scotland, Sir George Graham, so dubbed for his services to Scottish football – though how fully he served it might be open to question. Self-served, in many opinions, might be nearer the mark, for the same George had no qualms about using his powers as secretary of the SFA to manipulate his supposed masters to a point where he was virtual dictator of football in Scotland for more than two decades.

He unashamedly created power lobbies within the SFA structure and used them to his own requirements and notions. This had been proved in 1950 when he vetoed the Scotland team's participation in the World Cup because they couldn't go as British Champions. This

165

was merely stubborn short-sightedness but the confrontation over the Eire flag was prompted by nothing less than naked bias and petty obduracy. Fortunately for Celtic, Graham was to come face to face with a mirror image of himself in Catholic dress – Bob Kelly, clothed in the white robes of righteousness.

This other future knight had at last found a cause worth fighting for – the saving of his beloved Celtic. So, in 1952, he took up his lance in the manner of any gallant knight and slew the SFA dragon by sheer logic, calm good sense and an unbending conviction of Celtic's correctness in the matter. Kelly was helped in this by support from an unexpected quarter. John Wilson, the then chairman of Rangers, correctly pointed out that Celtic could not be penalised if they hadn't broken any rule – and there was no rule stating that Celtic could *not* fly an Irish flag over their own stadium.

The whole unfortunate incident is only relevant to the McGrory story because of the effect it had in raising the standing of Bob Kelly as chairman of Celtic, to the detriment of McGrory's status as manager. Bob Kelly's quasi-messianic sense of right in all matters Celtic, and the way in which he held this position virtually single-handedly against all the mustered regiments of the Establishment, impressed everyone who was involved. Good sense eventually prevailed and the matter was allowed to die a quiet death after a series of tactical retreats that allowed the SFA to save what face it could – but it could not spare its blushes.

Flag-bearer Kelly claimed the day, to his own great satisfaction. Like all his generation of Catholics he was obsessed by the notion of bigotry. He had all the pent-up frustration of the marginalised and was all too ready to use that energy, aware that those who were not for him were against him. It was only as the years passed, and another generation of Catholics rose up around him, that Bob Kelly began to be aware that there were good Protestants too – but tell it not in Gath. The flag did come down – much later – but only to accommodate yet another League Championship flag as Celtic had run out of flagpoles. A fitting end to an unfitting episode.

Throughout the whole controversy, McGrory kept his pipe firmly clenched between his teeth. It was not his area of competence. He was happy to leave it to his chairman. The last thing he ever wanted was an argument with anyone, especially when deep feelings were involved. He found it hard to talk wages with players, never mind religion. The players rarely saw him upset. The only time he ever lost his temper was after a Charity Cup tie against Third Lanark in that same season when, following a 1–1 draw, Celtic got through on the toss of a coin. The team was celebrating this 'victory' in the dressing-room when McGrory burst in and silenced the room at once by his untypical demeanour. He was literally shaking with anger and eventually controlled himself to say quietly, 'You fellows should think shame of yourselves wearing that jersey.' He then walked out, closing the door behind him and leaving the dressing-room still in silence. It was Jock Stein who broke it by saying, just as quietly, 'He was right.' But then he added, 'But he'll no' say it again. Right?'

On this moment hung the big changeover within Celtic. Jock Stein, the stop-gap deputy brought up from a non-League side to a Scottish League side that was hardly much better despite the quality of some of its players, now took matters into his big, miner's hands. If there was hard graft to be done it would start from *now*. With the hour cometh the man, but there was hardly a moment to spare. Jock Stein knew what it had cost the quiet man he called the 'Boss' to come in and say just those few words, because Stein knew how much the jersey meant to McGrory. Things changed from the moment he'd shut that door on them.

Despite the fact that that same Celtic team actually won that year's Charity Cup, beating Queen's Park in the final 3–1 before 40,000 spectators, McGrory was worried about reports of supporter discontent. To him, they were the essential part of the club, it was they who kept it going – just as the same Celtic had once kept many of their fathers and grandfathers going. By 1952, the Charity Cup had had its time. It would soon go the same way as wartime rationing, which was still being phased out. The austerity years would have to be put away just as the war years were. Celtic would have to stop mourning for its glorious past and prepare for the future. This was the turning of the tide. Everyone at Celtic Park could sense it.

Coach Jimmy Hogan had come and gone before Stein arrived, but his was, nonetheless, a big influence at the club. He had given the players a glimpse of the football world beyond their local week-to-week preoccupations, but few listened. He had tried to tell them that what one did off the ball was often as important as what one did with it. When not in possession, you took up position. It was as simple as that, but it taught players to work for each other. It was teamwork, in other words. For the most part, the Hogan message fell on deaf ears but Jock Stein was quick to profit from this legacy, and Bobby Evans' international career was to prosper because of it. It was Hogan's instinct that changed Evans from a lively, but ordinary, left-winger to a wing-half, and later centre-half, of international class – indeed, a future Scotland captain. The enigmatic Englishman had the same high opinion of Tommy Docherty. Tommy, another Boys' Guild player, had been signed by McGrory from Shettleston Juniors in 1948 and was unfortunate in that his Celtic career coincided with that of Evans. Docherty had been signed as a forward but Hogan saw him, too, as a half-back. Unfortunately, this admiration for the player wasn't shared by chairman Kelly. The vociferous 'Doc' was not promoted as he deserved and soon afterwards left for Preston North End.

One wonders what voice McGrory had in these moves? He was the manager after all, but in this case he was caught between the omnipotence of his chairman and the prestige of a hired, but respected, coach. McGrory's less sophisticated football world of manager, team trainer and a variegated ensemble of eleven players on the field was giving way gradually to the demands of a new era in the sport where a squad was the thing and tactics the name of the game. This objective, intellectual approach was inimical to a man who was a natural, instinctive player and a compliant, undemanding manager, but it was right up captain Jock Stein's street.

The new approach was something the team could talk about, think about and even try out. Stein knew the ability that was there in the players that McGrory had signed like John McPhail, Bobby Evans, Bobby Collins, Willie Fernie and, of course, Charlie Tully. Each had more than his fair share of natural ability but the combination wasn't gelling and the approach was too hit and miss. There was no doubting the new will to win, but the way to win was still not clear and would have to be worked out painstakingly at training from the playing material available.

Even the best players lose form in patches or get injured. Unfortunately, little Bobby Collins broke his arm on the close-season tour of Ireland and the team had to do without his vital service until mid-December 1952. He came back into a different Celtic. There was a new spirit in the side and the latent talent was starting to show itself. It was in this season that Charlie Tully scored his fantastic 'two-goal' corner kick in a Scottish Cup tie against Falkirk on 21 February 1953. He scored the first directly from the corner but an over-fussy linesman had insisted the ball was not properly placed. Unperturbed, Charlie gave the returned ball to the linesman and asked him to place it himself. As soon as he did so, Tully hit it over into the crowded goalmouth – and scored again. It was an exact replica of the first goal. The crowd at Brockville that day knew that they had seen one of their great legends in mythic action. It inspired the Celtic team from a 2–0 deficit to 2–2, then with five minutes to go, centre-forward John McGrory (no relation) received the ball facing his own goal, turned on a sixpence and fired the winner into the top of the Falkirk net. He was so overwhelmed by his teammates' congratulations he had to receive trainer Alec Dowdell's attention, but his goal had done the name of McGrory proud.

The matter of the family name was something that concerned Jimmy McGrory as the latest signing for 'Team McGrory' now made it a family of four at Rowan Road. Elizabeth Marjorie Anne was born on 2 March 1953. However, it was another Elizabeth, the Princess Elizabeth, who was the centre of attention outside the McGrory household. She had now become Queen on the death of her father, King George VI and to celebrate her coronation in June 1953, a new national football tournament was arranged.

The FA and SFA worked jointly on this with a tournament to be held at Hampden featuring specially selected teams. Celtic were among those invited to take part but strictly on their name alone. They were there to make up the numbers and everybody knew that. However, this was the year that the veteran Stanley Matthews won the FA Cup for Blackpool and another 'oldie', Gordon Richards, won the Derby on Pinza. It was the year for the unexpected and this time Celtic were to provide the football surprise.

Knowing that the team needed strengthening, McGrory tried to buy goalkeeper Jimmy Cowan of Greenock Morton, but his offer of £4,000 was turned down. (Cowan later went to Sunderland for twice that.) However, Celtic were luckier in going for Neil Mochan, a centre-forward and former teammate of Cowan's at Greenock. Mochan was with Middlesbrough but they accepted £8,000 for him and, as a keen Celtic supporter, Neilly was glad to come to Parkhead. He signed on Friday, 8 May 1953 and next day he was playing against Queen's Park in the Charity Cup final, scoring twice and winning his first medal in his first match. His next three games were also to be played at Hampden in the Coronation Cup – and all before he even kicked a ball seriously at Celtic Park.

Goalkeeper John Bonnar had been bought as cover for Willie Miller after Rolando Ugolini had gone to Middlesbrough but his appearances had been fitful. Now he was chosen for the side to contest this big, prestigious tournament. As he was boarding the bus to take the team to Hampden, he looked around and quipped,

'Where's Jimmy Cowan then?' Bonnar didn't know it, but like Mochan, he was to be crucial to Celtic in the next couple of weeks. Another 'new' face was John McPhail, who was restored to the side at wing-half instead of forward. Since returning from the American tour he had put on a lot of weight and consequently suffered a dreadful slump of form. Now, trimmed down, he had found a new lease of life in the spring of the year by stepping back to left-half, where his footwork and his guile could be put to better use in linking with Tully. The Celtic team for the competition was Bonnar; Haughney and Rollo; Evans, Stein and McPhail; Collins, Walsh, Mochan, Peacock and Tully.

The other teams taking part by invitation were Arsenal, Manchester United, Tottenham Hotspur and Newcastle United from England and Rangers, Hibernian and Aberdeen from Scotland – and more or less in that order. The four English teams were League leaders or FA Cup winners in recent years and in Scotland, Rangers had just won the Scottish League – again – but Hibernian were the team of the moment. The Edinburgh side boasted a forward line of Smith, Johnstone, Reilly, Turnbull and Ormond – the Famous Five – every bit as good as Celtic's pre-war Exhibition Cup line-up. Like them, each Hibernian player was a star in his own right but combined, they were deadly. They had won the Scottish League the year before and were currently in great form. Now they were joint favourites with Arsenal to win the new Cup, and it was Arsenal that Celtic were to meet in the first round.

Some Arsenal players had watched Celtic play Queen's Park in the Charity Cup final and they left early with the feeling that their tie with the Glasgow team would be little more than a formality. The English club might even have got a bye because Celtic nearly withdrew due to dressing-room dissension caused by the players' bonus demands. Things were somehow smoothed over by an impassioned McGrory and the team took the pitch determined to show their real worth. For once, they got their act together and, spurred on by Bobby Evans, they all played to their potential, with even full-back Alex Rollo coming upfield with a run. They totally dominated the London team and ran out worthy winners, even though it was by the only goal in the match – Bobby Collins doing a Tully and scoring direct from a corner. Celtic not only surprised themselves, they astonished their delighted support. One fan described watching the match 'like finding a five-pound note in an old jacket pocket. You don't ask any questions; you just accept it.'

Manchester United, who had beaten Rangers, were the next to fall to this rejuvenated Celtic. Hibernian, meantime, were disposing of Tottenham Hotspur and Newcastle United so that an all-Scottish final was in prospect – a battle between the two green-and-whites, the Edinburgh and Glasgow offshoots of the same ancient stem – but there would be no quarter given here. The outcome would depend on how this new-shape Celtic defence would deal with Hibernian's Famous Five. Celtic's own forward potential was not even considered. Then Tully called off with an injury but, fortunately, they had in Willie Fernie, an exquisite ball-player and a high-calibre substitute.

More than 117,000 spectators, most of them Celtic supporters, turned up at Hampden on 20 May (a lovely, sunny Wednesday night) with at least 10,000 locked out by the police because of congestion at the King's Park 'Celtic' end. It was a memorable final, if only because of Celtic's first strike, 'Smiler' Mochan's wonder goal. Stein cleared out to Fernie on the wing, who then did the unexpected by not hugging the touch-line as before but immediately turning it in to Mochan on the centre circle. The centre-forward headed at once in the direction of the Hibs goal and their defence held back expecting him to continue forward. Instead, Mochan suddenly let fly from more than 30 yards out with his right – supposedly weaker – foot and the ball flew past Tommy Younger's despairing right hand into the roof of the net. Had he touched it, it would have broken his fingers. It is a goal that has since passed into Celtic's history along with Tully's corner kicks, Patsy Gallacher's somersault effort and Jimmy McGrory's famous headers.

In the second half, Hibernian threw all caution to the notorious Hampden swirl and turned up their forward line to full power. Celtic could only fall back to defend. With three minutes to go, Jimmy Walsh seemed to seal a Celtic victory when he scored but Hibs still pressed forward. This was the clash the purists had wanted to see and they were only denied by the new hero of the hour, Jimmy Cowan stand-in, Johnny Bonnar. The little man had grown at least six inches on each hand because he reached shots that seemed impossible and his solo display that night was in the same class as the Celtic legend that he had been bought to replace, Willie Miller. His was a one-man curtain drawn tightly across the Celtic goal and not all the wiles and tricks and power of Smith, Reilly and Ormond could prevail against it. Even when, for once, he was beaten, there was John McPhail to head off the line. Still the Hibernian attack persisted

171

and still the Celtic defence held out. With the last shot of the match, Lawrie Reilly shot strongly but again Bonnar got his fingers to it and, as he turned the shot away at the base of the post, the final whistle blew. The whole Celtic team rushed to pick Bonnar up. He had had the night of his life and Celtic had won the Coronation Cup. Willie Ormond was later to say, 'That Celtic team were a puir bloody lot . . . but we couldnae get wan by that bugger Bonnar.'

After the tensions of such a match, especially the siege that was the second half, the Celtic support hadn't the energy to move from where they stood for a long time. Many didn't sleep that night. They didn't need to; they had had their dream 90 minutes and they didn't want to forget it. They had seen their team rise from mediocrity to mastery in a matter of weeks and they still couldn't believe it. Jimmy McGrory was manager of a team that had beaten the best in Britain.

After all the rejoicing, there was a moment of sadness. On 17 June, just weeks after the memorable night, the great Patsy Gallacher died at his home in Scotstoun at the age of only 60. McGrory's great hero, he had inspired not only him but a whole legion of players and many thousands of fans on the terracing. He was a 'milestone' Celtic player, as Jimmy Quinn was before him and Jimmy McGrory after him and what Charlie Tully was at the time of Patsy's death. Gallacher's was the kind of name that identified an age and his funeral was a mark of the standing in which he was held by all in football. If not quite in the same hysterical level as John Thomson's passing, it did bring many together who had not seen each other for years. One such reunion was that between Jimmy McGrory and Willie Maley.

Maley was now an old man of 85 and had been virtually a total recluse since leaving Celtic in February 1940. He had made no effort to contact McGrory or Kelly since the death of Tom White in 1947, but funerals, like weddings, have a way of bringing people together. Maley now gave all his time to charitable pursuits like the promoting of a sanatorium in Kingussie. The Big Fella had sold off all his business interests and shrunk his life to the minimal opportunities still open to him, although he had been seen from time to time as a guest of the Rangers at Ibrox. Now here he was seeing Celtic faces again. The emotion of the reunion showed plainly.

McGrory, of course, could bear no grudges and made every attempt to build bridges. The austere Kelly, remembering his father's affection for Maley in the early days, also sought reconciliation. As a result, a charity match was arranged between Celtic and a Bohemians of Dublin Select XI in aid of the 'Willie Maley

Testimonial Fund' with the receipts to go to his nominated charities. The game was scheduled for 10 August 1953 and so it was that the old Boss, flanked by former players Joe Dodds, Willie Loney and Jimmy McMenemy, walked on to the turf of his beloved Celtic Park. The crowd roared as they saw him. He raised the famous homburg and stood for a moment in the centre circle, looking around him at a place that must have been drenched in memories for him, then he walked slowly off the field with his three old players and disappeared back into his self-imposed anonymity.

The boost that Celtic had been given by the Coronation Cup was sufficient to propel them forward into the next season with great expectations but a reaction set in and they just could not get going. They lost out in the Glasgow Cup and the League Cup and then someone at Celtic Park had a brainwave. They put the bustling Sean Fallon in at centre-forward and played Mochan out on the left wing, bringing Fernie inside. The reshuffle worked to such an extent that the team had a 13-match unbeaten run and Neilly Mochan ended the season with 25 goals. This saw the team shoot up the League table and by the time they had played their way to another Scottish Cup final after a tough replay against Motherwell, they were already top of the League, five points clear of Hearts. If they could win this final they would have completed the rare League and Cup Double, a redoubtable feat they had achieved three times before in their history – 1907, 1908 and 1914.

Celtic's opponents once again were Aberdeen, and the team sent out to try and give the club its finest year since 1938 was: Bonnar; Haughney and Meechan; Evans, Stein and Peacock; Higgins, Fernie, Fallon, Tully and Mochan. In a sense, nothing could stop them now, and sheer exuberance carried them through against a determined Aberdeen. The score was 1–1 when Fernie, after leaving a trail of defenders behind him, eventually found Fallon in the goalmouth, who took the pass and side-footed the winner from close range. After 40 years, the Cup and League Double was theirs.

As a reward, and very untypically, Celtic splashed out and took the team to the 1954 World Cup finals in Switzerland. Fernie and Mochan had been picked for Scotland and were competing at this level for the first time, so their teammates were there to cheer them on. As it turned out, it was sympathy that was needed, for Scotland were beaten by Austria 1–0 and by Uruguay 7–0. Also in the Scottish team was a former Celtic player from the Hogan era, Tommy Docherty. Tommy, for all his future wanderings, would always

173

remain a Celtic man at heart, and the tongue that had so often got him into trouble at Celtic Park was to earn him a very comfortable living in later years on the after-dinner speakers' circuit.

The Swiss trip was not only a generous gesture on Celtic's part, it was to prove a shrewd move by Kelly in exposing the players to the highest standards in the game and to the latest tactical developments. One senses the hand of Stein here. McGrory was allowing the big man more and more off-the-field authority. It was already obvious that Jock was working, in his own quiet, methodical way, towards something. He was taking an even greater part in training routines and, like Patsy Gallacher, his was the dominant dressing-room voice before every match. And the players listened.

Perhaps in reaction to the wonderful season of before, Celtic lost out as champions to Aberdeen but there was a nice touch when Aberdeen came to play at Celtic Park in 1955. The announcer asked the home crowd to welcome the Dons as champions, and the Celtic support responded splendidly, giving Aberdeen a prolonged and deserved ovation. What pleased the home support even more was that they beat the new champions 2–1 in the April sunshine, both goals coming from John McPhail, now restored to centre-forward. Having been runners-up in the League, and having reached the final of the Scottish Cup, they imagined that their chances were good against the lower-placed Clyde at Hampden on 23 April.

This was the first Scottish Cup final to be seen on television, and that doyen of English football commentators Kenneth Wolstenholme was brought up from London to 'voice' the match to Scottish viewers. One can hardly think of anyone less appropriate to commentate on the action between a team from Parkhead and another from Bridgeton, but at that time Scotland had not yet grown its own Archie Macpherson.

Of the two sides, Celtic were streets ahead in class, having at least half a dozen players in their line-up of proven international quality. Clyde boasted only two caps, Haddock and Ring, the latter who ought to have been a Celt, as he was in the author's year at St Mungo's Academy in 1947 and, like the rest of us, was an ardent Celtic fan. One other interesting minor fact about the Celtic team that day was that their now recognised half-back line of Evans, Stein and Peacock was known to the Celtic support as 'The Brothers' – because each of them was believed to have been a Freemason.

Perhaps because of the television coverage, the crowd at the final was smaller than usual – a fact which assisted Bob Kelly's view that

174

television coverage would eventually change the face of football. How sadly true. However, more than 100,000 fans turned up on the day to roar on Celtic as they laid siege to the Clyde goal from the kick-off. It took half an hour before they scored, through Walsh. Clyde did well to hold out for the rest of the game but it was Celtic who then, in the last half-hour, went inexplicably on the defensive until two minutes from the end when a Robertson corner kick, assisted by the notorious Hampden swirl, was missed by Bonnar, so giving Clyde the equaliser.

In the replay, Celtic made some puzzling changes, bringing Fallon (Kelly's man) back to centre-forward and dropping Bobby Collins, a proven Cup battler, for no apparent reason. Sharpshooter Mochan was also sidelined. The result was that Clyde had all the confidence in the world against a reordered Celtic. They easily contained the plodding Fallon and the cumbersome McPhail. In a breakaway attack in the second half, Tommy Ring, of all people, scrambled in a goal and this proved to be the winner. Clyde had won the Scottish Cup. Bonnar, the hero of the last final, was the villain of this one, but really the defeat was a team effort, or rather, it was due to a managerial blunder in tinkering with a good team.

A poignant domestic coda to the Cup final was the reaction in the Celtic-mad Ring household when Tommy, the Clyde goal-scorer, went as usual to his mother's house after last Mass on Sunday. His brothers wouldn't speak to him. From being the replay hero with a Cup medal in his pocket, he was now the 'baddie'. Family peace was only restored when Tommy said it would never happen again. It didn't. When Celtic next met Clyde in the following season's Glasgow Cup, and with Collins and Mochan reinstated to the side, Celtic won 4–0. Presumably by then Tommy Ring had been restored to his usual place at the family table.

The question that would preoccupy the Ring brothers around that table and other Celtic supporters like them in the '50s was: who was choosing the team every week? It seemed to the ordinary fans that the management were picking numbers out of a hat, selections often being made just hours before a game. It didn't make for any kind of consistency and badly affected team morale. Everyone suspected the pervading Kelly influence and one wonders at the effect this had on McGrory's confidence as manager.

The manager of a football club is not unlike the chef in a hotel kitchen. He is given, or selects, his various ingredients and using his experience and/or skill he concocts his dish and sends it out to the dining room for the delectation of the patrons. In McGrory's case, the analogy might be extended to include chairman Bob as the maître d' who comes into the kitchen and not only adds seasoning as he likes, but picks the vegetables himself. And some right turnips he chose.

It was undue boardroom influence that had so disheartened Jimmy McStay in the war years, but McGrory was more resilient. Or was he merely more compliant? The 'tandem' control exerted from the manager's office via the boardroom didn't work because it so often threw Celtic out of their winning ways by eccentric selection, random changes and player favouritism.

McGrory was always available to the players but chairman Kelly also made his presence felt, standing at the tunnel during training taking in each player with those gimlet eyes and unnerving many, even the most experienced. It was noticed that Tully and McPhail always exerted themselves on the running track whenever Mr Kelly was present but as soon as he left they resumed their usual roles as spectators of the training routines. Jimmy McGrory was a popular and much-admired manager, but there was no hiding who the real 'Boss' was.

At least Jimmy was still head of his own house, and on 20 October 1955, unto him a son was born. James Hubert Gerard McGrory came into the world and made the family complete. Belltrees rang with the noise of a new baby and a happy family. Incidentally, at the christening of James McGrory Junior, his godparents were a certain chairman and his wife, Josephine – Bob and Joey to the McGrory family. That says something about all parties concerned. For Mr McGrory Senior, now turned 51, life was more than just a game of football – but only just.

TWELVE

Paradise Retained

In football, nothing is inconceivable.
Always expect the unexpected.
Tony Woodcock, footballer, The Independent, 2005

On 9 February 1956, Hugh McGrory, Jimmy's oldest brother, died at his sister Lizzie's house at 94 Bellgrove Street in Dennistoun. Hugh was yet another instance of a little life lived out in the shallows, hardly disturbing the water around him. He hadn't played professional football, but he had survived the trenches in 1916, and that was the big event in his life. A shy bachelor, he laboured anonymously for most of his 66 years. Jimmy registered his death, knowing that his big brother's small existence could so easily have been his, but for football. He always insisted he had been lucky, but at this time, he was riding that luck somewhat.

In the mid-'50s, conditions at the club were not what they might have been. This is evident in an account given by Peter Sweeney of his visit with the well-established Sarsfield Celtic Supporters' Club to Celtic Park just after the great League and Cup Double of 1954. As published in *Oh, Hampden in the Sun . . .* by Peter Burns and Pat Woods, it sadly illustrates the contrast between the recent great deeds on the park and the grubby and depressing lack of imagination and style backstage at Parkhead. It also indicates the diminished status of former icon, Jimmy McGrory, in the scheme of things, effectively being reduced by Bob Kelly to little more than an office minder and

occasional caretaker. This is an edited version of what Mr Sweeney
wrote:

> Some members suggested that we have a visit to Celtic Park.
> Our first surprise came with the reply agreeing to our visit. It
> was written on a piece of ordinary notepaper by Jimmy
> McGrory. There were more surprises to come. About 20 of us
> met outside the main entrance to Celtic Park and were then
> invited through by an official. Most of us were going through
> that door for the first time. We were left in a dismal and
> poorly lit entrance hall for a few minutes. On the walls were
> several portraits of people like Brother Walfrid and some
> giants who had worn the hoops. They all looked very sad.
> Eventually Jimmy McGrory appeared to welcome us. Most
> wanted to see the Trophy Room. Here the disappointment
> started . . . all the trophies were there . . . but the presentation
> was very bad – there was a hole in the carpet and you could
> have written your name in the dust on some of the cabinets.
> All the trophies were needing some attention. One member
> asked where the Coronation Cup was. Jimmy didn't know,
> but said we could help him look for it. We found it on the
> floor behind the door we'd just come through. It was a sorry
> sight, tarnished and still bearing the green and white ribbons
> from the day it was won, but they were faded and wrinkled.
> As the tour continued, things didn't improve. The chairman's
> office looked like a scene from *Steptoe and Son*. The manager's
> office was tiny and bare. The director's room was a joke – odd
> chairs, maybe they were antiques! The treatment room was so
> small that the trainer, who had a young player on the table,
> had to step aside so that we, one by one, could 'peek' round
> the door. The dressing-rooms were so impoverished, it
> prompted one of our members to say, 'I've seen better
> facilities at a junior club.' Our tour ended with a cup of tea,
> then Jimmy said training would soon be over and we could get
> some autographs. Personally, I had seen enough and made my
> excuses, as did several others. Outside the ground we were
> saying to each other, 'What did they do with the money?'

That was a question many supporters were to ask; and quite rightly,
for they regarded it as *their* money. There were rumours about
discrepancies between given attendance figures and the actual

number of people coming through the gates. Some gates were allowed to pass people through free of charge, like friends and families of the players. It was all so slapdash and old-fashioned that everything was open to question and suspicion. It wasn't a new broom that was needed here but a battery of vacuum cleaners. Even the ground itself looked sad; it had been in a state of decline for years. Celtic was in a miasma of its own making and there seemed to be no way out but down. It was uncanny, too, how the fortunes of the club should have descended so quickly from sublime superiority to stumbling mediocrity in so short a time. Then, for the first time ever, Jimmy McGrory was booed by his own supporters.

It was the practice of Celtic to hold a public trial match every year before the start of the season between the Probables (Greens) and Possibles (Whites). These summer evening matches were always well attended, and this year everyone could see there was an abundance of young talent in the club but supporters rarely saw these players as the season developed and they wanted to know why. As McGrory took his seat in the stand beside Kelly, some supporters showed their discontent by booing. It startled the manager but, once again, it was Kelly the supporters were really aiming for. They knew the score.

The two men were joined at the hip in their wholehearted love of everything Celtic but, where McGrory was modest and unassertive in its display, Kelly was exactly the opposite. He held his quirky views on players strongly and would not be gainsaid. Whatever McGrory thought, his opinions washed against the massive bulwark of the chairman's absolute self-certainty and so he just ebbed away into ineffectiveness. Of course McGrory ought to have spoken out, but he wasn't that kind of man. He merely puffed on his pipe and blew smoke rings around his private misgivings, if he had any. It wasn't in his nature to push or speak out, as he was the first to admit. As far as he was concerned, for passivity, read loyalty.

Celtic supporters sensed this and as if to give him some reassurance of their deep loyalty to him personally, they packed the Kelvin Hall on 2 September 1956 to tell Jimmy McGrory exactly what they thought of him. On this kind of occasion, of course, the compliments fly but one gets the feeling there was a unanimous sincerity in all the comments made. In the programme for the event, Cyril Horne, the sports journalist from the *Glasgow Herald*, made the point that while McGrory's prowess as a manager did not compare to his fame as a footballer, it mustn't be forgotten that, under his management, Celtic won all the major domestic honours available in the game, as well as several that were unique in themselves, like the St Mungo and Coronation Cups. If he were not as famous a manager as he was a player it was because he was 'too decent' to be a ruthless manager, and not self-seeking enough to protect his image. 'If these traits are faults then he is to be commended for them. Jimmy McGrory will always be remembered as a footballer but it should not be forgotten that he was also a gentleman.'

Willie Maley followed in the same vein, except that he paid tribute to Barbara McGrory as the nurse who had attended to him in hospital during the recent operation for the removal of his right eye. Even with one eye, Maley 'saw' in McGrory the ideal player, hard-working, tough and an inspiration to his teammates. Like himself, he was 'once a Celt, always a Celt', and even when he ceased to be a star player, he still remained part of the Celtic management team, 'keeping that spirit that told him that the game is never lost until it is won. That is the characteristic of the club as well as of the man.'

Bob Kelly reminded his audience that he had seen nearly every game Jimmy McGrory ever played and what remained his outstanding quality throughout his career was, in his opinion, his keenness and enthusiasm. 'I have known Jimmy for over 30 years and every year increases my admiration for him, for he is a man of outstanding character, blessed with an innate sense of sportsmanship and loyalty. Anyone who can call him friend is indeed fortunate.'

Why call him a manager, one is tempted to ask, if he isn't allowed to manage? There is no record of Jimmy's reaction to all this, except that he was amazed that so many people should even bother to arrange such events for someone like him. And he meant it. He returned to his desk the next day gratified that there was still a strong feeling for him among the supporters but in order to keep that respect, he had to find a forward line, particularly a centre-forward. Had it been necessary, he might even have turned out himself. He had hoped for something from young Jim Sharkey but that brilliant prospect had a personality problem – in Bob Kelly's eyes – and soon departed for Airdrie. Jock Stein's playing career had also ended due to a stubborn knee injury which left him with a lifelong limp so, fore and aft, the good ship Celtic was in danger of foundering.

The League Cup had never been lucky for them – they had never even got to a final. However, they did so in the 1956–57 season. After a midweek replay against Partick Thistle before a low crowd of 31,000 they won largely due to a bravura performance by Charlie Tully, who served up one of his best displays in one of the worst

Celtic teams ever to win a national trophy. One major bonus was the two-goal debut of Billy McPhail, a younger, slimmer version of the recently 'freed' big brother, John, but the remainder of the season only laid bare the failure to sustain a challenge for the championship – a failure which would haunt McGrory until the end of his managership. They could not even make amends in the Scottish Cup when crass defending lost them the semi-final against Kilmarnock.

This playing fragility led to tensions within the squad and these mounted as game followed game and a winning blend refused to emerge even though they bumbled their way to the final of the League Cup. Feelings in the dressing-room ran high as the final drew near and culminated in the bizarre dressing-room incident on 17 October which saw Tully and Evans resort to fisticuffs. Teammates had to rush to pull these two great talents apart as they fell to the ground like wee boys wrestling in the playground. It was squalid, it was embarrassing, it was demeaning for all concerned, but more importantly it was symptomatic of the strain the players were working under in the lead-up to that history-making League Cup final.

Not that footballers didn't fight amongst each other from time to time. They were healthy young men, brimming with testosterone, who had to get it all out somehow if they couldn't do so in the course of their field activities. Many a training argument was settled in the tenement back-courts around Celtic Park but until now, there had never been a serious fight in the dressing-room. After-match recriminations perhaps, actual blows, no. One spectator of the Tully–Evans bout that day observed dryly that it was a good job both men made their living as footballers, as they would never have made it as boxers.

Not that anyone at Celtic Park was making a fortune playing football, though money bought a lot more than it does now. Tully would be on top whack and at this time it was £16 a week for a first-team player with £3 for a win and 30 shillings (£1.50) for a draw. It was not big money for the huge crowds they drew in to the ground. Most of the supporters, ordinary working men, doing a bit of overtime every week, would take home a sum not far from that amount in their pay packets. It is almost impossible to believe that top footballers existed on this pittance and still managed to dress nattily and even run a car – although it must be said that not many did. Most still caught the bus or tram to work. Cars were for the select few.

The ubiquitous agent had yet to dip his long fingers into the football pie and pull out the plums for some but spoil the taste for most. In those pre-Bosman days the average player was bound, like a slave, to a contract that gave all the rights to his employer. This largely accounted for the autocracy of old-time chairmen like Tom White and Bob Kelly. They knew they held the reins and they shamelessly drove the horses hard, thinking that they were lucky to be within such shafts. The players urgently needed someone to speak out for them but the only agents they would have known were the little insurance men in raincoats who went round collecting anything from a penny to a shilling a week up the tenement closes so that the tenants would have enough put away to buy themselves a decent funeral. People had different priorities in 1957.

All this, however, must be put aside because, having tasted from the League Cup the year before, the Celtic team of that season, no matter their fluctuations in form, decided that they liked it and wanted more. Their section that year had included Hibernian, who beat them at Easter Road, but in the return match Willie Fernie was retained at right-half, Billy McPhail at centre-forward and a new left-wing was formed with Sammy Wilson and Bertie Auld. These changes worked and Celtic won 2–0. This allowed them to proceed to their second successive final against their natural nemesis, Rangers, to be staged at Hampden on Saturday, 19 October 1957.

So much has been written about this momentous occasion that it seems otiose to add any further comment, but since it took place within the managerial reign of Mr McGrory, it would seem to have a place by right within his story. Anyway, it's too good a football tale, from the Celtic point of view at least, not to mention it again; and when will any other Celtic team score seven goals in a final?

The event has passed from contemporary fact through all the gradations of reality to myth and now it exists in that world of memory where even the actuality has an unreality about it. But then perhaps what is really true is only what we remember. It is a dream to be recollected and dreams belong to the upper levels of the imagination. That's where the magic lies. This game is one of those that belong in that epic category. The actors in this fantasia were:

Celtic – Beattie; Donnelly and Fallon; Fernie, Evans and Peacock; Tully, Collins, McPhail (W.), Wilson and Mochan.
Rangers – Niven; Shearer and Caldow; McColl, Valentine and Davis; Scott, Simpson, Murray; Baird and Hubbard.

Celtic historians Peter Burns and Pat Woods devoted a whole book to the match and the events surrounding it – *Oh, Hampden in the Sun* . . . I recommend it to the reader as a full, encyclopaedic account of the incredible Celtic occasion. For the purposes of this book, however, a precis is now offered, with thanks to those two indefatigable authors.

It turned out to be a lovely sunny day and Celtic even won the toss. Bertie Peacock decided to go with the sun behind them. Simpson kicked off to Murray to start the game for Rangers and that was the last they saw of the ball for a while. It had been nearly 30 years since the Old Firm had last met in a major final and it must have seemed that long at least before Simpson got into the action again. Fernie showed signs of things to come when, after only ten minutes, he took the ball from his own half-right into the Rangers penalty area, trailing defenders behind him. No goal came from the run, but he had fired the Celtic engine and it wouldn't miss a beat from then on.

McPhail's head flicks and general dexterity at centre-forward were disconcerting the giant Valentine, and Charlie Tully emulated Fernie with another run which saw him hit the post with his final shot, with Niven stranded. Celtic supporters, who knew their team only too well, wondered if this was going to be a day of outfield superiority and no goals, with Rangers getting the winner in the last ten minutes. It had happened so often before. But not this time. A Celtic goal had to come, and it did in 23 minutes through Sammy Wilson. This was a signal to flood the King's Park end of the ground in green and white. Tully might have made it two immediately afterwards but was penalised by referee Mowat for hands. The pressure continued and then, a minute from the end of the first half, another Celtic goal. Wilson pushed the ball out to Mochan on the left, who started off along the by-line brushing off Shearer and McColl to fire an unstoppable cannonball from an impossible angle, which almost burst the roof of the net. This was one of the *great* goals. Hampden erupted unevenly and the interval gave one end a chance to catch their breath and the other an opportunity to wonder if what they had really seen had happened. Rangers supporters had been badly trained for defeat – even at half-time. Had they but known . . .

Part Two resumed as a replay of Part One, with Fernie setting off at a canter through the Rangers defence and his cross won a corner off Shearer. Mochan took it and the clearance came to Collins, who once more lofted a pin-accurate cross to McPhail and with a nod of that dark head Celtic were three up. This was not a position they were used to against Rangers. However, Evans was injured by a fierce tackle and while he was off the field, Beattie in the Celtic goal was beaten by a Simpson header which flew in at the top corner. This setback only spurred Celtic to greater efforts. They were in almost total command. McPhail had totally mastered Valentine and Tully, on the right wing, had swapped his jester's stick for his assassin's dagger and was 'killing' Caldow on the left. Davis had to fall back to help out and this left room for Fernie to run riot down the middle. With Mochan running Shearer ragged up and down the left touch-line and Collins and Wilson waiting to pounce on any chances around the box, this Celtic forward line was unbeatable. They knew it was their day. And then the goals came . . .

Again it was Billy McPhail with a powerful shot from close in following a Rangers goalmouth tangle and that was number four. Sammy Wilson then scuttled down the right wing to send over a cross, which Neilly Mochan met on the volley, and Celtic went nap. Number six was as effective as it was direct. Beattie's kick-out was aimed deliberately at the head of McPhail, who was sprinting towards the Rangers goalmouth. He evaded one tackle neatly and then calmly placed the ball past the advancing Niven and into the net for his hat-trick. It was another 'King Billy' who ruled Hampden Park that day and this only roused the Rangers fans to a fury of invective – so much so that they started fighting amongst themselves and the mêlée caused the Rangers fans to spill on to the track in order to avoid the trouble. Police were on to the scene of the disturbance like commandos and dragged three angry and despondent supporters away. They might have been glad to go, for Rangers' troubles were by no means over.

The Celtic half-back line of Fernie, Evans and Peacock had grown in confidence as the game went on and they were now almost disdainful of the Rangers forwards, thus giving their own attack all the time and space in the world. The score might easily have been ten, as some newspapers were to say the next day, but Celtic insisted on playing at their own one-touch pace, ensuring that football quality could win over brute strength if given the chance to play. The Hungarians had shown this and now eleven green-and-white Magyars were having a field day.

Rangers were now shambling all over the field in a state of shock and Celtic weren't playing against them but *with* them. This was typified by Shearer's ungainly rush at McPhail, which brought the elegant Celtic forward down in the penalty area. Captain Bertie Peacock gave the ball to Willie Fernie to put the 7–1 seal on the match and on his own classy performance. Fernie smoothly obliged. A master craftsman had been at work all afternoon, playing with such style he might have been wearing white tie and tails. Now he added the final, finishing touch to a game which he had helped fashion into a work of football art. The final whistle blew Rangers into unaccustomed depths, and Celtic and their following into heights of ecstasy where they still hover, unbelievingly, to this day.

They had seen their team of extraordinary talents suddenly come together in an afternoon and magic was in the air. The support took a long time to disperse from the Hampden slopes and, walking home, they were already rehearsing the stories of this day that they would tell their children. It would have taken Shakespeare's *Henry V* to find the right words – in an appropriate Glasgow accent:

> This day is called the feast of Celtic,
> He that outlives this day, and comes safe home,
> Will stand a tip-toe when this day is named,
> And rouse him at the name of Celtic . . .
> Old men forget; yet all shall be forgot,
> But he'll remember with advantage
> What feats he did that day. Then shall our names,
> Familiar in his mouth as household words,
> Billy McPhail, Tully and wee Collins,
> Fernie and Evans, Wilson and Neilly Mochan
> Be in their flowing cups freshly remember'd.
> This story shall the good man tell his son . . .
> Celtic Seven, Rangers One!

Agincourt itself could not have roused the supporters to a greater fervour. The team celebrated in Ferrari's Italian Restaurant in the centre of Glasgow, much in the same way previous sides had in Willie Maley's Bank Restaurant. Tully and Evans made their peace and McGrory beamed at everyone through his pipe smoke. After all, he had signed up the whole team. It was a night he would remember. Even Bob Kelly permitted himself a smile. He also made a nice gesture in sending a car to Stein's home in Hamilton to bring Jock to the party as he was nursing his ankle injury and had listened to the game on the radio.

The match had also been televised but, in one of those Scottish BBC mysteries, the film had been 'lost' on the day and Celtic supporters were deprived of living their fantastic idyll all over again.

185

Celtic supporters went wild with fury in front of their television sets and it is rumoured that not a few dear-bought receivers were permanently damaged when this fact was announced. Several even reached the window on their way out of the house but restraining hands and women's voices saved the hundreds of pounds of investment about to be lost. From the BBC's point of view in 1957, BBC Scotland had no editing facilities at Queen Margaret Drive so everything had to be done through Lime Grove Studios in London. Telerecording then involved television cameras taking in the scenes at Hampden and beaming these pictures down the line to London, where a telerecording machine photographed the screen and sent the edited images back up to Glasgow for relaying on to the Scottish *Sports Special*.

Regrettably, an operator in London, when changing over film, had accidentally left the lens cap on the camera used for recording the second half. As a result, the entire second half was black. Celtic supporters blamed Peter Thomson and his team in Glasgow, who were thought to have a Rangers bias, but they, in fact, were helpless in the face of the London malfunction. As McGrory might have said, it was just one of those things, but had it been recorded the film would have become a collector's item. Fortunately, a Celtic-minded camera enthusiast did take film of the action from the main stand that day so a record does exist, but, more importantly, a whole generation of Celtic fans had the encounter printed in their minds' eyes – and such images are indelible. The event left a powerful mark on a huge swell of the male population in Glasgow that had green-and-white affiliations and this was still evident in the months that followed the actual game. Something very big had happened and a new hero had entered the Celtic pantheon: Billy McPhail.

Jock Stein had said Billy had two weak knees and was injury-prone. Now everyone had seen him glide past the heavy artillery tactics of a Rangers defence who were made to look leaden by the grace and agility of this former St Mungo Academician. It was no accident that this player had played for Queen's Park, the last bastion of the gentleman in Scottish football. His was a kind of Corinthian attitude, in that the game was all and the result was not the absolute end of things. He had plied his early professional trade with the modest Clyde, only because they made him a better offer than Celtic, but he never lost his essentially cavalier attitude to the sport. He never confused his playing strip with his business suit.

He could afford to be superior to the ordinary needs of the

professional because he was sustained by a solid hairdressing business and, later, a restaurant off Great Western Road in Glasgow. Billy was an atypical football player in the '50s. He didn't need the game as many did. The game needed him. It needed a player who could 'soar among the pigeons' to reach a cross and still evade a rough tackle by a sleight of foot that was typical of his big brother, John. Billy came in at Celtic's front door just as John was preparing to leave by a side door that led him into journalism. Jackie Gardiner of Queen's Park had said of the younger McPhail that he was 'God's Gift to Football'. If this might be thought excessive, it must be weighed against the Celtic supporters' reaction after the League Cup final that he was an instrument of Divine Intervention sent to restore Celtic as God's own team.

Alas, no football team is forever. Even those who played out that glorious day in the Hampden sun have to yield to their mortality. Unfortunately time does tell but, in this case, the process was hastened by the usual Celtic mix of diffidence, short-sightedness, insensitivity and petty mismanagement. A playing dynasty was allowed to crumble almost before the season was out and the chance of a lasting immortality was gone. All the songs had been sung, the parodies aired and a golden time passed even while the sweet taste of it was still on everyone's lips.

This team ought to have won everything in sight that year but instead they spiralled down to a 6–0 defeat by Middlesbrough, an English Second Division side, in a friendly that summed up how their season ended. There was surely something wrong at a club where such a peerless collection of fine players and promising youngsters should not come to deserved fruition and maturity on the field. To paraphrase Shakespeare again, there was 'something rotten in the state of Celtic' and blame must be laid squarely at the *Steptoe and Son* boardroom at Parkhead.

Bob Kelly had never really come back to earth since his high stand on the Irish flag business and his success in that cause had given him a liking for the beleaguered martyr image. He thought he was fighting alone to save Celtic whereas, by his blinkered despotism, he was gradually strangling it. Good players were allowed to drift away for the sake of a few pounds a week, ordinary players were encouraged to stay and play badly for the jersey. The greats grew old and tired and there was no one of like quality standing by to take their places. What was missing was a voice that would have stood up to Kelly and protested, who would have demanded that he leave

187

football matters to football minds. This was the moment for McGrory to stand up for himself but, to him, self-assertion was first cousin to vanity. He chose to stay quiet, thus leaving the field clear for his titular superiors.

Field is the word. There was a big battle to be won here for the identity of the club that was much more important than any rhetoric over a flag. Celtic was a public football club before it was a private platform for one man's idiosyncratic theories and self-defeating experiments. The irony was, no one could have loved the club more - or had greater pride in its achievements but in this instance, love was not all, and we all knoweth where pride goeth. Having reached such extraordinary heights so recently, any fall would be made to look the more dramatic. Practical efficiency plus vision was needed and an even greater irony was that they already had on their books the man who personified those very qualities – Jock Stein.

That, however, left the question of what to do with Jimmy McGrory, the titular manager and still a famous name to many – and everybody's uncle at Parkhead. It was unthinkable that such a good man, who had given his life to Celtic, should be coldly sacked, so the matter was put to one side – for the time being – but it was not to go away. Meantime, it was Kelly rules – OK?

The loss of McPhail, Tully, Fernie and Collins to injury for long spells didn't help, nor did the transfer of the last two in order to pay for the floodlighting at Celtic Park. The playing pitch may have been illuminated but the players seemed to have been left rather in the dark. The truth was something seemed to have died at the heart of this great club. It was a time of dying. Ironically, in another part of the city, an old man was dying who, in his prime and for all his contentiousness, was just the kind of figure Celtic needed at this time. He was about to join a great raft of Celtic names who had recently passed away and funerals became a part of Jimmy McGrory's working routine – Joe Cassidy, Tommy McInally and Bill Struth, the Rangers manager, all died and now it was time for the Big Fella.

Willie Maley died on 2 April 1958, during Holy Week, the final week of Lent, in a nursing home in Mansion House Road, Glasgow, not far from his flat at 17 Hyndland Road. His son, Charles, registered the death, and Cyril Horne, in the *Glasgow Herald*, appropriately registered its impact on the football world:

> Celtic FC was his life. Many of the players who served under
> him had mixed feelings about the discipline Mr Maley

exerted, but I do not know one who did not concede that he
had been correct. He was not merely, however, a man of stern
discipline and distinctive judgement in football matters. There
was no greater sentimentalist, no kinder man. The good deeds
that he did were known only to a few outwith the recipients.
[But] it is unlikely that Celtic will ever have a greater Celt.

David Potter, in his already-cited autobiography of Maley, tells of the
same Cyril Horne who, on the day of Maley's funeral from St Peter's,
Hyndland, to Cathcart Cemetery, passed the time by picking a
Scotland team from among the mourners. They were: Harkness
(Hearts); Campbell (Queen's Park) and Hilley (Celtic); Wilson
(Celtic), Meiklejohn (Rangers) and Geatons (Celtic); Connolly
(Celtic), McMenemy (Celtic), McGrory (Celtic), McPhail (Rangers)
and McLean (Celtic).

It is only fitting that such a team of all the talents should have been
there on that day but think of the Celtic team he could have fielded
had he had the pick of all the ages in his tenure as manager –
Thomson; McNair and Doyle; Wilson, Lyon and Hay; Delaney,
Gallacher, McGrory, McInally and Quinn. There is a testament of
talent indeed and every one of them signed by him for Celtic.
Without Maley there would never have been a Celtic as we know it
and, therefore, no Jimmy McGrory.

At the end of this *annus mirabilis* for Celtic, acknowledgement was
made to the real status of its manager. Hugh Taylor, at the end of
1957, edited the *Scottish Football Book No. 3,* which featured a review of
Jimmy McGrory's playing career under the heading – 'They Spelled
it "McGlory"'. Mr Taylor wrote:

> . . . Across goal comes a fast low cross. In a flash, the centre-
> forward is flying through the air, head first, arms spread like
> a swallow diver. His head meets the ball. As he flops full
> length on the turf, he looks up. And sees the ball nestling
> cosily in the back of the net. The crowd roars, applauding a
> brilliant and spectacular goal.
> . . . But almost every time this happens there will be a
> veteran spectator who remarks: 'Aye, he took that just like
> Jimmy McGrory . . .'
> To those of us who had the privilege of seeing him in
> action, gasping as he leapt high in the air, twisting his powerful
> neck and flicking the ball almost as fiercely as most forwards

could do with their feet past a helpless goalkeeper, James McGrory of Celtic was the greatest header of a ball of all time.

McGrory played in Celtic's golden age. He was fortunate that he had as colleagues some of the most bewildering ball-workers of all time. But without McGrory's dash, urge, power, shooting – and, above all, heading ability – the great Celtic teams in which he played would not have been complete units.

How I wish we had a modern McGrory today. There was nothing subtle about his methods. He had the physical attributes and the power to SCORE goals. That was his job. And he did it supremely well – better, to my mind, than any centre-forward before or since.

If the modern leaders developed their talents like McGrory, on the old-fashioned lines of shooting and heading whenever a chance appeared, there would be much more excitement in the game. And centre-forwards would become the heroes of all boys again.

This illustrates exactly the psyche of boys who follow football and the mystique they attach to the men who play at centre-forward. Yet Jimmy McGrory himself would be the first to tell you that there was no mystery about it. If there was a secret at all, it was never to give up – no matter how hopeless it looks or what little time is left. *You never know.*

THIRTEEN

Changing Hands

> I have noticed the change in players over the past few years
> – a sort of disenchantment with the game, a lack of sparkle.
> One finds oneself looking around the dressing-room more
> like an officer looking at his men in the trenches in the First
> World War. Which ones will crack – and which will have the
> nerve left to go over the top?
>
> Dr Neil Phillips, FA official, 1972

In August 1960, Celtic were in France to play Sedan FC in an
abortive competition called the Anglo-Franco-Scottish Friendship
Cup. James Sanderson, a journalist with the *Scottish Daily Express,*
wrote a series of articles on Celtic. One of these centred on Jimmy
McGrory and the following is an extract:

> The stocky, thoughtful-looking little man, puffing blue clouds
> from his pipe into the windless air, stood watching his Celtic
> players training at the magnificent Rheims Stadium in France.
> A player broke off, trotted across the luscious green turf and
> said respectfully: 'Will we knock off now, Boss?' Quietly, the
> pipe-smoking man nodded his head and turned to walk down
> the yawning tunnel leading to the luxurious dressing-rooms.
> A few yards away, three of France's greatest players – Kopa,
> Fontaine and Plantoni – stood talking and laughing. A Rheims
> official said to me: 'The world hasn't seen many footballers

like these. All France is proud of them.' The official obviously
had never heard of the little man who had just walked down
the darkened tunnel; a man to outrank any Kopa, Fontaine or
Plantoni. Today it is hard to peer into the past and imagine
that this quiet, well-groomed man was the menace of his day;
that he was lionised and idolised by thousands, respected by
all who knew him and feared on the field . . . Today Jimmy
McGrory is back in his beloved Parkhead as manager. But
thousands who only know him as a living legend can hardly
believe that the quiet, pipe-smoking man is THE Jimmy
McGrory.

Not long after this article appeared, Bob Ferrier, son of a famous
Motherwell football father, wrote about McGrory for Charlie
Buchan's *Football Monthly* September 1960 issue. McGrory was
obviously still newsworthy:

If the true merit of a centre-forward be goals scored then
Jimmy McGrory is the greatest centre-forward of all time. In
the Scottish League, First Division, he scored 410 goals in 15
seasons – an average of 27 per season [for correct figures see
'McGrory Statistics' on page 249]. In all first-class matches in
that time, he scored a staggering 550. Bloomer, Quinn,
Gallacher, Ferguson, Dean, Camsell, Lawton, Nordhal,
Kubala, Kopa, Hidegkuti, di Stefano – in the light of these
names it would be a bold man who would insist that McGrory
was the greatest centre-forward of all time but as a goal-scorer
he remains supreme . . . He speaks quietly, never blustering or
ranting at his players. Some people say that this is no quality
for a football manager. He dresses conservatively in dark
suits, wears a Homburg-style hat and now, nearing fifty,
would pass for any successful city executive, even to the
habitual pipe. In his personal life he is completely different
from the dynamic figure we, who saw him play, retain in the
memory. His life centres around the presence and existence of
the Celtic club and the only paradox is that he lives in Ibrox,
near the Rangers' ground. Under a powerful chairman,
Robert Kelly, Jimmy McGrory has concentrated on the
administrative side of the club rather than plunge into policy-
making . . . but like all managers, he must compromise with
the material available at a given moment.

ABOVE: Four legendary Celts at Parkhead prior to Jimmy McGrory's testimonial match against Rangers in August 1934. From left, Jimmy Quinn, Willie Maley (then Celtic manager), Jimmy McGrory and Patsy Gallacher, who acted as linesman.

BELOW: Three of the best: Jimmy Quinn (Celtic), Alan Morton (Rangers) and Jimmy McGrory (Celtic). Morton, a former Rangers player, was linesman at McGrory's benefit. Jimmy couldn't play due to injury.

ABOVE: McGrory is presented with a grandfather clock in Ireland.
He is the only one in the gathering who is properly dressed.

BELOW: McGrory commiserates with an
Aberdeen player after Celtic's Cup final win.

ABOVE: McGrory the manager – behind a desk for the first time.
(From the James McGrory collection)

BELOW: McGrory (at rear) in what he called his first 'proper job':
a factory storeman in Ayrshire during the Second World War.

ABOVE: The first Mr and Mrs Jimmy McGrory
attend a function at Glasgow's City Chambers.
(From the James McGrory collection)

BELOW: The second Mr and Mrs McGrory with
Chairman Kelly. Did McGrory have to ask his permission
to marry? (From the James McGrory collection)

TOP LEFT: Jimmy McGrory with pipe and wife on the doorstep at 'Belltrees'. (From the James McGrory collection)

TOP RIGHT: Playing Happy Families in the garden.
(From the James McGrory collection)

ABOVE: Team McGrory is completed with the arrival of James McGrory Junior seen here on his mother's knee. Little sister Elizabeth takes Daddy's hand while big sister, Maria, stands tall behind her wee brother. (From the James McGrory collection)

TOP LEFT: Jimmy is making sure the Scottish Cup is in the bag.
(From the James McGrory collection)

TOP RIGHT: Yet another testimonial; this time, Yankee-style, in
Kearney, New Jersey, in 1967. (From the James McGrory collection)

ABOVE: Jock Stein with Jimmy McGrory and Mrs McGrory on the
team bus after the 1965 Scottish Cup win in which the retired
manager had been a great help in taking the team to the final.
(From the James McGrory collection)

TOP: After 1969 Scottish Cup win. (From the James McGrory collection)

MIDDLE: Jimmy McGrory opens the new stand in 1971 at Celtic Park. Jock Stein and the Celtic Board look on. (From the James McGrory collection)

BOTTOM: Goal-scorers of the club unite. Bobby Murdoch, scorer of Celtic's 6,000th League goal, is congratulated by Adam McLean, who scored goal number 2,000, while Jimmy McGrory (3,000) and Jimmy Delaney (4,000) look on. (From the James McGrory collection)

ABOVE: The retired Jimmy McGrory holds up his famous size six football boots. (From the James McGrory collection)

BELOW: A last puff. (From the James McGrory collection)

It says much for McGrory's own status with the players that he kept any authority at all. What is certain is that the chairman never meant it at any time as a blatant insult to his manager. He liked and admired McGrory but Kelly thought that everyone knew that he (Kelly) acted only in Celtic's interest and not his own. His bias was always towards attitude rather than to basic skills. This was clear from comments he made in the *Celtic Handbook* at the time:

> Some of the finest Celtic teams of the past have been reared and coached at Celtic Park, and it should delight all who have Celtic's interest at heart, that unless there are unforeseen circumstances, we shall be fielding in the forthcoming season in top-class football in Scotland, a team composed entirely of players who have joined us from no higher a grade than juniors. Our policy of creating a team of players imbued with the Celtic spirit and tradition will continue, but that does not mean to say we shall not engage more seasoned men if the necessity arises.

This is exactly what Rangers had been doing for years – and doing well – and this was why they dominated Scottish football and totally eclipsed the latter-day 'do-it-yourself' Celtic. The Rangers management wasn't afraid to buy at the top end of the market and 'season' their team from time to time with classy players who could bring on their younger colleagues. This is how McGrory himself had been brought on in the game and others, like Chic Geatons, after him. Chic, in his direct way, put his finger on the problem. There was no questioning that the talent was there but it was not being 'managed' properly. Writing in the *Weekly News* on 8 October 1960, the former wing-half and trainer/coach looked no further than Bob Kelly:

> The question I ask myself is: If Celtic are at the mercy of one man's whims and fancies, is there anybody around with the courage to stand up and insist on a new deal for the club? It is all wrong that the chairman should take over so much managerial direction; the chairman should chair the directors, the directors should direct and the manager should manage.

This echoes 'Rex' of the *Sunday Mail's* cry for an old hand to lead the band of young talents that everyone could see was developing at

Parkhead, but Jock Stein had already done this with the reserve team, which won everything in sight at their level. It might have been supposed even then that Stein himself might be groomed to succeed McGrory in due time, but Kelly made it clear in remarks he made that the latter 'might have gone as far as he could expect to go at Celtic Park', and in any case, 'the club is not yet ready for a Protestant manager'. Kelly had already earmarked Sean Fallon, by now serving as coach, for that post – because Fallon was a good Catholic.

This was the kind of thinking in the boardroom that put the brake on advanced ideas on the park. That they should even consider training a carthorse to take the place of a warhorse when they already had a pedigree stallion in the stable is beyond any understanding. Stein got the message and, in March 1960, cantered off to become manager of Dunfermline, who were struggling to avoid relegation – but not for long. Big Jock was to work the first of his miracles in Fife. No reproach is at all intended to Sean Fallon's attitude to the club or McGrory's proved enthusiasm but if they provided, with Bob Kelly, a triumvirate to restore Celtic, it was a Holy Trinity on a par with the wartime Five Sorrowful Mysteries.

What was patently required was an objective, scientific appraisal of playing assets and the best use that this clutch of young bloods might be put to in competitive games. What is often overlooked, however, is that these players were the cubs who would become the future Lisbon Lions and every single one of them was a McGrory signing.

Meantime, in 1961, Tottenham Hotspur won the Double in England, where Bill Nicholson, a stolid player but an astute manager, had built a young team around Danny Blanchflower, much in the way that Celtic might have done around Pat Crerand. Spurs had topped the Football League and won the Cup at Wembley with the kind of football that the Celtic colts played naturally but erratically. McGrory had lost Tully to time, Evans to injury and Fernie and Collins to club parsimony. Alf Ramsey was to take Ipswich Town to the Football League Championship in 1962 on little more than tactics and the smell of liniment, but the financial constraints imposed on McGrory made it hard for him to hang on to the young players he was already bringing forward in the first team. Pat Crerand was a typical case in point. As McGrory himself explained to Gerald McNee in 1975, the situation in the early '60s was not always of his choosing, and, of course, he could look no further than his own chairman. Being McGrory, of course, he could always see both sides:

> Sir Robert Kelly was one of the greatest men I have ever known inside or outside of football. He was a director for 40 years, ruled the club for a quarter of a century and in his last days he was appointed the very first president of the Celtic Football Club . . . [but] he could be one of the most difficult men to understand and the best example I can give is the transfer of Pat Crerand to Manchester United in 1963.
>
> Sir Robert had something against Paddy Crerand – for what reason I could never find out. Some blamed it on the fact that Pat ran about with Jim Baxter of the Rangers but that wouldn't have caused a transfer. Anyway, whatever the reason, Sir Robert told me he wanted Crerand sold. I told him I was against the move and that we couldn't afford to lose a player of Pat's ability. All I was told was to fetch Crerand and accompany Sir Robert to the Cathkin Hotel near his home in Burnside, and there we met Matt Busby, the Manchester United manager.
>
> We found that every last detail had already been agreed between them, including the transfer fee, and the papers were all ready for Pat to sign. Matt Busby left the three of us together for a while and then came the scene that shattered me – Pat Crerand suddenly burst into tears, and said to me – 'I don't want to leave the Celtic. I don't want to go.' Sir Robert immediately got up and left the room, leaving me with the player. I was nearly in tears myself.

Given a scene like this, it is difficult to see McGrory at this stage as anything other than a lackey with no voice of his own. It contrasts markedly with a similar set-up more than 30 years earlier when Maley tried to sell McGrory to Arsenal without the help of *his* chairman, Tom White. McGrory simply refused to go. It would appear that Pat Crerand wasn't given that option. Like every other player of the day he was a bonded slave to the club. If he didn't sign, he didn't play – and no play, no pay. Professional players who were discontented had been known to sit out a whole season. All the cards were on the employers' side – and they were clubs.

The irony is that, from 1963 onwards, Crerand went on to great things in Europe with Manchester United in the company of Bobby

Charlton, George Best and the rest, but one has the feeling he took his boots to Old Trafford but left his heart at Parkhead. It has been the story of so many Celtic greats. Bertie Auld was another who earned the Kelly frown and was exiled to Birmingham – although he was to get an unexpected reprieve and grabbed the chance to become part of a new chapter in Celtic history – but in 1963, those palmy days still lay ahead.

McGrory, as always, was acting according to his own lights. He was a hired hand and he had to acknowledge *his* paymaster. For him, there was a due order in things and the survival trick was to know where you were in the pecking order and act accordingly. His working-class background had ingrained in him the fact that he was an employee, and his employer was the Celtic Football and Athletic Club. It was as basic as that. All his life he had depended on that weekly pay packet but he had never presumed on it. He was that way as a player and he remained in this attitude as a manager. What else could he do? He knew his place, and was glad to be in it.

The position gave him prestige and standing and nicely reflected the glory of his playing career. Whatever the daily ups and downs, he could not have been happier in his work. If he had his way, he would stay at Parkhead until they carried him out. Just like his old boss, Willie Maley, he could think of no other way of life. He carried on a tradition of total service to Celtic and saw nothing wrong with that. He was at the ground early each day and was always there at the end of each training night. That's how things were done in the Maley days and he would try to preserve that spirit of complete dedication to the job in hand. Comforted by his wife and young family, strong in his own Catholic faith, rested by annual Highland and Irish holidays and secure in his standing with Celtic supporters, Jimmy McGrory was impregnable in his modest self-belief.

This is a long way from ego. Being totally lacking in personal ambition, he saw no reason to 'rock the boat' unnecessarily, and so he allowed it to drift more than many others would have done in his place. As he saw it, as long as the teams were sent out and they gave of their best in every game played, he was doing his job at Celtic. Whether matches were won or lost, that would be as Fortune decreed and he would live with it. Everything was always in accordance with the effort put in and he expected no more from his players than their best efforts – just as *he* had done. He was always optimistic. It was always, for him, 'a great day for shooting' – which was about the total extent of his coaching advice.

It is extraordinary to compare this passive, fatalistic managerial attitude with the pugnacious belligerence of his playing persona a quarter of a century before. On the field in those days he was all daring, adventure and risk but now, operating under the shadow of 'he who would be king', he was cautious, accommodating and safe. Perhaps that's what the years do to any personality, but duality is a very Scottish trait and most of us have to live with our other selves. It should also be borne in mind that Jimmy McGrory grew up virtually fatherless and tended to lean in his adult life towards patriarchal figures. Canon Lawton loomed over his boyhood, Willie Maley towered over his playing days and now, as a football manager, Bob Kelly was ever looking over his shoulder. Added to all this, the shadow of Jock Stein was hovering around him. It's a wonder the essential McGrory was given any chance at all. Yet he had his moments, as some results show, even in the lean years that lay ahead.

In that notorious biblical span, the seven years of famine between 1958 and 1965, their record was reasonable enough, finishing well up the League table most years, getting to semi-finals and finals in the two cup competitions but the truth is, they won nothing except the Glasgow Cup (twice) and the Charity Cup (twice). The most painful loss, however, was the 1961 Scottish Cup final, when Jock Stein's resurrected Dunfermline beat them, helped by the heroics of goalkeeper Eddie Connachan, whose boyhood hero, ironically, had been Celtic's Willie Miller.

In September 1962, the Kelly Kids (Stein's former reserve team) played a Celtic Park friendly against an ageing Real Madrid containing di Stefano, Puskas and Gento, to name only three of their greats, but the Celtic team now boasted names like McNeill, MacKay, Murdoch, Johnstone, Lennox and Hughes and their time was almost imminent. It was just before this game that director James Farrell first noticed signs of McGrory's being 'nervous' and 'ill at ease'. This may only be Mr Farrell's lawyer's way of couching the observation in euphemistic terms, but he was certainly worried about McGrory's professional deportment at times. Did Farrell see the first hairline cracks in the rock-like edifice that was Jimmy McGrory? Certainly the director had to advise his manager to go and lie down at one point. He thought he might have had one glass of sherry too many. Can one wonder? The strain the man must have been under was massive. Only someone of his equanimity could have withstood it so long. He had never drunk as a player, why should he start now?

What did the odd glass of sherry matter? Would they have preferred he sip holy water?

The continuing Kelly influence was evident in the decision to release the club captain, Bertie Peacock, to play for Northern Ireland in a friendly against Italy when his experience and ability might have been used to better effect against Dunfermline in a cup replay which Celtic lost 2–0. The Kelly hand was seen again in the omission of the young Jimmy Johnstone in the 1963 Cup final replay when Rangers humbled Celtic to the tune of 3–0. Little 'Jinky' had been the hero of the first match, yet he was left to look on at the next. Perhaps even more pernicious was the chairman's insistence that, after beating MTK Budapest 3–0 in the European Cup-Winners' Cup in the spring of 1964, Celtic 'entertain' the Hungarians with good football rather than defend their lead. As a result, they lost on aggregate 4–3, when they might easily have won through to their first European final three years earlier than they did. Such experience would have been invaluable. Instead, it made supporters sick.

It was illness that prevented McGrory taking Barbara to the Royal Garden Party at Holyrood Palace in Edinburgh on 2 July 1963. Had he gone, who knows what royal favour may have come his way. 'Sir Jimmy McGrory' was not entirely out of the question for one of Scottish football's most likeable men, not that such thoughts would ever have entered his head. He had enough to think about from day to day at Celtic Park. In August 1963 the long-suffering Celtic supporters demonstrated their impatience with the club chairman after a miserable draw against Queen of the South in the League Cup. There were loud calls for Kelly's resignation and when he didn't appear (he was at the reserve game in Dumfries) police had to be called to disperse the demonstrators. Noticeably, once again, their antipathetic chants did not include the name of McGrory. The fans were angry at the way good young players were being allowed to flounder and were disheartened at losing to teams of much lesser talent, not to mention the continuing humiliations heaped upon them by Rangers.

In August 1964, McGrory's general stability wasn't helped by the bizarre episode of his being sent to Spain to secure the services of Alfredo di Stefano, the Real Madrid legend, who had been released by the club and was open to offers. The only one he wasn't in the least interested in was Celtic's offer of £200 a game to come to Parkhead but that didn't stop the Celtic Board from flying out

McGrory, with Spanish-speaking John Cushley, a reserve centre-half, as interpreter. The spectacle of one of the great centre-forwards of all time pursuing another who was clearly not interested in meeting him is not an edifying one.

The Celtic offer to the Spanish star was good for the time. Players like Johnny Haynes of Fulham were the British top earners at £100 a game, but meantime, there were signs that goals might come from sources nearer home. It was a McGrory signing, a fellow Garngader's son, Steve Chalmers, one of the beleaguered babes of that era, who now started scoring. He was immediately dubbed 'di Steviano' by the supporters and justified the name by getting five against East Fife in the League Cup. Shades of McGrory himself. Steve's feat was almost a one-player vindication of the much-scorned youth policy, as were most of the other young players now jostling for first-team places. Stevie, however, was in the McGrory mould – energetic, irrepressible and full of running. No ball was impossible unless it was out of play or in the net. He gave the same effort in the barren years as he was to do when the prizes started to come. A great Celtic servant, and likeable with it.

Billy McNeill, who had by this time replaced Bertie Peacock as captain when Bertie returned to Ireland, remembers Jimmy McGrory as Mr McGrory:

> He was always Mr McGrory to me – and to all the other players. A lovely man with a pipe. Quietly spoken, never in a bad temper, always had time for everyone, even the very young players who came in for training at nights. We all respected him as a man and for his record. Which is something. It still stands. Always smartly dressed in a suit with collar and tie, it was hard to tell he was such a dynamo of a player in his day. But then a player changes as soon as he runs on to the park. Mr McGrory would have been the same. He didn't just love Celtic – he *was* Celtic.

That has been said so often about him. Billy McNeill told the present writer that although Mr McGrory had signed him for Celtic in 1957 ('I was ecstatic about joining up at Parkhead. A dream come true'), it was Jock Stein who had brought him to McGrory's attention. He had seen the 17-year-old Billy play for the Scottish schoolboys against England and thought the soldier's son had a football future. After playing against Billy McPhail in Celtic's public trial that year, the other Billy (then called Willie) had broken into the first team during the pre-season Irish tour. Now here he was, already into his future, as the young captain of a young Celtic waiting to welcome another Big Fella back to Paradise.

Murmurs were being heard. 'Celtic are finished,' muttered the disenchanted, but McGrory himself was 60 as the New Year of 1965 beckoned. It was clear that a gap was widening between an elderly manager and his group of very young players. They certainly looked for something other than enthusiasm from their boss. Worse still, the discontent was spreading to the support and attendances were dropping. As far as they were concerned, they could see the trophy famine extending into infinity. Like all Scots, McGrory imagined if he could get through the winter, all would be well. It was one of the worst winters in years, so literally and metaphorically it was a hard time for all concerned.

Then, suddenly, in the way these things happen, it all changed on the afternoon of 30 January 1965. This was the day the young Celts suddenly 'clicked' as a unit and ran on to the ice rink that was Celtic Park and skated home against Aberdeen to the tune of 8–0. It is believed this transformation happened because morale was sent soaring by the rumour going round Parkhead that the Messiah had come back to earth – Jock Stein was returning to Celtic.

Meantime, Jimmy McGrory just got on with the job of being Celtic manager. One of his duties at Celtic Park was to take a No. 9 green tram to Glasgow Cross and, at the Bank of Scotland branch in Trongate, pick up the week's wages in two leather bags and bring them back to the ground for distribution. A recent addition to the payroll was the Coronation Cup hero, Neilly Mochan, who had returned to Celtic Park as the new trainer. They went through a lot of trainers at Celtic Park and 'Smiler' was the latest. Also added, in January 1965, was another returnee, Bertie Auld, who had come back from Birmingham on McGrory's telephone call after Mr Kelly had relented and ended Bertie's reluctant exile. It was also the end of a McGrory signing saga with Auld. He had signed him first as a junior in 1955, loaned him to Dumbarton in 1956, brought him back in 1957 then sold him to Birmingham City in 1961. Now he was back yet again. At any rate, a pay packet had been made up for him this Friday and was with the others on the table in Mr McGrory's cubbyhole cum office ready for his smiling distribution at lunchtime. It was a ritual he enjoyed.

Jimmy McGrory would always remember that he only ever got £8 a week in his playing days, even though he actually signed for £9 and didn't find out until a pre-Scottish Cup final dinner organised by the *Scottish Sunday Express* in April 1963, that every other first-team player in his time got £9. He overheard an ex-teammate, Peter Wilson, telling someone. McGrory had never known. Anyway, he wouldn't think it any of his business. He felt a bit put out at first but then, typically, he rationalised it by remembering the number of times he was paid for pulling on that green-and-white jersey. The truth was, he would have played for nothing.

The payroll routine was interrupted one fateful morning when the chairman, Bob Kelly himself, came in and, without any ceremony whatsoever, told Jimmy McGrory that they had appointed a new manager and that therefore his services were no longer required at Celtic Park. The shock was so great, and so unexpected, that McGrory couldn't say anything. For a moment, he thought he would burst into tears, but he held on and, regaining his composure, asked the chairman quietly; 'Is it big Jock?'

'Yes.'

'I thought so.'

There was another pause before McGrory went on, 'It makes sense – you couldn't have made a better choice. There's no one quite like him – but I'll tell you this, he won't work for my wages.'

The chairman assured him that 'everything was taken care of'. McGrory must have thought back to the Cathkin Hotel when Kelly had said 'everything was taken care of' with regard to another 'Celtic-minded' individual, Paddy Crerand. Now, here he was, being dealt with in the same summary manner. It was a shock, and he had to admit privately that it hurt as much as any injury he had ever received on the field. He remembered, too, that Willie Maley had been pushed out at the end in 1940, as had Jimmy McStay in 1945. In comparison, he was being dealt with softly. These thoughts may have been in his head but as it had all happened so suddenly, he didn't know what else to say. So he said nothing.

Kelly, who seemed to be quite cool about it all, went on to assure him that the Board hadn't forgotten him and things had been reorganised at the club so that they could offer him the new post of Public Relations Officer in recognition of his long service. His salary would continue at the same level and his duties would be 'as found'. McGrory felt some relief at knowing he wasn't being thrown out on to the street at his age, but he was no fool and knew it was nothing more than a sop to his feeling, a salve to his hurt pride. Celtic had always boasted that they had never sacked any of their managers but

Maley's 'retiral', McStay's 'resignation' and now his sudden sideways 'promotion' to 'PRO' were all the same kid glove drawn over some cruel, bare knuckles. He was, in effect, being sacked – and he knew it. So must Kelly, and he was glad to leave McGrory to it – and let the new situation sink in.

Robert Kelly was no fool either and realised that there would have been a public outcry had he abruptly dismissed his manager in the ordinary way. He knew McGrory was no ordinary manager; he was an icon, and idols cannot be toppled without risking accusations of blasphemy. To a man of strict moral principle like Bob Kelly, that was anathema. The PRO solution was an act of appeasement and it would allow for a smooth changeover as soon as was convenient to all parties. McGrory, as Kelly well knew he would, recognised the change as the best thing for Celtic, and accepted it, although he did feel that his team were on the verge of a breakthrough and that the good times were just around the corner. They were, but they would happen 'under new management'. Now the only question bothering the Celtic ex-manager was, what was he going to say to Barbara?

When he did tell her, he made it sound as if it were the best thing that ever happened to him. Barbara wasn't so sure, but Jimmy insisted. After all, he was getting too old now to gad about Europe looking for players and fixing up hotels and air flights. Football was changing fast and was becoming global. More matches would take place in Europe and a British League was not out of the question one day. McGrory could see all this in 1965 but he knew, too, that his years would prevent his seeing it all come to pass. But Barbara wasn't interested in hearing all about that. She was only concerned, like any wife, about the effect the change would have on her husband. She needn't have worried. Jimmy McGrory was nothing if not adaptable. Hadn't he shown that throughout the Kelly years?

He also realised that the whole face of football had changed. The modern manager was a new animal. He wore a tracksuit instead of a soft hat and one can be sure he never stayed behind a desk licking pay packets. Administration was a full-time job, just as coaching had become. It would take two men to do the job in future and big Jock Stein had the energy of two men. He could cope. He thrived on the responsibility and was always ready to try new ideas in football; always on the lookout for new tricks to work on. He had studied the Hungarians when he was a player and, when he was Dunfermline's manager, he had gone to Italy to see at first hand the methods used by Helenio Herrera at AC Milan.

That was Jock Stein, a football autodidact always on the lookout for learning, soaking up knowledge because the chance had come late and was, therefore, all the more appreciated. He had once been a miner and was making sure he would never go down a pit again. Instead, he would hew a football team out of a squad of young hopefuls he had known as cubs. The lounge-suited, affable Jimmy McGrory, who had been in football all his life, was handing over a bright young team to a tracksuited manager who was in nappies when McGrory first put on a Celtic jersey.

Stein, while a player, had been only too aware of the Kelly restraints that McGrory had worked under while manager. So constricting were these that Jimmy was, in a sense, driving the Celtic bus with the handbrake on. No wonder he couldn't get very far. Yet he might have been a good manager given a free hand. He was respected by the players and loved by the supporters. To many he could still do no wrong, but he was never given the chance to prove it as a manager as he had as a player. Chairman Kelly had seen to that. Now that the McGrory position had been settled, the only question was how Stein would deal with Kelly. The two men got on well. Even after Stein left Celtic Park, they had met from time to time on football matters. Stein was cannily keeping the Celtic lines of communications open – just in case. He wasn't a fool either. Some think he was allowed to leave Celtic Park just to gain managerial experience so that he might then return to Parkhead when McGrory retired. Bob Kelly himself said as much:

> He left Celtic because, like everyone else, he had to learn his trade, but there was always an understanding that he would return. I want to emphasise this is not a panic change. We are doing this when the team is winning and when we think we've got a good team.

This, however, was not the Stein scenario. As always, he had sought out his own experience. After he'd won the Scottish Cup for Dunfermline in 1961 he went on to Hibernian to guide them to the Summer Cup in 1964. He had sticky fingers for trophies. While at Easter Road, he had been headhunted by Wolverhampton Wanderers, who had sacked their player and manager of long standing, Stan Cullis. Shades of McGrory. Stein met with Kelly in the North British Hotel in George Square to discuss this offer informally and it was then that Kelly, on his own initiative, invited him to consider becoming Celtic's manager. The chairman wondered if

Stein might work in tandem with chief coach Fallon, as co-manager. Stein wisely asked for time to think about it.

What he did was to sound out the views of Desmond White, the secretary-director, and talk to Hibernian, who had the grace not to stand in his way. Nor had Bob Kelly when they next met. It was obvious that Stein was going to be manager on his own terms and had no intentions of becoming a Kelly front-man – or of sharing with anyone. It is not known if he talked to McGrory. A press conference was called for the day after the 8–0 drubbing of Aberdeen to announce the appointment. On his first day as manager of Celtic, 9 March 1965, Bob Kelly shook big Jock warmly by the hand and said, 'It's all yours now.' Stein was to make very sure it was. The first thing he did was to seek out McGrory and tell him that as far as he (Stein) was concerned, he (McGrory) was still 'The Boss'. It was a nice touch by the big man. He had given McGrory his place – which he hadn't had for years.

If everyone was thrilled at the prospect of the Stein scene, they were just as happy for McGrory. He was coming to terms with it himself. As he said, what had been done was done for the good of the club. He had to keep telling himself this. It was merely a case of changing hands. Now it was a matter of all hands on deck as the good ship Celtic sailed on into new waters and towards a bright horizon. McGrory was happy to be still on board. The only difference was that, instead of a compass, he'd been handed a lifebelt.

FOURTEEN

Public Relations

Change is not made without inconvenience,
even from worse to better.

Richard Hooker, 1554–1600

During the great Celtic phase now imminent, it could be said that the McGrory Story gave way to the Stein Song. If the door to the new PRO's office wasn't closed to the big events, it was only slightly ajar. There was no deliberate intent in this. Stein himself could not have been more respectful to his old boss and he made sure everybody else was, but there was a definite drifting away by the older man from the centre of decisions. He was still acknowledged as the living ghost of Celtic's past, but he was far from dead yet and strove to make himself useful about the place.

There was, of course, the usual Celtic Supporters' Association rally to mark his new appointment and this one took place on Sunday, 7 March 1965 at the Green's Playhouse Cinema in Glasgow. What an irony that this should be the venue, with its Green associations of such recent memory. Fred and Bert were still alive at this stage but Jimmy saw less of them than before, although there was the occasional Green family get-together for Christmas at Craigie Hall, to which the McGrorys as a family were invited. The McGrory children were often driven to school by the Greens' chauffeur and lunched from time to time with Bertie at the Playhouse, so the connection was not being allowed to wither.

The principal speaker at the Playhouse Rally was Jack Harkness, then a respected journalist with the *Sunday Post*. He began with the story of the cuff links, which occurred when Hearts were guests at Celtic Park for the opening of the new Grant Stand on the first day of the season in August 1929. In those days, the teams didn't leave the field at the interval and Jack enjoyed sharing an orange in the centre circle with his fellow goalkeeper, the young John Thomson, especially as Hearts were leading 1–0. Jack continued:

> Seven minutes from time we were still leading when, in a tremendous do-or-die finish, McGrory flashed a couple of balls past me – both with the head. After the game, I heard that a wealthy Celtic supporter had gone into the Celtic dressing-room, taken off his magnificent gold cuff links and handed them to Jimmy as a present; one pair for each goal as a token of his great relief in Jimmy's saving the day for Celtic on such an auspicious occasion. He never thought of coming into the visitors' dressing-room and giving me his tiepin for my contribution in making Jimmy's feat possible.
>
> He scored 550 goals in his career and I think half of them must have been against me. For fifteen years, that head of his has mesmerised me. I don't know what his neck muscles are made of but he could head the ball harder than many players today could kick it. I've played against all the great centre-forwards, Hughie Gallacher, Willie McFadyen, Dixie Deans, and take it from me, McGrory was easily the best of them all. He knew all about jet propulsion before it was invented. How else could he have reached those crosses from Connolly and McLean?

Next was the story about McGrory and the goalpost. Paddy Connolly had sent over a fierce ball from the touch-line. Jack went on:

> I could see that it was going to go past the far post and I decided to let it go. Suddenly, out of the corner of my eye, I could see McGrory in a flying, horizontal position making an attempt to get his head to the ball. I also realised that his head was heading straight for that far post. I dived towards Jimmy and managed to push him a few inches to his side so it was his shoulder, not his head, that crashed against the post. When the trainer came out to attend to him, he said to me, 'Thanks

Jack, I didn't realise I was so near the post.' The Celtic supporters behind the goal thought that Jimmy was complaining to me about stopping him getting to the ball, and there were calls for a penalty. When this was denied, I got the full treatment – and I don't mean from the trainer, either.

But Jimmy mentioned the incident to Mr Maley and at the next home game he inserted a little notice in the matchday programme under the heading 'Jack's Best Save' and the true facts were set down. When I returned to Celtic Park for the next Hearts game, I got a hero's welcome from the Celtic supporters.

And he got it again from the same supporters on that Sunday night in the cinema. He concluded:

If character, charm, willingness, frankness, integrity, politeness and modesty are essential parts of the job then Jimmy is assured of success, because my good friend, James Edward McGrory, is endowed in abundance with the lot.

The Playhouse rose to him, just as spontaneously as when he himself went for a Connolly cross and as gallantly as Jack himself once leapt to make the save. McGrory was now formally installed in public relations.

Stein completely revitalised the same players who had stumbled and crumpled only weeks before. All he had said to them was, 'I promise to do my best for you but, in return, you have to do your best for me.' And they did, rollicking through the rounds of the Scottish Cup, despite a replay in the semi-final with Motherwell, to reach the final against Dunfermline, who had beaten Hibernian, who, in turn, had knocked out Rangers. Stein was now in a position to plan against a side he had built up and for a team he had just begun to build. To 'tinker with' might be truer. He felt he was just taking them up the straight. They'd been over all their hurdles. The team that Stein sent out to take them over the finishing line on 24 April was John Fallon; Young and Gemmell; Murdoch, McNeill and Clark; Chalmers, Gallagher, Hughes, Lennox and Auld.

In their eagerness to impress Stein, the new Celts started in a rush and got themselves into a fankle. After only a quarter of an hour, Melrose lobbed the ball into an empty Celtic net after a defensive mix-up. Fortunately, on the half-hour, Bertie Auld equalised with a brave header – which put him in the net as well (shades of Patsy Gallacher). But then Dunfermline's McLaughlin put them ahead again with a long shot. Stein's former pupils were doing him proud. He must have taken his new class to task in the interval because they came out determined in the second half and once again it was Auld who brought them level after a neat exchange with Bobby Lennox. This fired Celtic and in the last quarter they bombarded Dunfermline. With less than ten minutes to go, Celtic got yet another corner and Pat Crerand's cousin, Willie Gallagher, ran to take it. As he placed the ball, he saw Billy McNeill start his run from the back so he sent over a high cross which met the Celtic captain leaping high into the air in the Dunfermline penalty box and, with a force and precision that would have delighted Jimmy McGrory, the ball landed high in the net beyond Jim Herriot in the Pars goal. A hundred thousand Celtic fans roared their relief and Billy was lost in a mound of green and white. Everyone in the ground knew it was the winner. With that goal, the Stein era could really be said to have begun. He was to say later, 'It would not have gone as well for Celtic had they not won this game.' There was only one way for this team to go now and that was up. The lean years were over at last and the club had worked up an appetite. This Celtic team was hungry. The new order was now in place and the Celtic PRO retired quietly to his office as the new Celtic began to grow under his feet.

McGrory might have been excused had he sat back at his PRO desk to bask in the glory of the incredible epoch that now got under way, but his innate modesty would have forbidden any such reflection. Nonetheless, these young men, with the exception of Joe McBride in 1965 and, later, Willie Wallace in 1966, had all been signed by him and had developed under his eye at Celtic Park. As one commentator put it: 'It was a McGrory team hardened and honed to success by Jock Stein.' McGrory himself was quick to acknowledge this. In an interview given to the *Scottish Daily Express* on 21 May 1965, he told Jack Webster:

> Jock Stein is absolute boss of the team and in my view that is a good thing. Of course, he can have the advice of the directors but he is in sole control and, as far as Celtic are concerned, he was just what the club needed, somebody to put some 'go' into the team. The players had the ability but not the consistency and Jock brought along that something else which he had all along and I cannot pinpoint. Whatever it is, it makes the players pay attention. They are with him.

As the interviewer pointed out, these were brave words from a man who might have been expected to feel differently but they were true of a man of his probity. It could now be seen that the handover had been not only necessary, but beneficial. Having got over the hurt by the manner in which he had been so brusquely told of it, his essential fair-mindedness asserted itself and he was happy for the club that was so dear to him. He knew that football was a rough trade at best and all the sentiment was with the supporters – but that's what he was at heart – a supporter. He ended the interview with the wry comment: 'Anyway, I've been long enough in the game to realise that football's a rat race. I'm quite happy to be handing over this job to a younger man.'

In all the Celtic excitement, little notice had been given to his 'other' team, Kilmarnock, who had won the League title by beating Hearts at Tynecastle. One of the first to send congratulations to Willie Waddell and his team was McGrory from behind his new desk. In 1945, he had sent his hopes to Kilmarnock that they might rise high in Scottish football and here they were, 20 years later, League champions. Waddell, of course, was soon to go on and become manager at Rangers and ultimately, the supremo at Ibrox and lead them into Europe. Meantime, Scott Symon, the McGrorys' good neighbour over the wall from Belltrees, was holding the redoubtable blue fort, and with the help of Crerand's pal, Jim Baxter, Willie Henderson and young John Greig, Rangers ruled the roost in Scotland. Since the famous 7–1 defeat in the sun seven years before, they had beaten Celtic regularly and remorselessly . . . but all that was now to change.

Another League Cup final presented itself on 23 October and Celtic fielded the team that had beaten Hibernian after a replay. The side included the two recent arrivals, Ronnie Simpson (a Stein reject from Hibernian) and Joe McBride, his first signing, from Motherwell. The team was already beginning to have a leonine look. A crowd of 107,609 turned up at Hampden to watch Simpson; Young and Gemmell; Murdoch, McNeill and Clark; Johnstone, Gallagher, McBride, Lennox and Hughes face the all-conquering Rangers. John 'Yogi Bear' Hughes gave an early hint that he was on form down the left wing and it was he who scored first with a penalty against McKinnon for handling. He then added a second with another penalty. To get one penalty against Rangers was an event for Celtic, but to get two was unheard of and even though Rangers got one back in the second half, Celtic got the League Cup.

This was the game notorious for the half-lap of honour. When the Celtic players came out on to the track to parade the Cup, the Rangers supporters broke out from their pen and made to attack them. Luckily, the police were on hand and shepherded the Celts back to the pavilion. Just as well, for had any of their players been harmed the Celtic supporters would have invaded the field from the other end and who knows who might have been injured, even killed. Not surprisingly, laps of honour were banned for all future Old Firm finals.

By the New Year, both teams were level on points in the race for the League title and when they met at Parkhead for the traditional Ne'erday game, it was like a cup final all over again, such was the tension at the ground. It was, as they say, a game of two halves, with Rangers winning the first and Celtic romping away with the second to the tune of 5–1, with Steve Chalmers getting a hat-trick. By this time, a new chant rose from the Celtic terraces – 'Jock Stein! Jock Stein!'

From here on, however, the difference in management practice became more apparent. Method was applied instead of relying on the weather and hoping for magic. McGrory had favoured the 'team' approach, aspiring to an eleven that would cohere and blend as a unit through playing and touring together. The players would work their way into the team and, once established, would stay in their positions so as to establish continuity (allowing for the Kelly eccentricities from time to time). It could be seen that McGrory preferred an agile goalkeeper in the John Thomson or 'Sonny' Hunter mould, two sturdy backs who stayed back, like Bobby Hogg or Peter McGonagle, and a stopper centre-half like Jimmy McStay or Willie Loney, the 'Obliterator'. In the centre he would have hard-working wing-halves (the Peter Wilson or George Paterson type) making a box with two clever inside-men (like Patsy Gallacher or Charlie Tully) with a spearhead centre-forward like himself fed by fast wingers on either side such as Delaney or McLean. That would be a team for McGrory and it would be a good one too.

Stein, on the other hand, favoured a 'squad' from which the basic team is chosen, with a handful of top-class players always hovering on the fringe so that he could permutate changes according to conditions, opposition strengths and current form. He knew that not all players could be at their top level *all* the time. For Jock, it was 'horses for courses' and the stable was kept on its toes as team selection was made a game at a time. In this way, no one ever got stale and everyone was anxious to play – and to play his way in every single game. He told them they were good and he treated them as if they were good, and being good, they responded effectively. This was how great teams are made and at Celtic Park the making was already under way.

Jock Stein was a thoroughly modern manager and Celtic had a lot of running to do to keep up with him. He took the whole squad on the American tour of 1966, from which they returned unbeaten and with morale high. There was an excitement in their play and with it a growing confidence. The side was on song and making lovely music as they glided from game to game. Put another way, this Stein Machine was beginning to fire on all cylinders. It suddenly dawned on everyone at Parkhead that such was the power in this engine it could go a long way – all the way, in fact.

By the New Year of 1967, they were comfortably ahead in the League and finals were approaching on all fronts – even in Europe. Could they keep it up? The answer was, they got better. The squad had refined itself to a team of exceptional quality, described by one English sportswriter as: 'an exhilarating team that sought to blend athletic speed and combativeness with imagination, delicacy of touch at close quarters, and surges of vitality'.

The key man of the team was the direct Bobby Murdoch at right-half working in cross-tandem with the wily Bertie Auld at inside-left and these two operated the engine room supported by John Clark and Willie Wallace in the alternative left-half and inside-right positions. It was a Stein parallelogram as opposed to a McGrory square box. Billy McNeill was a commanding centre-half with the knack of coming forward to score vital goals and at the back were two mobile full-backs in Craig and Gemmell, who also came forward at every opportunity (*à la* Duncan MacKay from earlier seasons). Both backs could match any winger for speed. Jim Craig, in particular, had been a long jumper of some merit while a dental student at Glasgow University. Little and large were on the wings with Jinky Johnstone on the right (coming into his own as unique football property) and John Hughes on the left – when it wasn't Jinky's best pal at the club, Bobby Lennox. Presiding over all in goal was the man they called 'Faither', the oldest player in the club, Ronnie Simpson, son of a Ranger and a professional for ever it seemed, but now enjoying the finest phase of his long career. These, then, were the men and their hour was almost upon them.

While all this energy was building up at Parkhead, McGrory

accepted an invitation from the famous Kearney branch of the Celtic Supporters' Association in New Jersey to be their 'honoured guest' with old teammate Joe Kennaway on 1 April 1967. While the team was preparing for a Scottish Cup final against Aberdeen, he crossed the Atlantic once more to be fêted in the American way. He took the chance to see old friends and family over there, like Harry's daughter, Moira, who now lived in New Jersey. He knew it was something Harry himself could not do. It was a rare chance for McGrory to give family priority over football. He made sure, however, he was back in time for another Hampden final on 29 April. With no disrespect to Aberdeen, this was almost taken for granted, and the Scottish Cup was duly won 2–0. Now the only trophy left was the big one – the European Cup.

The team meaning to deny them was no less than the giant Inter Milan under Helenio Herrera, the man whose methods Stein had gone to study. Now we would see who was the Master. No British club had ever got to the final before, never mind won it, although some had come close. Now, this bunch of little-known Scots, hitherto ignored throughout most of Britain until then, was the cynosure of all sporting eyes as they lined up in the long, dark tunnel beside the massive, tanned Italians, who were amazed to hear an unprepossessing line of Scotsmen lustily bellowing out 'It's A Grand Old Team to Play For'. There was no operatic retort from Milan.

What happened after that at the Lisbon Estadio Nacional has gone into football history (see *One Afternoon in Lisbon* by Kevin McCarra and Pat Woods) and from there to legend and from there to myth, so that there is little need to recount it here, but a few facts beg for mention. As always, Jock knew what he was doing. He was tending his men. Stein came into his own on that day, showing his true size under the burning sun. He handled his charges with infinite care, like a nurse one moment, warning them about sunburn, like a mate at other times, wondering how much overtime the fans would have to put in to pay to get to Lisbon and then like a fond father as kick-off time drew near, sending them out on Thursday, 25 May almost nerveless to 'play their ain game'.

Somehow, even at one down they knew it was going to be Celtic's day. And it was. Craig hared down the wing and passed exactly into the path of his partner, Gemmell, whose pile-driver brought them level. Five minutes from the end, with the score still 1–1, Murdoch fired in one of his specials, Stevie Chalmers stuck out a leg to divert it past the brave Sarti in the Milan goal and Celtic had won the

European Cup. Stein immediately limped on to the field to embrace Simpson, who was crying. They were joined by Billy McNeill, who was exultant, and by a kilted fan who had vaulted the moat and was hysterical. This little huddle of four set up a monument to the moment when the Lions of Lisbon had roared and the beautiful city which gave them their name braced itself for a Celtic carnival.

Billy finally made his way to the heights of the main stand to collect the trophy and when he lifted it above his head, the stadium turned green and white in the evening sun. When he eventually got it to the dressing-room, Jock Stein handed it, as a gesture, to Jimmy McGrory, who immediately burst into tears like the good Celtic supporter that he was. As he said to Gerald McNee, 'It was the first time in all my years in the game that I had cried.' Jimmy forgot that he had once cried for John Thomson, but he went on: 'What a thrill it was to see young boys like Murdoch, McNeill, Johnstone, Craig, Gemmell, Clark and Lennox coming of age. What a thrill to see the club I had served all my life reach the pinnacle.' He added that he hoped he would live long enough to shed more tears into the European Cup. He did, but they were to be tears of a different kind a year later.

He also cried for the death of his remaining brother, Harry McGrory, who had had a heart attack just before the Celtic party left for Lisbon. Harry was the brother that Jimmy thought was a better footballer than he was but ended up as a factory worker in Bishopton – and glad of the job. Harry was 65. It cannot be said that the McGrory brothers were long-livers. Jimmy was now 63 and he would be the last survivor of Henry McGrory's family, but in 1967, he was still going strong – and still rapt in all things Celtic.

After such an *annus mirabilis* it was only natural that they would all feel the reaction in 1968. Some of the Celtic travelling support took that long to get back from Lisbon. Others went by car and came back by plane – and vice versa. It was that kind of party. They were on such a high that it was hard to come down to earth again. Yet in the following season, the League Cup and the Glasgow Cup were won and the Championship retained, which would have well satisfied everyone not long since, but now they lived at a stratospheric level of expectancy and this could prove dangerous.

For Celtic, it was still as welcome to beat Rangers as it was for Scotland to beat England. Stein tried to downplay this emphasis on Old Firm encounters but their impact went too deep in the blood of both camps for it to be ignored. His own father, a Rangers man, could never honestly wish him luck when Celtic played the Ibrox side. All he could say was: 'Have a good game, son'. Stein admitted as much to Archie Macpherson. Both father and son recognised that Celtic was, in Macpherson's apt metaphor, 'a green-and-white ship sailing on an ocean painted blue'. This was just a fact of life in Scottish football.

World football was a different matter and Celtic had their eyes opened after they were 'refereed' out of the first round of the European Cup by Dynamo Kiev, when Murdoch was inexplicably ordered off and a good Lennox goal was disallowed. Worse was to follow when the South American team, Racing Club from Buenos Aires, came to Hampden to play in the first leg of the Inter-Continental Cup, then recognised as the unofficial club world championship. The South American tactics were plain. Intimidated by Celtic's football skills, they determined to kick, elbow, knee, spit and jersey-pull the Scots out of their composure. This they did so competently that Jimmy Johnstone had to have his hair washed at half-time to remove the spittle and Billy McNeill sported a black eye he had received when heading the winning goal. It was a cruel, callous, cynical display of professional fouling at its highest, or lowest, level. Celtic ought to have withdrawn from the field for reasons that were all too obvious.

If only they had done so. The second game in the concrete Avellaneda Stadium in Buenos Aires should have more appropriately taken place in Alcatraz, it was such a criminal farce. The less said about these South American confrontations the better. They weren't football matches, they were little wars fought against marauding thugs masquerading as sportsmen before their own people, who drove them on for the dubious honour of their nation. After two tries they got the result they wanted and a dire reputation for criminal activity on the football field. A battered and bloodied Celtic team could only troop on to the plane home, glad to have survived.

For a full account of these distasteful events see *The Story of Celtic* by Gerald McNee. As Gerry points out, it wasn't that Celtic had lost a game of football in a faraway country; they had lost control and in so doing had lost all self-respect. Even though the consequent inquiry by the SFA's secretary, Willie Allan, put the blame entirely on Racing Club, he had to note the lack of discipline shown by the Celtic players. They ought to have been complimented for their restraint.

McGrory was not party to all this. He had a heart attack in 1968.

For the first time in his life, he was seriously ill. All the pent-up feelings of the previous quarter-century suddenly demanded release and a heart attack was the result. It had to come out somehow. While he was convalescing in Glasgow during 1968, Robert Kelly sent his famous telegram to UEFA protesting over the invasion of Czechoslovakia by Russia and forces of the Warsaw Pact. He threatened to withdraw Celtic from the European Cup as a gesture. This created all kinds of ructions in the political and football worlds and caused East to be separated from West in future international fixtures between clubs. It was an astonishing action by a provincial football club but it was quite in keeping with Celtic's standards and Kelly's own high principles. It also helped to sweeten the sour taste left by the South American debacle.

Given this foray into the political arena, it was no surprise when, in the New Year Honours List of 1969, chairman Kelly was given a knighthood for services to Scottish Football. It is understood that Lady Kelly was delighted. It was also an honour for Celtic and an acknowledgment of the high status they had now won for themselves in European football – despite Montevideo and all that. No such honours came McGrory's way, despite his eligibility for an award for bravery in the field and conspicuous gallantry under fire while in office.

Instead, he sat back to watch 'his boys' put the bad Argentinian memories behind them and win their third title in a row – thus making them eligible for the 1969–70 European Cup. Gloriously, after a titanic struggle with Leeds United, then England's top team, they got through to yet another final. This time their opponents were a workmanlike Dutch side from Rotterdam, Feyenoord. Like everyone else at Parkhead, McGrory believed they could do another Lisbon.

Graham Williams interviewed him just before the final, which was to be held at the San Siro Stadium in Milan. He found that for the first time in nearly half a century, McGrory would not be attending a Celtic game. A heart attack of two years previously made him a little chary of flying these days and, in any case, at sixty-seven he preferred to watch the game in the comfort of his Ibrox home in the company of Barbara and their three children, Maria, Elizabeth and James McGrory Junior. Young James was now scoring goals at centre-forward for the Celtic Boys Club, but he was already finding that being Jimmy McGrory's son meant dealing with high expectations. 'I hope he's good enough to play for Celtic one day,' said his father. 'He couldn't pick a better club.' Well, what else would you expect the Celtic PRO to say? Young James had no comment. Graham Williams continues:

Today, still with the dark, swept-back hair and strong, determined features that dominated Scottish football for so long, Jimmy McGrory is Public Relations Officer at Parkhead. He attends headquarters every day and handles much of the office work. The man who scored more goals in his career than any other Scot, and who is officially tabbed by the club as 'the greatest living Celt', will endure the final in front of the TV set ten days from now. Was he nervous about the game?

'You would think I would've got over nerves by now, but I haven't. I've found that the longer you're connected with football the worse it gets. I was at the last final in Lisbon and when it was all over I cried like a child.'

I pointed out that the majority of that side was already at Parkhead when Jock Stein took over from him in 1965. McGrory shook his head.

'No one can take away from the success Mr Stein has had as a manager. He may have said himself that he just took them in the run-in to that first Cup win, but the credit is all his.' He laughed, 'Frankly, I was getting a bit tattered and torn by then and Jock has a way with the players I've rarely seen before. He's so devoted to the game, I wonder he gets any sleep. Mind you, he's a hard man. Hard, but scrupulously fair.'

Was it fair that such fabulous sums are lavished on modern players in wages and bonuses when he himself never got more than £8 a week as a player and his highest ever bonus was £15 for a Scottish Cup win?

The bespectacled McGrory answered at once without a trace of envy, 'I think it perfectly right that players should be paid well if the club is doing well. They make the money for the club, why shouldn't they share in it? I never had a full-time job apart from football simply because there was no work to be found. It was the Depression, and there were six in my own family out of work. I thought I was well paid for the time, and I had to help out.'

He still expressed his pleasure in being connected with football.

'It would be a poor nation without it,' said this most sincere and pleasant man. 'The men would all go mad, as they do in the close season anyway.'

And I left him, this easy-going but once so famous

personality who is so obviously content with his lot – 'My job at Parkhead is very agreeable. I work in the office, mainly in the mornings. There's no pressure on me.'

All the pressure was now on his successor. Stein had to maintain the exhilarating momentum of the earlier seasons now that Championship No. 5 loomed. This was duly accomplished and so Celtic were favourites to win their second European Cup and, what was worse, they believed that they would. For once, Stein had underestimated the opposition and, as a result, this Celtic team, with seven of the Lisbon side in place, had not the mindset they had in 1967. This is all the more ironic, because in the semi-final against Leeds United at Hampden they had won one of the most exciting and hard-fought encounters ever seen on that famous ground. Stein had said of the final to come: 'If they play as well as they did against Leeds, I'll be delighted.' I myself was at that game, crushed high on the terracing at the Aikenhead Road end, and can verify the quality of the Celtic side – especially Jinky Johnstone, who was superb and tormented Cooper, the Leeds left-back.

As the day of the match approached their confidence grew to such an extent that they almost sauntered on to the San Siro pitch on 6 May 1970. Hadn't they beaten Leeds convincingly and the Portuguese champions, Benfica, on Billy McNeill's correct guess of a coin? Their luck was in; the European Cup was surely meant for them again this year. It was just a matter of avoiding going Dutch in Milan. So they thought.

Within half an hour, they were one up through a Gemmell thunderbolt but Feyenoord equalised with a soft header and the match went into extra time with Celtic visibly wilting. This deflated Celtic side needed an original spark so Auld was replaced by George Connelly, but to little avail. Feyenoord got the winner two minutes from the end and the Celtic players sank to their knees, hardly able to look each other in the face. They knew that the Cup ought to have been theirs on form and quality, but football matches are won on the day.

Back in Glasgow, Jimmy McGrory slumped back in his chair at Belltrees, took off his glasses and wiped his eyes with his hankie. He wasn't crying this time. He was sad. He shook his head in disbelief. This was not supposed to have happened. With a sigh, he lifted up his beloved pipe. And sighed again. Even his pipe had gone out.

FIFTEEN

Extra Time

> Sure it's a grand old team to play for,
> Sure it's a grand old team to see,
> And if you know its history,
> It's enough to make your heart go
> Oh-oh-oh.
>
> Celtic supporters' song

One wonders if he was still sitting in that armchair on Saturday, 2 January 1971 when Celtic were leading Rangers 1–0 with seconds to go in a League match at Ibrox. Rangers supporters were already leaving down the steep exit on Stairway 13 at the Rangers end and someone stumbled and fell as Rangers equalised with the last kick of the game. The roar of the crowd might have been the last thing heard by 66 Rangers supporters as they died among the pile of tumbling bodies on the stairway.

Did McGrory hear from his window the wail of sirens as police cars and ambulances sped towards Ibrox and did he think of John Thomson and wonder why so many sad occasions are linked to that imposing stadium so near his home? Spectators coming away from the ground on that terrible night couldn't remember the score. It didn't seem to matter. The disaster hung like a pall over the rest of the season. Another Championship and Cup Double came to Celtic by the end of it and by then the new bonds created by the tragedy had already begun to fray. Blood had been spilt but blood will out

218

and before long all the old hatreds reasserted themselves between the two sets of supporters. As Archie Macpherson said, it seems to be the way of things in Scottish football. Why? For God's sake, why?

On a lighter note, the next Celtic trophy was won on television. This was the BBC's *Quizball*, in which a selection of British football teams competed in a quiz programme for a cup presented by the BBC. The format was that each club sent teams of three players plus a 'celebrity' supporter to vie with each other in general knowledge in a series of programmes transmitted weekly. The Celtic team consisted of Billy McNeill, Jim Craig and Willie Wallace. The present writer was fortunate enough to be selected as the guest supporter and was glad to share in the fun and the prizes. Billy's general knowledge was excellent and Jim Craig had extraordinary knowledge of every kind of sporting trivia. Mine was the arts and literary territory and 'Wispy' Wallace contributed a winning smile. He hardly spoke at all when we went to air. He made a try at one question – 'Who was Edgar Wallace?' The questionmaster thought he might even have been a relation. Dear old Wispy replied, 'Is he the racing correspondent of the *Daily Record*?'

The whole exercise was a trivial pursuit in every sense, but it was good fun and Celtic supporters all over Britain loved it. Especially when the same team won it twice in successive seasons – and were thenceforth banned from competing again. It all served, in a superficial way, to underline Celtic's propensity to win cups that are up for permanent possession. The two *Quizball* trophies are now a small part of a distinguished collection. It was while on this programme that I learned that Jim Craig's nickname on the park was 'Cairney' because of my involvement in a previous BBC television series in which I played the eponymous *This Man Craig*.

Meantime, the team that had boasted all three *Quizball* players, the Lisbon Lions, was formally disbanded after a sentimental last get-together arranged by showman Stein, now John Stein CBE. On May Day 1971, on the last day of the season at Celtic Park, he fielded the complete side against Clyde, with the exception of Ronnie Simpson, who had retired through injury. Nevertheless, Stein, with his usual sure touch for the theatrical, had Simpson lead the team out for the warm-up before giving way to Evan Williams, newly signed from Wolves. The old Lions won 6–1 and Bertie Auld was carried shoulder-high from the field, going straight on from there to Hibs. Gemmell moved to Nottingham Forest, Hughes and Wallace to

219

Crystal Palace and Chalmers and Clark to Morton. It was like breaking up the Crown Jewels.

By now, the former jewel in the Celtic crown, Jimmy McGrory, had reached his allotted span in the first years of the new decade and his proper title might have been Celtic's 'Grand Old Man'. It was considered appropriate, therefore, that he should be invited to officially open the reconstructed grandstand, then the only seated area at Celtic Park. The ceremony took place on 1 September 1971, prior to Celtic's match with the South American club champions Nacional of Uruguay. Sixty thousand supporters present showed their respect to their all-time favourite player as he stood by the plaque with its curtain ready to be drawn. When it was, it read:

> This reconstructed grandstand was opened by Jimmy McGrory on 1st September 1971 and on this date Celtic played Nacional of Uruguay, the Champions of South America.

It was fitting that McGrory should perform the opening ceremony since he was a survivor of the Celtic team that had played Hearts on the first day of the 1929–30 season at the opening of the then new 5,000-seater stand which replaced the original Grant Stand of misty memory. He may have remembered, too, that to build the 1929 new stand he had almost been sold to Arsenal. It is surely extraordinary for one player to have been a witness of these key events in the development of one club. His position as a Celtic institution was by now virtually unassailable and everyone acknowledged that. The only one to have any doubt about his status was the man himself.

In the match programme, chairman Desmond White, who had once wanted to replace him with Matt Busby, described McGrory as 'one of the great centre-forwards of world football' who had had 'a wonderful career' during which he 'deservedly gained the reputation of being one of the gentlemen of football'. The tribute ended with the assertion that 'so long as Celtic are discussed so will the name of Jimmy McGrory be mentioned'. Standing beside Jock Stein during the pre-match ceremony, and flanked by the tall Desmond White, he looked even smaller than his 5 ft 6 in., but his stature was such, and his pedigree as a player so obvious, that he had little need to rely on any complimentary address. His deeds spoke for him.

He may just have been starting to show the first signs of age. The Humphrey Bogart face was now drawn and bejowelled under the permanent glasses, but the spirit was as willing as ever and he stood there, an honest man, still all-square to the world. What memories must he have had as he felt his favourite turf under his feet? What emotions must he have triggered in the thousands of supporters who watched a soberly dressed old man pull a cord to reveal the plaque permanently inscribed with his name? In the game that followed, the then Celtic team beat Nacional, 3–0. Unlike a certain Argentinian club, the Uruguayans did not have manslaughter in mind and they helped put a proper football seal on a very special day.

Oddly enough, in all my own comings and goings at Celtic Park during this period, I never met Jimmy McGrory – I never even saw him. Yet he was there all right. He must have been. A new Celtic Park was towering all around him as Parkhead was being prepared for the New Age. For the first time the traditional stepped terracings to east and west were being covered. The only thing that troubled McGrory in all the renovations was that smoke detectors were being installed and the smoke from his ever-present pipe had set them off several times, much to the annoyance of the East End fire brigade who came clanging up to the main door, sirens wailing, to be met by a very apologetic public relations officer. After one such false alarm, a fire officer said to him, 'It's a good job you're Jimmy McGrory.'

However, if I didn't meet Mr McGrory, then I met his chairman. In the early '70s I was attempting to establish a Scottish Football Hall of Fame in Scotland and I asked Sir Robert, among many others, for his idea of the kind of Scottish player that should be included in such a display. His reply was to send me his Scotland XI – which my files show was: Brownlie (Third Lanark); Hutton (Aberdeen) and McNaught (Raith Rovers); Meiklejohn (Rangers) Young (Rangers) and Mackay (Tottenham Hotspur); Jackson (Chelsea), Walker (Hearts), Gallacher (Newcastle United), James (Arsenal) and Morton (Rangers). It is obvious that he knew the football of his time but it is also noticeable that he didn't select McGrory.

Only weeks later, on Tuesday, 21 September 1971, Sir Robert Kelly died at his home in Burnside after a long illness where he was tended, at his own request, by Barbara McGrory. It was almost as if he had allowed himself to become ill now that Celtic was in capable hands. He no longer had the purpose that had driven his life so he just yielded to cancer and let life go. The Requiem Mass at St Columbkille's, Rutherglen, was conducted by the Archbishop of Glasgow, the Most Reverend James D. Scanlan. It was attended by nearly everyone in Scottish football including Celtic's public relations officer. The last time he had been in this church he was wearing plus fours for the first time to go rambling with John McMenemy from Springfield Road. He remembered he had walked all the way back to the Garngad – the back way. How much simpler everything had seemed then, when all that was worrying him was wearing plus fours.

Now everything worried him. Changes were swirling round him all the time. He seriously wondered if he had anything to offer the new world of football as it was gradually emerging. His world, his standards, his ideals didn't seem to have a place in the rush and scurry of the modern game. His kind of open, direct game, a spearhead feeding off speedy wingers and astute inside men backed by a strong defence was now under the threat of overall game tactics and the permutation of a given pool. Stein had shown how well this worked but what would happen to football as McGrory and his like had known it for nearly 60 years? There was no place for the kind of manager he had been. The job was too complicated for one man. It would now be divided between administration and coaching. Soon there would be a bigger team in the pavilion than there was in the park and many of the suits would never have kicked a ball.

Would the British League come as he and Bob Kelly had thought? Would there be a World League one day – teams jetting round the globe for inter-continental games? Thank God, he'd never see it. The simple game got less simple every day. Money counted more than ever. Managers can buy success these days. Yet money isn't everything. You can't buy magic, at least the kind that Patsy Gallacher once showed – or Jimmy Johnstone still did. All you can do is hire the boots and hope that they can play. The trouble is the feet belong to a man, and that man has all the failings, foibles and fantasies that any man has – especially a young man. It's a gamble all round.

Jimmy McGrory firmly believed that Scotland would always be a power in football, no matter the FIFA rankings or latest results because as a nation, albeit small, we produce good players and occasionally, a great one, like a Denis Law, a Kenny Dalglish or a Jim Baxter. Alas, the conditions are no longer there to produce a Jimmy McGrory. The distractions are too many for young boys today.

He was always proud of the fact that, at one time, Celtic boasted the youngest team in Scotland, and these were the boys who not only became the Lisbon Lions, but were also the players who achieved 'Nine in a Row' – that remarkable run of successive Championships from 1966 until 1974. This glorious Stairway to Paradise was hailed as a Jock Stein creation. He was certainly the engineer-in-charge, but the honest labourers of Irish stock who put in the foundations were a certain James Edward McGrory, who was foreman, and the site supervisor, Sir Robert Kelly. They were the ones who were covered in muck for years before the pillars went in to take the team to the heights. Teams must come and go in the course of things; that's the nature of football. It was, after all, a young man's game – and the young Celts were ready and waiting.

Dalglish, McGrain, Hay, Connelly and Macari were already lined up at the dressing-room door and Dixie Deans from Motherwell was hustled in through the transfer window. These were the men who would help clinch Championship No. 7 in 1971–72, thus beating Celtic's own record of six in a row dating from 1905 to 1910. They also won the League and Cup Double for the fourth time in six years and only lost out on penalties to Inter Milan in the European Cup. So it looked as if, by 1973, the Celtic waves were to continue beating on the shores of success, but those same sands could be treacherous, and they had learned it was fatal in football to take anything for granted.

McGrory had no regrets about his career. He had no regrets about life, but he was beginning to wonder how much actual useful time he had left. There has never been a Celtic name of his triple status as player, manager and PRO, but he was beginning to feel more and more out of things in the new Celtic Park. His loyalty was as strong as ever but he wasn't sure it was a quality reciprocated by the present Board of Directors. He had the uneasy feeling he was being tolerated rather than utilised, yet, ostensibly, the wheels were still turning smoothly.

With the League Championship attained yet again, the Scottish Cup of 1972 was won in great style against Hibs. Dixie Deans got a wonderful hat-trick in the 6–1 victory. It brought to mind a certain Jimmy McGrory. It was obvious to many though, that Jimmy was beginning to look tired. Even the giant Jock Stein was starting to feel the strain and was experiencing heart problems, so much so that he had to take time off in December 1972 to go into hospital for observation. The team carried on, of course, under Sean Fallon, but it was as if it were driving on automatic pilot. McGrory was not consulted now. He became as much of a spectator to events around him as any fan sitting in the enclosure that was emerging as the modern Parkhead Stadium.

When Bobby Murdoch reportedly scored Celtic's 6,000th goal in February 1973, a photograph was later taken of him in the company of all the other great Celtic scorers still extant. McGrory, as scorer of goal 3,000, was in the picture along with the other thousand-stage scorers like Adam McLean (2,000) and Jimmy Delaney (4,000). Frank Brogan, the scorer of goal 5,000 was absent from the group as he was by then playing for Halifax Town, as was, naturally, the scorer of goal 1,000, old-timer, Davie Hamilton (d. 1950), who had netted his against Port Glasgow Athletic in 1905. Given the length of time involved and the absence of wartime records, these statistics may be dubious by the strictest statistical standards but they served as a good guide to the prowess of the players concerned and the occasion did show that McGrory still featured among the record-makers.

The group photo taken, however, shows how much thinner he looked and the famous neck muscles appear scraggy. This is perfectly natural and inevitable, but it's still sad to realise that our sporting gods are human. This was emphasised even more when a much younger man, George Connelly, one of the few modern Celtic players of true genius, walked out of Celtic Park and out of football to return home to his native Fife and voluntary obscurity. This was a tragedy for both young man and club. He had been with them since he was 15 and had promised so much, but, in the end, the peripheral stresses were all too much for him and he opted for driving a taxi around Dunfermline.

Gentleman Jim McGrory might well have thought of walking out in the mid-'70s. The almost cynical appropriation of the game by television companies and assorted corporates only underlined the difference between the 'haves' and the 'have-nots' in a sport-now-turned-entertainment medium. Similarly, the gulf between players was just as marked – and it wasn't just a pound a week differential. Scores of players were unbelievable millionaires but the great majority, comparatively, were on poverty row. These absurd conditions only served to highlight the value that players like McGrory had to a football club in his day.

Given the social and cultural differences between then and now, it was still evident that McGrory had *enjoyed* his football and *played* it throughout his 15-year career. He did not report to a daily activity merely because he was required to do so by contract. He *loved* his job and it showed. Hence, the balanced mental attitude, the unflagging enthusiasm and the sheer stamina that made him as potent a striking force in his last game for Celtic as he was in his first. More so, because he had added guile to his armoury and the sheer weight of match experience told in his favour. It is a fact that he was scoring better than ever in his final season, possibly because he was in a good team again, and had he remained free of injury and completed that season, he would have set a season's scoring total that would have been unsurpassable.

When he left the field for good, he left it as he had begun in it, as a sportsman; but, 50 years later, today's star football athlete has became a businessman in a coloured jersey with his website on his undervest and his mobile phone in his bootbag. It was appropriate that the new player now had a number on his back and his name above it. He is as much a product as the name he endorses. If the agents had their way, they would also advertise on the rest of the jersey space so that teams would run out on to the park looking more like Formula One racing cars than football players.

In Mrs Thatcher's selfish '80s, Celtic did not as yet boast any millionaires in their ranks but you can be sure there were few playing for the equivalent of McGrory's £8 a week. He, meanwhile, could only sit back and watch from his innocuous seat in the stand helpless and, for the most part, bypassed. He was only brought to mind again when Dixie Deans threatened his match goal-scoring record by scoring six against Partick Thistle in November 1973.

At the end of that season, Celtic won their ninth Scottish League Championship in a row by drawing with Falkirk at Brockville and a new pinnacle had been attained – but at a cost. After a heavy defeat by Rangers at Ibrox in January 1975, they gave up the Championship chase in a manner that the old Celtic teams would never have done, and not only Celtic supporters were sorry. Ian Archer, the doyen of Scottish sportswriters spoke for many when, after a further defeat at Easter Road on 22 February 1975, he wrote in his *Glasgow Herald* column:

> The crown lies shakily on Celtic's head. One little nudge and it will roll in one huge clatter, down the steps of the throne from which they have ruled this Scottish kingdom for the past nine years. There should be much sadness abroad in the land. Coming back from the capital by train, looking into the deep-set eyes of Celtic supporters who seemed to have fought a long campaign in the desert rather than attended a football match, you were in touch with grief. This last decade has established Celtic as one of the great clubs of the world. Not

as lastingly famous as the unique Real Madrid, not as individually talented nor explosive as Ajax of Amsterdam. But more friendly and better loved than Inter, more attractive than any English club since the last revival of Tottenham Hotspur. They trod more new paths than any Scotsmen since Dr Livingstone left Blantyre.

Billy McNeill retired in May 1975 after winning another Scottish Cup medal against Airdrie and was carried off the field on the shoulders of his teammates to become manager of Clyde two years later. David Hay had already left to join Chelsea strictly for the money, and his was a big loss to the team. An even greater loss was suffered when, on 5 July 1975, Jock Stein nearly lost his life in a car accident while returning from holiday and was out for the whole of the 1975–76 season. It was like the London Philharmonic losing Sir Thomas Beecham and certainly Celtic never 'played' as well under the lesser baton of assistant, Sean Fallon. Rangers took advantage of the situation and scooped the treble that year – League Cup, Scottish Cup and Championship. It was an ominous echo of former times.

The Lisbon Lions were no more. They were the last Celtic side to play as a team and now an assortment of individual talents were sent out to blend as best they could on the day. These were the forerunners of the modern-day mercenaries who, in many cases, were merely boots for hire, and in too many cases, these boots were also made for walking. Over the next few seasons, players of any real calibre still at the club would leave on the high road that took them to the money in England and elsewhere and there was nothing that Jimmy McGrory could do about it.

He had by now dwindled into something of a Celtic irrelevance and stood outside the main door each match day, with coat, hat and pipe, looking more like a monument to himself than an active executive in a thriving public concern. He seemed to be kept in reserve by the directors for the sole purpose of welcoming visiting dignitaries and celebrities who were, nevertheless, always keen to meet him. It was a demeaning, subservient role and if it hurt, he didn't show it, having a smile for everyone. When film star Sean Connery, for instance, a former footballer himself with Bonnyrigg Rose, a junior team from the Edinburgh area, visited Celtic Park, McGrory asked for the actor's autograph. Connery refused, adding that he would only give it if McGrory would first give him his. This was a neat compliment by the actor. He knew McGrory's real status, even if McGrory didn't.

This was underlined even more when, during public tours of Celtic Park, parties of schoolchildren would be told by their teachers, much as beaming grandfathers would tell their grandsons, that the nice man who showed them round the place was the great Jimmy McGrory, at one time described as 'the greatest menace to goalkeepers in the history of football'. It must have been hard for the children to relate the avuncular guide who stood before them in his pinstriped suit to the terror of the goalmouth. His picture was there, of course, but to the young they were pictures from the history books. A living legend is harder to deal with than a name on the page or a picture on the wall.

Jimmy McGrory, himself, was not finding it easy. He didn't seem to know what was going on at times. He was vague and not at all like himself in day-to-day activities around the ground. He walked slowly and, sometimes, even unsteadily. Sean Fallon was reported to have commented that his old boss was 'hitting the sherry' behind closed office doors. This was perhaps what director James Farrell had also suspected a few years before but, as will be seen, this was no more than what might be called a 'sherry trifle'. His problems with balance were due more to his gradual physical decline than to any covert drinking. He may have had recourse to a glass or two as part of his PRO duties but it would be grossly unfair, and totally wrong, to accuse him of alcoholism. Drink was never his problem. He had seen too many retired players lose their way in the licensing trade. Jim Baxter, for one.

McGrory's occasional vagueness could be more accurately attributed to the cumulative effect of all those famous years of heading a cannonball at speed into goals. If not quite full-scale Alzheimer's disease at this stage, a definite dementia had taken hold. According to his own doctor, he was 'punch-drunk, due to continued blows to the head over a long period – just like a boxer'. Recent studies have shown there is a correlation between this kind of repetitive head action over a sustained period and the outward signs of a mild senility, or more acutely, Alzheimer's disease.

Jim Kennedy, the Celtic left-back prior to the Tommy Gemmell era, died of Alzheimer's in December 2003. Centre-forward Billy McPhail had also suffered in this way and, shortly before his death in April 2003, was unsuccessful in a Scottish court action to prove that his condition was due to repetitive heading of a football.

However, in England, the coroner's verdict following the death of Jeff Astle, a well-known centre-forward with West Bromwich Albion in the same period, upheld the cause of final illness as being due to his many years as a professional footballer, particularly in his heading of a heavy leather ball throughout his career. It may now be seen as a professional footballer's risk.

As recently as 2004, this was confirmed by Alan Birkbeck, a senior engineer at Glasgow University, who asked a one-time professional player to kick footballs against a wall in order that their velocity might be measured with a high-speed camera. He found that the balls, which had been soaked in water to simulate the conditions in which matches were often played on old grounds that were little more than mudheaps, were squashed to half their diameter on impact with the wall. The effect on the skull would be similar – 'It was like having ten bags of coal dropped on your skull. It's the weight and the speed it's coming – and you stick your head in the way of it.' McGrory did just that for nearly 20 years. Dr Ron Thomson of the University's Mechanical Engineering Department commented:

> We wanted to see if there was anything in the claim that repeated heading could lead to brain damage and the answer was yes. We were surprised at how great the force of the new ball we used was. If subjected to these forces repeatedly I would be worried.

This totally validates the work of R.D. Archer. Professor Archer was an Australian aeronautical engineer noted for his work on shock waves focusing, especially, in its medical applications. This led him in later studies to consider the damage done to the human brain by repeated 'small impacts, which soccer players experience when heading a ball'. This work was ongoing at the time of his death in 2004 and its conclusions would appear to justify a connection between the condition and the behavioural patterns exhibited by McGrory. It is certainly a more credible hypothesis than an increased appetite for genteel sherry.

During 1974 and 1975, Gerald McNee interviewed Jimmy at Belltrees for the McGrory autobiography *A Lifetime in Paradise*, which Gerry edited and published as a small volume with McGrory himself in 1975. Gerry remembers that interviews with the old player were difficult because his memory was almost gone and he had to be prompted by the latter's questions arrived at from research through old records and newspapers. When asked about his eight goals against Dunfermline, Jimmy retorted, 'But you should have seen the ones I missed.' Again, when complimented on three goals in three minutes against Motherwell, he removed the pipe from his mouth to mutter, 'Jeez, was I that good?'

Gerry McNee told the present writer that, in the two years of regular evening visits to Belltrees, he never found the seventy-two-year-old McGrory to be other than patient, courteous and helpful. He also remembers that the old man, unfailingly, no matter the weather, would get up and put on his hat and coat to walk the writer to the bus stop on Dumbreck Road. One wonders if McGrory might have had difficulty finding his way home again.

He did not attend every Celtic match as before. He found it more and more difficult to cope with the travelling. By this time, the Premier League had happened in Scotland. Some say it was created to break the hold Celtic had had on the old League for a decade. Rangers – who else? – won the initial Premier League title, but then Jock Stein returned, Sean Fallon left and Celtic won the second. They also won the Scottish Cup in a final that was the first to be televised live. This allowed viewers to see Dalglish's last game for Celtic as it happened and King Kenny moved his kingdom to Liverpool for a then British record fee of £440,000 and to even greater acclaim by the Kop.

The same Liverpool team provided the opposition for Stein's testimonial match in 1978 but this was followed soon after by his resignation. He was only 55 but he had had his first trophy-less season since 1965. His 13th season had not been lucky for him but, frankly, Jock Stein hadn't been the same man since his accident. Besides, a ready Celtic successor was waiting in former captain Billy McNeill, then managing Aberdeen with John Clark as his assistant. An offer was made to big Jock to take charge of Celtic Pools. This would give him a seat on the Board, but the big man was unimpressed. Chairman Desmond White, who did not always see eye to eye with Stein, made a statement at the time in the *Celtic View*:

> It is a truism that, no matter how talented and successful the manager, there comes a time when the pressures and strains start to take their toll. As well as knowing better than most just what these pressures entail for a man at the top, Jock Stein suffered serious physical injury as an innocent victim of a major road accident. These factors combined to bring home

to him several months ago that the time was now opportune
for the directors to consider seriously the appointment of a
successor.

This was on a par with the gloved mailed fist shown to Jimmy
McGrory in 1965. It was acceptable to Jimmy, but for Stein it was like
trying to fit a whale into a goldfish bowl. However, Jock sincerely
welcomed Billy to his new role. To be fair to Celtic, they were
worried about the continued strain on Stein's health, particularly
with his heart history, but they could not see that his heart was in
football – not in money-raising or ticket-selling. In August 1978 he
took himself off to Leeds to replace Jimmy Armfield as manager
there. Armfield had stepped in when Brian Clough was sacked only
45 days after replacing Don Revie, Stein's old friend, who had
become manager of England in 1974. Similarly, Stein left Elland
Road after only 44 days to become Scotland's manager – the job he
was destined for.

Jock was to take a good Scotland team to the World Cup in 1982
and was building towards the next in 1986, when, after a qualifying
decider at Ninian Park, Cardiff, on 10 September 1985, where
Scotland secured their passage to Mexico, he collapsed on the
trackside and died on the dressing-room table. With his going, it was
as if the floodlights had been switched off in the Scottish game. It's
been struggling in the dark ever since.

Billy McNeill was a natural Celtic manager. Like McGrory, he was
Celtic through and through. 'Ours is no ordinary club,' he had once
said – and he meant it. His long playing career gave him a close link
to both McGrory and Stein and thus preserved a valuable continuity.
A surge of loyal feeling rushed through the club again and swept
them up in a tide which was to carry them to further triumphs before
the decade ended. In the meantime, the Celtic PRO of nearly 13
years was now almost 75, and failing; Barbara knew it was time for
him to leave Celtic.

So, one January afternoon in 1979, Mr McGrory tidied his desk,
picked up his hat and, after taking a polite farewell of everyone at the
ground, walked out of the Celtic door as unostentatiously as he had
arrived in 1922 – and that was that. He could leave with his head
high and a memorable span of virtually 50 years' service to the club
behind him. He had wanted to stay on with Celtic until the day he
died and when he left Parkhead in that winter twilight he knew that
dying was all there was left to do.

SIXTEEN

Injury Time

> For when the One Great Scorer comes
> to mark against your name
> He marks – not that you won or lost,
> but how you played the game.
>
> Grantland Rice, *Alumnus Football*, 1941

On hearing the news of Jimmy's retiral early in the New Year of 1979, his old friend, Father Coleman, offered up a Mass in New York. 'In thanksgiving,' he said, 'for being given such a wonderful Celt as Jimmy McGrory.' Celtic FC, in contrast, gave him the parting gift of a new pipe. They should have given him a pipe band. Even a hundred pipers an' a' would hardly be enough to honour the end of a fantastic football career. If the bright fire of his player youth had dimmed to the grey ash of public relations, he nonetheless didn't deserve to see nearly fifty glorious years go up in a pipeful of tobacco smoke.

The Celtic Supporters' Association, however, didn't let the event go unnoticed. They could be relied on to make an appropriate gesture to their favourite son and organised their 34th Rally in his honour at the Kelvin Hall on Sunday, 4 March 1979, which drew a capacity audience. Jimmy was astonished at the huge turnout. His daughter, Maria, said he had whispered to her before it started, 'Who have they all come to see?'

'*You*, Dad,' she told him.

'Goodness,' he exclaimed.

The Celtic Board were led by the chairman, Desmond White, who presented Jimmy with a silver salver inscribed 'To the One and Only Jimmy McGrory'. Billy McNeill suitably led out the full back-room staff from Celtic Park and players, past and present, added to the vast assembly gathered to pay tribute to someone who'd given his all to them for 50 years. In the official programme for the evening, Harry Andrews of the *Scottish Sunday Express* wrote an article – 'King of the Golden Days' – which placed McGrory nicely in the context of his time:

> I saw Jimmy against the background of his great contemporaries. They were golden days for Scottish football. I remember Jimmy best as the spearhead of a Celtic attack that saw him flanked on the right by the two Thomsons, Bertie and Alex; and on the left by Peter Scarff and Charlie 'Happy Feet' Napier. Over at Ibrox, Alan Morton, Sandy Archibald and Bob McPhail were in full flow. Motherwell were revelling in a forward line that read Johnny Murdoch, John McMenemy, Willie McFadyen and the glorious George Stevenson with Bob Ferrier on the left wing. There were stars like Benny Yorston and Alex Cheyne at Aberdeen, that super centre, Barney Battles, at Tynecastle and almost every club had an outstanding personality. But even in such company, Jimmy McGrory was a giant. I can still see that square-shouldered, powerful figure in a green and white jersey – though oddly enough, I still see him flying through the air, head ready to meet one of those crosses in which Celtic specialised from both wings. It would be quite wrong to think that Jimmy had only his headwork to recommend him. But it is equally true that he was probably the finest header of a ball that football has ever seen. [He] thrived on the fast-flying cross ball and there were few defenders – even of international standard – who could cope with the tactic.

During the interval, the President of the CSA, Peter Murray, presented Jimmy with a cheque and a clock to acknowledge the time he had spent with Celtic and the great times he had given the supporters. They hoped he would now have time to watch the game he loved from the comfort of his home.

Comfort was not immediately available. One early result of his retirement was retrenchment for the McGrorys. He had had no golden handshake to ease his departure, no nest egg to fall back on. His Celtic wages of £70 a month had hardly been a king's ransom and did not allow for much saving for old age. His earnings had been little more than crumbs from the Celtic biscuit tin. Barbara had to go out and work again as a private nurse in order to make ends meet. The three children were now grown up and independent but their mother and father still had to live. The children were angry, and still are, that a distinguished career such as their father's should be allowed to end on such a note of apparent indifference from an establishment he had helped to sustain for so long. He had, in truth, become something of a memorial to himself but the McGrory family couldn't help feeling it was one that had been left to stand out in the rain.

Yet there was never a syllable of complaint or self-pity from him. He had done his job, or jobs, as well as he could, as player, manager and front-man, and thought himself well rewarded in more ways than money. No matter that these roles had diminished in effectiveness as they went on, they were now behind him and he must get on with retirement. Of course he was old but he only wanted now the dignity of his end days and the means to see them out in a proud quiet. Instead, he and Barbara had now to count the pennies that fell from Paradise. Was his a fool's Paradise after all?

Celtic supporters, not to mention McGrory himself, would have been appalled to think that their former favourite was in any kind of discomfort or financial embarrassment, or that his personal affairs were subject to any public discussion. Had he been in any real hardship, he would have got much more than cuff links, that's for sure. There are still rich Celtic supporters. This proud man didn't need charity but Barbara McGrory felt, most strongly, that her husband had been shabbily treated by Celtic at the end and her son, James, is keen, for the sake of her memory, to clarify some anomalies that still persist in the later McGrory story.

For instance, what *did* happen to the £800 loan from 1935? James McGrory would like to know the answer to this mystery. He is a policeman, so he has a professional curiosity, but in his quiet diffidence and modesty, he is exactly his father's son. As a young man, he never thought of his father as any kind of celebrity just because he played for Celtic. The McGrory children, nevertheless, enjoyed some of the perks that this status gave him but, for the most part, he was just their father. They were brought up by Barbara as a conventional family with ordinary expectations – despite the fact that

233

they had, whether they knew it or not, an extraordinary father.

Today, James McGrory has no desire to muddy waters that have, in any case, long passed under the bridge, but he is anxious to complete the true picture of his famous parent. His own grown-up son, Jamie, is surprised that, even today, people still know his grandfather's name and want to know more about him. This book is only one way of telling them.

Jimmy was more or less confined to the house now and to his presentation clock, his radio and his television set. It was the nearest he could get to a football ground at that time – even though, sitting in his armchair, he could hear the roar of the crowd at Ibrox. On the afternoon of 15 May 1982, he might even have heard the roars from Parkhead as Celtic clinched the Championship, scoring just enough in a 3–0 victory over St Mirren to edge out Aberdeen, who were beating Rangers at the same time. The late Ian Archer, in his *Sunday Standard* column the next day, perfectly summed up the atmosphere at Celtic Park:

> What was remarkable yesterday was the extraordinary performance by the Celtic fans, who supported the side through a hard patch in the game and who wouldn't go away afterwards. They commemorated the championship in their chants to the late Johnny Doyle and while that may read rather morbidly, it was strangely moving and sensitive. At the end, Tommy Burns went over to where the invalid carriages are parked and shook hands with all those supporters – the act of a fine player and a proper gent. Maybe such actions, proving the affinity between those who play and those who watch, explain why this club has succeeded where others have failed. There is nothing wrong with passion in football and somehow Celtic have more of that commodity than most.

No one personifies that commodity more than McGrory, but nature was taking its course and it was downhill all the way. Barbara McGrory was having a hard time with her husband. The door had to be kept locked whenever he was left in alone in case he went out and wandered off. Barbara, even with all her nursing experience, was under a severe strain because of the constant vigilance required. It had all happened so gradually, but everyone could now see that there was something very wrong with him. He was getting increasingly vague and latterly it was unsafe to leave him alone in the house. He was finding the stairs more and more difficult and the open fire was an increasing hazard. With the children all away, the place was now too big for just the two of them and the upkeep was getting harder all the time.

In 1980, to save on the rates and also make it easier for Jimmy, Barbara sold Belltrees to a second-hand car dealer and moved herself, Jimmy and Tara, the dog, to a ground-floor flat at 30 Maple Road, just a few minutes away. It was here, not long afterwards, that Pat Woods visited the McGrorys and, at Barbara's request, began sorting and collating Jimmy's vast collection of photographs and football memorabilia. The present author is especially indebted to this very important body of research material. Pat has this personal recollection of McGrory at that time:

> When I first met him Jimmy was in failing health, but you could still see traces in his physique of the powerful build he had used to great effect as a player. It was a great honour to carry out the work on his behalf, for I had been brought up on my father's stories about Celtic, in which the great McGrory featured prominently, particularly the recollection of his stirring, inspirational role in the 1931 Scottish Cup final against Motherwell.
>
> When I was researching the history of the club, I was struck by the debt which Celtic owed to him during the inter-War period when the club was largely in the shadow of Rangers. Invariably, as you read the newspaper reports, you began to wonder who else was playing for Celtic, so important did his incredibly consistent goal-scoring and never-say-die spirit seem to the club and its supporters.

There is no more authoritative comment than that, but now, the subject of that encomium was unable to be trusted outside of the house because he would wander away and get lost and Barbara had to go out and find him. Altogether, the strain of being his round-the-clock carer was beginning to tell on her, and her children became concerned for both their parents. Barbara couldn't really manage him on her own. Something had to be done – and quickly.

On their doctor's advice, Jimmy McGrory was admitted to the nearby Southern General Infirmary during the first week of October 1982, and was given a bed in Ward 35 on the first floor. This step was taken by the children more to give their mother a rest than to give their father any hospital treatment. Barbara went up to her beloved Highlands and enjoyed some much-needed time in a private hotel while her husband lay back in his new bed, not at all sure where he was.

When word got out that Jimmy McGrory was playing out injury time at the Southern General Infirmary in Govan, his visitors were many. His son James, who was at his bedside regularly, had to submit to being mistaken for either of his two late uncles as his father talked to 'Hughie' and 'Harry'. However, there was often a long line of real visitors waiting at the end of the ward. Priests were prominent and the clerical queue was of Vatican proportions – and not all of them were there to give him Extreme Unction.

As always, Jimmy couldn't turn anyone away. There were St Roch's Old Boys like Jonny Connor and Garngad pals like John McFadyen, old Celtic players like Hugh Hilley from way back and players, not only from Celtic past and present, but old friends from other clubs, like Jack Harkness and Bob McPhail. These men were all getting on themselves and some took their time, leaning on sticks, to walk up the length of the ward to his bed. Bob McPhail never lost his fondness and admiration for his old rival and Scotland teammate: He was crying when he left. He knew that the big referee in the sky already had the whistle in his mouth and his hand on the watch.

Given his deep Catholic faith, Jimmy would not be too worried. He was, in a sense, already with God. Yes, the game was almost up for Jimmy McGrory. He wasn't bothered. He'd be glad to get to the big pavilion. He'd had a good game for most of the match. Who knows, there may be a whole other game to play, and God knows the next team he'll be in. As long as Patsy Gallacher was playing, he'd be OK. Tommy McInally would likely be in the opposition. Meantime, the old legs had given out and his wind was gone. He couldn't spring for those high balls now. He had nothing to be ashamed of – as a player. He knew in his heart he wasn't ideal executive material but he looked the part. He remembered Barbara's rushing out and buying him two suits at once with the money he got from the McNee book. One would have done, come to think of it.

Jack McGinn was one of his last visitors. Jack, who was by then commercial manager at Celtic, had called just to update Jimmy on events around the ground. Jimmy was always keen to know all the Parkhead gossip. Jack did most of the talking but then Jimmy never did say much anyway. When Jack was leaving, something made him stop at the end of the ward and look back. Jimmy was still smiling but he raised a hand and gave a slight wave. Jack knew it was a farewell.

Jimmy McGrory died at twenty past one in the morning of Wednesday, 20 October 1982 in the presence of his family. Barbara attested to the death certificate, which was signed by Dr D. Colin Drummond. The cause of death was given as 'old age'. He was 78. The man was gone – God rest him – but the legend of Jimmy McGrory was born from that moment – and that will never die.

'Jimmy McGrory is dead – long live Celtic.'

He had said he would die before he left the club. Well, he left them, and now he was dead. The surprise was that it took him three years. Celtic FC were never to be the same again with him gone. He represented, and took away with him, that special spirit he had inherited from Maley who had absorbed it from Brother Walfrid. They had all breathed a finer kind of air somehow and it hadn't survived the transition from a Victorian band of brothers to the more corporate identity the club was beginning to assume – including that contemporary callousness which trades under the name of cost-effectiveness. The Kelly and White regime at Parkhead did not allow their most famous player to go gently into his goodnight. As soon as he went through that Parkhead door in January 1979, it shut firmly behind him. Even the complimentary copies of the *Celtic View*, which Jack McGinn had always sent to Jimmy, were discontinued. The umbilical cord had been cut. From her flat in Maple Road, his widow could see her old house from the window. It was not the way she wanted to look back on her life with one of Scotland's most famous sporting names.

The McGrory family joked that they lived in a 'Green House'. Belltrees, after all, had been a gift from Marion Green. Now it was gone – and most of the Greens had gone too. The family, which had meant so much to their father in his first marriage and to the children of his second marriage in their growing up, was now widely dispersed throughout the UK, Spain and the United States. George Green's eleven children, a powerful team in itself, had carried on the good work he had started and had seen it grow into an empire of the sons and daughters, who in turn had passed it on to grandchildren, nieces and nephews who, in their turn, gradually dismantled the business, selling the twenty-four cinemas, one by one, as bingo halls to Mecca Entertainments before passing on to their various padded retirements. After all, they had been taught that the only way to succeed in business was to keep it in the family, although all monies from the Ann Jane Green Trust went to Catholic charities. Mrs Green herself had been a convert. George Herbert Dougal Green, the last-known Green descendent, became a multi-millionaire, and was last heard of in the United States.

Craigie Hall, the family home, came into the possession of Graham Roxburgh, a civil engineer with a passion for Charles Rennie Mackintosh, so it could be said to have found a good owner, and Glen Ard, Bertie's home, went to an Indian family for a suitcase of money. Tony Green, the affable son of cousins Doris and Richard, retired from managing the cinemas to run a prosperous pub in Paisley but Tony, now living in North Ayrshire, was only a boy when his Aunt Nona died although he remembers that she needed glasses for her slipstitch embroidery; and that the famous football player she had married once told him that what he was proudest about in his whole career was that he had never been pulled up for a foul on another player.

Barbara stayed on at 30 Maple Road until 1985 when she was to move to 18 Greenwood Road, Clarkston (where her daughter, Maria, now lives) not far from brother, James. Barbara would die in 1997 at Dumfries, at the home of her other daughter, Elizabeth. Life would move on, as it always does, and the past would distil itself into memories, and even most of these would fade. But some things – and some people – take longer to dissipate in the collective Scottish memory. James Edward McGrory comes into that category.

EPITAPH

Tho' Phoebus may forget to shine,
And man forget the Great Divine,
As long as soccer's tides shall flow
The world McGrory's name shall know.
> From *Tribute to James McGrory* by Neil T. Byars
> Published 21 October 1935, price 2d

Nothing underscored the importance of McGrory's life in football than the general reaction to his leaving of it. The passing of Jimmy McGrory was a public event of some importance and this was recognised by the space given to his obituary by the national press. The tributes by sportswriters and fellow footballers were fulsome and worthy as might be expected and, as they are on public record, they need not be repeated here but one eulogy deserves mention in print and that was Archie Macpherson's radio encomium on the night of McGrory's funeral. On the BBC's Scottish *Sportscene* programme, broadcast that night from Glasgow, sports commentator Macpherson paid a touching tribute to McGrory. Apparently, Archie had to press his producers to have the item included, but he insisted, knowing how meaningful McGrory's death was to all who love football – especially those in Glasgow. This extract is reproduced from the transcript of that broadcast:

> Long before I set eyes on Jimmy McGrory for the first time, I
> seemed to know him well. There were those old, rather faded

pictures you come across in books, of a sturdy player in the
hooped jersey, arms folded, rather stern-looking, solid and
determined. Or the ones of him in action, a distant figure
against a sepia background, from an age that seemed very
remote indeed. But any absence of information from these
imprints is more than made up for by another generation
spinning their stories of the great players and, inevitably, the
name of McGrory would come up. He who was not weaned
on these stories and did not hear of the prowess of the
McGrory head, which, we were told, could turn a leaden,
sodden lump of inanimate leather into an undetectable
missile, knows little of the football tradition. He did more than
score goals. He converted countless numbers of supporters to
the belief that football was all there was worth living for. And
in the '30s, that might not have been an unhealthy
supposition. When eventually I came into contact with him,
first as manager, then as PRO, that other, less public, side of
him came shining through the mists of football legend. It was
quite simply that he was the gentlest and kindest man I've
ever met in a sport more noted for turning saints into sinners
than the reverse. He also bulged football's history books with
enough statistics to ensure that the stories of his contribution
to the game and his legend will never be extinguished.

The funeral service was held on Friday, 22 October 1982 and was
paid for by Celtic. Requiem Mass was celebrated by Cardinal
Thomas Winning, then the Archbishop of Glasgow, at the tiny St
Leo the Great's Catholic Church in Beech Avenue just round the
corner in Dumbreck before a packed congregation of 400, which
included Billy McNeill, Jock Stein and Willie Waddell of Rangers.
Billy McNeill and James McGrory read the Lessons and all joined in
singing 'Abide With Me' at the end, the hymn sung at all Wembley
Cup finals. Ironically, Jimmy never got to play at Wembley.

The funeral itself was to St Peter's Cemetery, Dalbeth, and as the
funeral car came out on to the road from the church, there was
Calum MacDonald, his old teammate, standing in the street crying
his eyes out. The cortège, flanked by police outriders, travelled
through the city and came into the East End at Bridgeton Cross. It
stopped for a moment at Celtic Park and this was when young James
McGrory said, 'I realised for the first time who and what my dad
was. He was idolised. There were hundreds of people standing in the

street as we passed. Ordinary working people, many of them openly crying.'

The procession continued from Springfield Toll along London Road past Belvidere Hospital and Westhorn Park and on past the Celtic training ground at Barrowfield until it came to the gates of the cemetery where the looming figure of Jock Stein stood waiting. He bowed his head as the man he had always called 'Boss' passed by.

On 24 October, an old admirer, Harry Andrews, of the *Scottish Sunday Express*, wrote his piece under the headline 'The Nicest Celt Of Them All':

> I once saw Jimmy McGrory fly through the air and stick his head on a Charlie Napier cross. The sodden leather ball must have weighed a ton. Anyway, it hit the bar and landed back somewhere between the penalty box line and midfield. The crowd was silenced by the incredible power of that header . . . but McGrory was busy apologising to his teammates for missing the chance. And that was like the man. Jimmy was never convinced he had a talent above the average. When you pointed to his amazing scoring records, he handed the credit to the service he received from the rest of the side. It was not only that McGrory himself was too nice a man – surely there has never been a nicer – but also that he hated talking about himself and, in any case, could see nothing remarkable in his achievements. But, of course, his deeds spoke for him. Jimmy will live as long as football. And certainly as long as there is a Celtic Football Club.

In the *Sunday Standard* for Sunday, 24 October, under the heading 'How Gentle Jimmy Achieved Greatness', sportswriter Ian Archer engaged in a dialogue with Lisbon Lion Tommy Gemmell:

> Tommy: Just think of it, 550 goals. Can you think of how *difficult* that must have been? Look at it this way, we used to have a little practice at the end of our training sessions at Celtic which went like this . . . You would put a ball down at the end of the 18-yard box and drive it towards the goal. Not just push it but really hit it. Now we are talking about *good* players, the Lisbon Lions. You know, you were lucky to average three out of six. I bet you nobody could do better

than that. And then you think about McGrory, scoring all those goals with defenders all about him. It's quite incredible. And, it should be added, not with today's lightweight ball with that coating that keeps out the wet. He did it with those old leather jobs which, on a dreich November day, could weigh a ton. And he was wearing those big, old boots too.

Ian: Only the ancients remember him playing. Only the middle-aged and upward can remember his twenty years as manager of Celtic. Yet, the folklore surrounding a gentle, indeed diffident man, is substantial. He walked across the decades right up to our own times.

Tommy: He never said a lot . . . I knew I wasn't playing well. Nowadays, a manager would pull you into the office and bawl and shout and tell you to get back into the reserves until you had sorted yourself out. He didn't. He just puffed on his pipe and kept saying 'Well done, son.' He knew I knew I wasn't playing well but gradually, he built up my confidence. Oh, we were in awe of Jimmy alright. I remember being there for two years and I was still on £7 a week. I wanted a rise. I stood in front of him, my whole body trembling, and blurted out my case. Honestly, I didn't know if I would get the rise or the sack. He bumped me up to twelve.

Ian: Too kind, too good to be a manager, they said, probably correctly. He had signed all of the Celtic side which won the European Cup with the exception of Willie Wallace, but it needed the rigorous discipline of Stein to keep in charge a team who collectively did not see eye to eye with the new man's views about the need for an austere, almost monastic attitude to athletic life. Now another of those links to the past has gone, those days when hard and simple and honest men played the boys' game and when the terraces were blackened by mature citizenry seeking their Saturday afternoon entertainment while their wives tidied the home. Just think of all the things that were missing then – hooliganism, European football, strikers, home and away ties, all the jargon of a game which doesn't trust its own historical language. Dark, bad days lightened by the sight of a hero rising above a centre-half, twisting his neck and heading the ball past the helpless custodian. But Celtic did at least the right thing. They made a centre-forward their manager and that manager signed Jock Stein and Billy McNeill, so there was not just a continuity about the club but a genuine succession and that must be comforting to all who see in football still some sense of order in a small part of the world which has changed too much.

That sums it up for many, but space should be left for Gerry McNee, who, as the first biographer of McGrory, was in a better position than most to write about him. In the *Daily Express* on 23 October, he called him the 'best loved Celt of all':

> James Edward McGrory was laid to rest yesterday just a few hundred yards from his beloved Celtic Park but his memory and the legend he created will live as long as football is played in this country. Jimmy McGrory was a shy, unassuming man. To get him to talk about himself, never mind anyone else, was as daunting a task as goalkeepers faced in stopping his goal-scoring efforts. He always spoke fairly of people and always shunned controversy. Yet on the field he was a lion. Like Jimmy Quinn, his famous predecessor whom he resembled so much in build, he usually left it to fellow forwards to provide him with the ball. But when the passes weren't coming he could be a tireless forager. It was the size of his heart that made him a hero. That heart was also 22-carat. On the night his book was published he handed me a small leather box which contained his most treasured medal – for the League Championship of 1935–36. 'Here, I want you to have this,' he whispered quietly. We shall not look on his like again.

David Potter, like McNee, a Celtic writer of some distinction, has his personal McGrory memory:

> Born in 1948, I never saw McGrory play, but my father did, and he never tired of telling me about him and his phenomenal heading ability. I grew up watching a poor Celtic team of which he was the nominal manager [but] it was difficult to get angry with McGrory . . . we all knew where the power lay . . .
>
> My father and I got on to a train at Forfar in about 1964 to go and see Celtic play at Aberdeen. The team were on the

train and my father was struck by the fact that McGrory recognised him and nodded to him even though they had only met once briefly at a funeral some 13 years previously. My father went to his own grave in 1993 still happy about that. Such was the aura of the great Jimmy McGrory.

Graham McColl wrote in Celtic's official history:

Jimmy McGrory was a wonderful centre-forward, powerful and accurate with his head, mobile, capable of distracting defenders to create goal chances for his teammates, aware of everything that was going on around him and interested in only one goal; the next one. He also possessed the ideal physique for a striker, with the type of upper-body strength that looked as though he would be able to compete in a tug-of-war as a one-man team, and a mental attitude that placed the cause of Celtic above all else.

Ordinary football fans remembered him warmly. Ronnie Campbell of Leeds writes:

Many's a time I have stood at the front entrance to Paradise before a match and watched the portly man with the Crombie coat and Homburg hat knock out the ash from his pipe before striding through the front door. Thanks to James McAleer, my wonderful grandfather, sitting up in bed with his cup of tea, sucking his clay pipe, his pale cheeks turning crimson as he remembered Jimmy McGrory, it wasn't difficult to imagine that beneath those clothes there once was a superbly built athlete who graced stadiums around the country and scored more goals than any other Celtic player; indeed, more than any other player anywhere. I was in awe of him.

Ninety-three-year-old Tommy McMonagle was born on 19 May 1911 and was also a McGrory admirer – but the difference was that he was a Rangers supporter, and had been since 1919. He only gave up his Ibrox season ticket quite recently. Paul Craig, his grandson and present-day Celtic supporter, enjoyed a long conversation with him about McGrory during April 2004. This was McGrory as seen from the Rangers end:

Physical Appearance: His hairstyle was short back and sides. Most players were. He was barrel-chested, sturdy in appearance and had a very strong, thick neck. The player most like him today would be Alan Shearer of Newcastle. Occasionally he played with strapping on his knees, but this was normal in those days. It was a much harder, physical game then, but the game was *very* much slower. What I remember most is his bravery.

Demeanour on the field: He tended to stay up the park as a player, there was no chasing back into his own penalty area or anything like that, although he put himself about, no question of that. He never ever dived, or cheated . ... He was a fair player, never dirty. I don't remember him ever taking a penalty. Celtic's spot-kick expert was Charlie Napier. Goal celebrations were slaps on the back and handshakes – it was nothing like today. You never saw a player kiss his jersey.

Fan-worship: The Celtic fans revered him and Rangers fans respected him, no doubt about that. Bob McPhail and McGrory were great friends and great for Scotland. They just seemed to play together perfectly.

Money: I was an engineer with Smith's of Cook Street earning £2 18s a week during the '30s. Top players at the time were on £5 a week with £3 in the summer. I don't remember anybody being paid for endorsements. So the gap in wages wasn't as big as today.

Perhaps all these comments could be best summed up in Rangers chairman John Lawrence's remark to journalist John Rafferty in a 1971 interview, when Mr Lawrence said: 'He is the only man in football about whom I have never heard anyone say a bad word.' The man just did not have an enemy. Twenty years after his death, the *Celtic View* printed a two-page tribute to him for that anniversary, 23 October 2002. Joe Sullivan concluded:

To put it quite simply, before there was a record industry there was Jimmy McGrory. If there was such a thing as a goal machine then McGrory was at the spearhead of football's industrial revolution, a mechanism so well tuned he would leave all lying in his wake, so much so that mere statistics cannot do justice to what he means to Celtic.

The following little squib comes to mind:

> The goal machine, the goal machine.
> He was the greatest that ever has been
> If you'd ever seen him, you'd know what I mean,
> Jimmy McGrory – the goal machine.

A machine with a Scottish heart that ran on Irish blood. What better combination to drive a football engine that was assembled in a Garngad backyard to drive all the way to Paradise. Yet there was nothing mechanical about the man. He was a quiet, unassuming professional who transformed himself for 90 minutes on the playing pitch into a demon of daring, a hero for his own generation and beyond. He gave a lot of people a dream in the face of grim reality, hope in a time of hopelessness and a glimpse of the impossible when possibilities were limited.

He attracted poetic effusions from the public throughout his career, most of them pretty poor, but all of them well meaning. In *Hail! Hail!*, the magazine of the Celtic Supporters' Club of Perth, Western Australia, came 'McGrory's Farewell' by 'C.D. I.L.E.', probably dating from the end of his playing days in 1937 but it serves now as his requiem from the terracing:

> From the field a face is missing
> A face we'll see no more
> A credit to the football game
> And the colours that he wore.
>
> He wore the good old green and white
> He brought us fame and glory
> There'll never be another like
> The famous James McGrory.
>
> Around the slopes of Paradise
> We miss that mighty cry
> As through the air McGrory leaps
> To crosses hanging high.

We see it yet, we can't forget
As toward the goal it sped
In League or Cup, McGrory's up
With his million-dollar head.

You've played your last; your day is past
And we lift our caps to you
The hero of five hundred games
This is our fond adieu.

Farewell, farewell, McGrory bhoy
We cherish Celtic's might
And the finest lad that ever wore
The good old green and white.

In those lines an echo suddenly comes back from 1936 when Willie Maley, in his *Weekly News* article, said: 'I often think a cast of McGrory's head should be taken and added to the collection of trophies at Celtic Park. And one day, that idea of mine will become an accomplished fact.' Unfortunately, it did not, but his comment prompts a thought.

At the time of writing, the North and South Stands at Celtic Park are unnamed, so why not call one of them the McGrory Stand? After all, there is a Milburn Stand at Newcastle and his statue graces the approaches to St James' Park. Nat Lofthouse is named in a stand at Bolton's new stadium, as is Dixie Dean at Everton. Since a plaque on the wall of the present South Stand signifies that he opened its extension from the old Grant Stand in 1979, why can't Celtic name the South Stand in honour of their own legendary centre-forward, the most prolific goal-scorer in British football history? It is an honour much deserved and no more than justice to the memory of a much-loved player. It would also serve as a gesture of gratitude for an exemplary, lifelong loyalty.

Something of the same attitude has been shown by Steven Gerrard at Liverpool, who, as I write these words, has just turned down a move to Chelsea for untold millions in order to remain with the club he supported as a boy and has played for all his football life. It is an exact parallel of McGrory's career with Celtic, and what is more, Gerrard's refusal of Chelsea is a replica of McGrory's turning down of Arsenal in 1928. The only difference between the two players is £999,902 – which is the gap between Steven's weekly wage and

McGrory's. That, however, is a matter of a change of fashion and economics. It doesn't alter the fact that basically this is a matter of the heart.

Gerrard is quoted as saying: 'I love Liverpool so much. This is my club. My heart is with Liverpool.' This might have been the young McGrory speaking. As a player, he touched the heart and, as a result, a lot of hearts went out to him. This most uncomplicated of men caught our imagination. Here was no modern programmed robot responding to instruction, a homogenised soccernaut performing to order, a bland Beckham, more product than player. Personalities come and go in every season of football, and fame often lasts only as long as the next game – but heroes like Jimmy McGrory are forever.

McGRORY STATISTICS

Compiled by Pat Woods

Television coverage today makes it possible to identify goal-scorers clearly. Since McGrory played before this was possible, match reports have been scrutinised in order to try and establish accreditation in cases where discrepancies might arise regarding the scorer. In the table below, goal totals in parenthesis follow the number of appearances in each competition. Abbreviations for each competition are as follows:

L – Scottish League (top division in each season)
SC – Scottish Cup
GC – Glasgow Cup
GCC – Glasgow Charity Cup

SEASON	TEAM	L	SC	GC	GCC	TOTAL
1922–23	Celtic	3 (1)	1	–	–	4(1)
1923–24	Clydebank	*30(13)	3(3)	–	–	33(16)
1923–24	Celtic	–	–	–	2(1)	2(1)
1924–25	Celtic	25(17)	8(11)	2(2)	1	36(30)
1925–26	Celtic	37(35)	6(6)	6(6)	3(2)	52(49)
1926–27	Celtic	33(48)	6(9)	2(2)	–	41(59)
1927–28	Celtic	36(47)	6(6)	3(9)	1	46(62)
1928–29	Celtic	21(21)	6(10)	4(3)	3(8)	34(42)

SEASON	TEAM	L	SC	GC	GCC	TOTAL
1929–30	Celtic	26(32)	3(4)	5(4)	1(1)	35(41)
1930–31	Celtic	29(36)	6(8)	2(1)	1(2)	38(47)
1931–32	Celtic	22(28)	1	3(2)	2	28(30)
1932–33	Celtic	25(22)	8(8)	3(2)	2(3)	38(35)
1933–34	Celtic	27(17)	3(1)	1(1)	–	31(19)
1934–35	Celtic	27(18)	4(2)	1	1(1)	33(21)
1935–36	Celtic	32(50)	1	2	2(1)	37(51)
1936–37	Celtic	25(18)	8(9)	–	2(1)	35(28)
1937–38	Celtic	10(5)	–	1(1)	–	11(6)
TOTALS		408(408)	70(77)	35(33)	21(20)	534(538)

* McGrory was loaned to Clydebank for start of season 1923–24, being brought back to Celtic at end of that season in time for the Glasgow Charity Cup ties.

REPRESENTATIVE MATCHES
(McGrory goals in parentheses)

Full Internationals (all Home Championships)	*Score*
Scotland	
v. Ireland, Firhill Park, Glasgow, 25 February 1928	0–1
v. England, Hampden Park, Glasgow, 28 March 1931	2–0 (1)
v. Ireland, Ibrox Park, Glasgow, 19 September 1931	3–1 (1)
v. Wales, Racecourse Ground, Wrexham, 31 October 1931	3–2 (1)
v. Ireland, Windsor Park, Belfast, 17 September 1932	4–0 (1)
v. England, Hampden Park, Glasgow, 1 April 1933	2–1 (2)
v. Ireland, Celtic Park, Glasgow, 16 September 1933	1–2

Inter-League Matches
Scottish League

v. Irish League, Tynecastle Park, Edinburgh, 27 October 1926	5–2 (1)
v. Football League, Filbert Street, Leicester, 19 March 1927	2–2 (1)

v. Football League, Ibrox Park, Glasgow, 10 March 1928   2–6 (2)

v. Football League, Villa Park, Birmingham, 7 November 1928   1–2

v. Football League, Celtic Park, Glasgow, 7 November 1931   4–3 (2)

v. Football League, Ibrox Park, Glasgow, 30 October 1935   2–2

TOTAL

	Appearances	Goals
Full internationals	7	6
Inter-League	6	6
Representative total	13	12

CAREER TOTAL IN FIRST-CLASS MATCHES

	Appearances	Goals
Celtic	501	522
Clydebank	33	16
Scotland	7	6
Scottish League	6	6
Grand Career Total	547	550

BIBLIOGRAPHY

BURNS, Peter and WOODS, Pat, *Oh, Hampden in the Sun . . .* (Mainstream Publishing, Edinburgh 1997)

CAIRNEY, John, *The Scottish Football Hall of Fame* (Mainstream Publishing, Edinburgh 1998)

CAMPBELL, Tom, with WOODS, Pat, *The Glory and the Dream* (Celtic 1887–1980) (Mainstream Publishing, Edinburgh 1981)

CAMPBELL, Tom, *Rhapsody in Green* (Mainstream Publishing, Edinburgh 1990)

CAMPBELL, Tom and POTTER, David, *Jock Stein* (Mainstream Publishing, Edinburgh 1998)

CAMPBELL, Tom with WOODS, Pat, *Celtic Football Club, 1887–1967* (Tempus 1998)

CANNING, Tommy, *The Will to Win* (Mainstream Publishing, Edinburgh 1988)

CRAMPSEY, Bob, *The Scottish Footballer* (Blackwood & Sons, Edinburgh 1978)

CRAMPSEY, Bob, *Mr Stein – A Biography of Jock Stein CBE, 1922–1985* (Mainstream Publishing, Edinburgh 1986)

CRAMPSEY, Bob, *The Scottish Football League: The First Hundred Years* (The Scottish Football League, Glasgow 1990)

DOCHERTY, Tommy, *Call the Doc – An Autobiography* (Hamlyn, London 1981)

FORSYTH, Roddy, *The Only Game* (Mainstream Publishing, Edinburgh 1990)

GALBRAITH, Russell, *The Hampden Story* (Mainstream Publishing, Edinburgh 1993)

GREIG, Tom, *My Search for Celtic's John* (Ogilvie Writings, Glasgow 2003)

HAMILTON, Ian, *The Faber Book of Soccer* (Faber & Faber, London 1992)

HAYES, Richard, *The Football Imagination* (Arena Books, London 1995)

HUTCHISON, John, *The Football Industry* (Richard Drew, Glasgow 1982)

INGLIS, Simon, *The Football Grounds* (Willow Books, Collins, London 1985)

JARVIE, Grant, with WALKER, Graham, *Scottish Sport in the Making of the Nation* (Leicester University Press, Leicester 1994)

JOANNOU, Paul, *Wembley Wizards* (Mainstream Publishing, Edinburgh 1990)

LAMMING, Douglas, *A Scottish Internationalists' Who's Who, 1872–1986* (Hutton Press, Cherry Burton, Beverley 1987)

MacBRIDE, Eugene and O'CONNOR, Martin with SHERIDAN, George, *An Alphabet of the Celts* (ACL & Polar Publishing (UK) Ltd, Leicester 1994)

MacDONALD, Kenny, *Scottish Football Quotations* (Mainstream Publishing, Edinburgh 1994)

MALEY, Willie, *The Story of the Celtic, 1888–1938* (Original 1939 Edition, Facsimile, 1996)

MARSHALL, Stuart, *Celtic – Football Legends, 1888–1938* (Stenlake Publishing, Catrine, Ayrshire 1998)

McCARRA, Kevin, *Scottish Football – A Pictorial History* (Third Eye, Polygon, London 1984)

McCARRA, Kevin and WOODS, Pat, *One Afternoon In Lisbon* (Mainstream Publishing, Edinburgh 1988)

McGRORY, Jimmy, edited by Gerald McNEE, *A Lifetime in Paradise* (Jimmy McGrory and Gerald McNee, Glasgow, 1975)

McNEE, Gerald, *And You'll Never Walk Alone* (Impulse, Aberdeen 1972)

McNEE, Gerald, *The Story of Celtic, 1888–1978* (Stanley Paul, London 1978)

MURRAY, Bill, *The Old Firm* (John Donald Publishers, Edinburgh 1984)

MURRAY, Bill, *Glasgow Giants* (Mainstream Publishing, Edinburgh 1988)

POTTER, David W., *Willie Maley – The Man Who Made Celtic* (Tempus, Stroud, Gloucestershire 2003)

RAFFERTY, John, *One Hundred Years of Scottish Football* (Pan Books, London 1973)

ROLLIN, Jack, *The Guinness Book of Soccer Facts and Feats* (Guinness Superlatives, London 1978)

SOAR, Phil with TYLER, Martin, *The Encyclopedia of British Football* (Marshall Cavendish, London and New York 1971)

TAYLOR, Hugh, *Great Masters of Scottish Football* (Stanley Paul, London 1967)

WALVIN, James, *The People's Game* (Mainstream Publishing, Edinburgh 1994)

WARD, Andrew, *Scotland – the Team* (Breedon Books Sport, Derby 1987)

JOHN CAIRNEY'S PREVIOUS BOOKS INCLUDE:

Miscellaneous Verses
A Moment White
The Man who Played Robert Burns
East End to West End
Worlds Apart
A Year Out in New Zealand
A Scottish Football Hall of Fame
On the Trail of Robert Burns
Solo Performers
The Luath Burns Companion
Immortal Memories
The Quest for Robert Louis Stevenson
The Quest for Charles Rennie Mackintosh